AF352248

Currency Internationalization

Currency Internationalization: Global Experiences and Implications for the Renminbi

Edited By

Wensheng Peng
Chang Shu

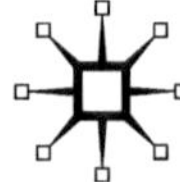

First published 2010 by
PALGRAVE MACMILLAN

Palgrave Macmillan in the UK is an imprint of Macmillan Publishers Limited, registered in England, company number 785998, of Houndmills, Basingstoke, Hampshire RG21 6XS.

Palgrave Macmillan in the US is a division of St Martin's Press LLC, 175 Fifth Avenue, New York, NY 10010.

Palgrave Macmillan is the global academic imprint of the above companies and has companies and representatives throughout the world.

Palgrave® and Macmillan® are registered trademarks in the United States, the United Kingdom, Europe and other countries

ISBN-13: 978-0-230-58049-7   hardback

This book is printed on paper suitable for recycling and made from fully managed and sustained forest sources. Logging, pulping and manufacturing processes are expected to conform to the environmental regulations of the country of origin.

A catalogue record for this book is available from the British Library.

A catalog record for this book is available from the Library of Congress.

10 9 8 7 6 5 4 3 2 1
19 18 17 16 15 14 13 12 11 10

Printed and bound in Great Britain by
CPI Antony Rowe, Chippenham and Eastbourne

Contents

Figures

Tables

Boxes

Foreword

On 15 and 16 October 2007, the Hong Kong Institute for Monetary Research (HKIMR) held an international conference entitled 'Currency Internationalisation: International Experiences and Implications for the Renminbi'. Representatives from the International Monetary Fund, the Bank for International Settlements and a number of central banks, and academics from China and overseas participated in the conference. The presentations given at the conference form the basis of this book.

An international currency is one that is widely used outside its home country. Essentially, the classical domestic functions of money – as unit of account, medium of exchange and store of value – are transferred to the international level in the form of, for example, trade invoicing, reserve holdings and exchange rate anchor for other currencies. What factors contribute to the use of a currency as an international currency? First and foremost, an international currency must be perceived as sound, and market participants must be willing to hold it as a store of value. It should also be convertible so that it may be acquired by non-residents.

Clearly, many currencies meet these criteria, but few emerge as international currencies, so there must be other factors that matter. One such factor has to do with size. A large and competitive economy, which is open to international trade and finance, will naturally generate many foreign exchange transactions with at least one leg in the home currency. Size also matters in terms of the presence of an open and developed financial market which supplies assets denominated in the local currency, for which there is demand among international investors. It is also argued that the international use of a currency involves network externalities. That is, an international currency, like domestic money, derives its value because other economies are using it. As a result, there is inertia in favour of continuing to use the currency that has served as the international currency in the past.

Indeed, historically only a few currencies have acquired international-currency status. In the post-Second World War period, the US dollar has been the dominant reserve currency, despite periodic speculation and discussion about the loss of its international pre-eminence, usually associated with episodes of US-dollar exchange-rate weakness. In recent years, the euro has become the second most widely used international currency, with some predicting that the euro will rival the US dollar, leading to a "bipolar" system in the future. In a way, the emergence of the euro as an international currency can be considered as an extension of the internationalization of the Deutsche Mark, but the introduction of the euro certainly increased the 'habitat' of the currency. It seems to me that the significance of the major currencies in international trade and financial transactions does vary over time, albeit slowly.

In Asia, there are indications of an increasing use of the renminbi outside Mainland China, although this is from a low base and pretty much limited to regions that are closely linked to mainland China. Spending in renminbi by mainland residents outside mainland China has been on the rise, particularly in some Asian countries. In the border trade between residents of China and some of its neighbouring economies, the renminbi is often the preferred currency for settlement. Most notably, since the launch of renminbi banking business there in 2004, Hong Kong has become the first place outside the mainland to have banks providing renminbi deposit taking, exchange, remittance and card services. A further major breakthrough was the issuance of the first renminbi bonds in Hong Kong in July 2007. There have been seven issues so far, all of which have met with very keen investor demand.

It should not come as a surprise to keen observers of the global economy that the international role of the renminbi will gradually increase over time. Already the third largest economy and the third largest trading partner in the world, China continues to rise rapidly as an important force in global trade and production. Meanwhile, the renminbi is gaining flexibility within a framework established in July 2005 and continuously refined since then. Significant steps have also been taken to gradually liberalize the country's capital account transactions. Being the currency of an economy of such growing strength and progressive financial liberalization, the renminbi is surely going to become a major currency in the region and the world, and possibly, in the fullness of time, a reserve currency.

The international use of a currency is ultimately determined by market forces, but in the case of the renminbi, policy restrictions on the capital account convertibility play a role. The pace and form of liberalization of such restrictions are governed by the overall development and reform strategy of the country, not necessarily by a desire to promote the international use of the currency. But liberalization of the restrictions may lead to an increased use of the currency in international transactions, which entails risks as well as benefits to the home country. There are a number of important benefits. First, the economy derives seigniorage, because non-residents' non interest-bearing claims on it are denominated in its own currency. In broader terms, the domestic financial sector will benefit from an expansion of the international trade and financial transactions that are conducted in the domestic currency. Second, it brings convenience for the country's residents, reducing transaction costs and avoiding exchange-rate risks. Third, it increases macroeconomic policy flexibility by allowing borrowing in the international market in the domestic currency at prevailing interest rates. However, internationalization of a currency also brings costs associated with the impact of the international demand for the currency on domestic monetary conditions.

In particular, increasing international demand for a currency coupled with expectations that it will appreciate may add to the pressure on the currency. In the 1960s and 1970s, the Japanese and German authorities were particularly worried about the possibility that if assets were made available to non-residents, an inflow of capital would exacerbate upward pressure on their currencies. In some ways, Mainland China have the same concern today. Thus, for a large economy like China, the international role of the domestic currency, and the concerns associated with it, would inevitably form part of the authorities' consideration when determining the pace and forms of financial liberalization and opening.

An increasing international role of the renminbi would have implications for other economies as well, particularly in Asia. Since the reform of the renminbi exchange rate in July 2005, we have already seen some signs of an increasing impact of renminbi exchange-rate movements on other regional currencies. If the renminbi is increasingly used in regional trade and financial transactions and its exchange rate flexibility rises over time, variations in the exchange rate of the renminbi against other major currencies such as the US dollar will have an increasing impact on the region. This is a challenge for the regional economies, one that we perhaps should start to think about how to address now, when the emerging international role of the renminbi is at an early stage. This calls for increased cooperation by the governments and regulatory authorities in the region to promote financial integration and strengthen the regional arrangements to increase our collective capacity to deal with internal and external shocks.

From Hong Kong's point of view, we see an international role of the renminbi as providing important opportunities for developing our financial market and strengthening our role as an international financial centre. China is in the unique position of having two financial systems within one country. Elsewhere I have argued that these two financial systems should develop a 'complementary, mutually assisting and interactive' relationship to develop in the longer term an integrated, much larger financial market for the country as a whole, and to promote Hong Kong as an international financial centre of global significance. Initiatives have been taken in a number of areas to increase financial integration between Mainland China and Hong Kong. In particular, the development of renminbi business in Hong Kong has provided it with the first renminbi market outside the mainland and built up the capacity of our financial system to conduct renminbi-denominated transactions. Continuing to develop financial intermediation in the renminbi will add to the breadth and depth of Hong Kong's financial markets, and is essential to the maintenance and development of our role as an international financial centre.

The benefits are mutual. As an international financial centre of China and with close cooperation between the mainland and Hong Kong monetary and regulatory authorities, Hong Kong is in an ideal position to provide a reliable testing ground for renminbi convertibility and its increasing international use.

The two-day conference on renminbi internationalization was held at an opportune time, since it is important to discuss a range of relevant policy questions at this early stage. Among the papers presented at the conference, those on the experiences of the euro area, South Africa, Australia and Korea considered the external use of their currencies, shedding light on issues relevant to the international role of the renminbi. Five other papers focused on some key issues in the process of an increasing use of the renminbi in international trade and finance, including the determinants of external use of the renminbi, its interaction with financial market developments and monetary policy, and the potential role of Hong Kong. A final paper presented empirical work suggesting that renminbi exchange rate movements had already started to affect exchange rate dynamics in the region. I am glad that through this conference, we have gathered together these thought-provoking papers on the subject contributed by a group of prominent Chinese and overseas researchers, central bankers and practitioners.

Joseph Yam
Chief Executive of the Hong Kong Monetary Authority

Notes on Contributors

1. Christian Thimann
Christian Thimann is Head of the International Policy Analysis Division at the European Central Bank. Previously he headed the ECB's division in charge of EU neighbouring regions and dealt with issues related to EU accession. He joined the ECB in 1998 from the International Monetary Fund, where he worked on European and Asian economies. He holds a PhD in Economics from the University of Munich and an MSc in Economics from the London School of Economics.

2. Johan van den Heever
Johan van den Heever has served as Head of the Research Department, South African Reserve Bank since 2006. He joined the bank in October 1987 and in 2003 was appointed as Senior Deputy Head responsible for Economic Reviews and Statistics. Prior to joining the bank, he lectured in the Economics Department at the University of Pretoria from 1980 to 1987. He completed his doctoral studies at the University of Pretoria with a thesis on macroeconomic stabilization policy.

3. Robert N. McCauley
Robert N. McCauley serves as the Chief Representative at the Bank for International Settlements' Representative Office for Asia and the Pacific in Hong Kong. Before joining the BIS, he worked for 13 years for the Federal Reserve Bank of New York, serving at times as chief economist for the interagency committee of bank supervisors that rates country risk. He taught international finance and the multinational firm at the University of Chicago's Graduate School of Business in 1992.

4. Kyungsoo Kim and Chi-Yong Song
Kyungsoo Kim has served as a deputy governor and general director at the Institute for Money and Economic Research, Bank of Korea since 2007. He has also been Professor of Economics at Sungkyunkwan University, Korea since 1988. Before joining the SKKU, he was Professor of Economics at Tulane University, USA between 1984 and 1988. He gained his PhD at the University of Pennsylvania, USA in 1984.

Chi-Young Song has been Professor of Economics at Kookmin University, Seoul, Korea since 1998. Before joining the university, he served as a research fellow at the Korea Institute of Finance, Korea between 1994 and 1998. Dr Song obtained his PhD from Brown University, USA in 1994.

5. Hongyi Chen and Wensheng Peng

Dr Hongyi Chen is Senior Economist at the IMF Sub-office in the Hong Kong SAR. Previously, he was a senior manager in the External Department at the Hong Kong Monetary Authority, monitoring the developments in the Chinese financial market and financial policy. He obtained his PhD from Columbia University, USA.

Dr Wensheng Peng is presently Head of China Research in Barclays Capital, responsible for macroeconomic and financial market research on China. He worked as senior manager in the Banking Development Department, then as division head in the Research Department and External Department of the Hong Kong Monetary Authority from 1998 to June 2008. Prior to joining the HKMA, Dr Peng worked as an economist with the IMF in Washington, DC for five years, covering mainly emerging markets in Asia. He graduated with a BA in economics from Nankai University in China, and MA (Econ) and PhD degrees from the University of Birmingham, UK.

6. Wen Hai and Hongxin Yao

Wen Hai is a Vice Chancellor and Professor in Economics in Peking University. He is also the Dean of the Graduate School Campus in Shenzhen and Dean of the university's HuiFeng Business School, and has served on various academic committees and editorial boards. Prior to his returning to Peking University in 1995, he taught in the University of California at Davis and Forte Lewis College, US. Prof. Hai obtained his BA from Peking University, and MA and PhD in Economics from UC, US.

Hongxin Yao has been a professor in Business School of Shantou University, China since 2008. Before joining the university, he served as a visiting professor at Akita Prefectural University, Japan from 2004 to 2005 and as a postdoctor in HSBC Business School of Peking University between 2006 and 2008. Prof. Yao obtained his PhD in management in Southwest Jiaotong University, China.

7. David Li and Linlin Liu

David Daokui Li is Mansfield Freeman Professor of Economics in the School of Economics and Management, Director of the Center for China in the World Economy and Dean of the Finance Department in Tsinghua University. Before joining Tsinghua University, he worked in the Hong Kong University of Science and Technology. Previously, he was an assistant professor at the University of Michigan at Ann Arbor, and a research fellow at Stanford University's Hoover Institute. Prof. Li obtained his BA from Tsinghua University, and his PhD in Economics from Harvard University.

Linlin Liu is a macroeconomy researcher at CITIC Securities Company. Her research areas include labour economics, international economics and the Chinese economy. Liu holds a PhD in economics and a BA from the School of Economics and Management, Tsinghua University.

8. Shusong Ba

Prof. Shusong Ba is a Professor in Finance, PhD advisor and Member of Standing Committee of the People's Republic of China's Central Government Youth Federation. Since August 2003, Prof. Ba has served as the Deputy Director-General of the Financial Research Institute in the Development Research Centre of the State Council. He obtained his PhD in economics from Peking University, where he also completed post-doctoral research. He has also received a research fellowship from the Development Research Centre of the State Council.

His co-authors, **Bo Wu, Ping Yuan, Miao Wang** and **Zhuqing Yin**, are Masters and PhD candidates.

9. Haihong Gao

Prof. Haihong Gao joined the Institute of World Economics and Politics, Chinese Academy of Social Sciences in 1989, and is currently Director of the institute's International Finance Section. She has led a number of research projects sponsored by China's Ministry of Finance and Social Science Fund. She obtained her BA and MA degrees in Economics from Peking University, and her MSc degree in International Money, Finance and Investment from Durham University in the UK.

10. Chang Shu

Chang Shu joined the Hong Kong Monetary Authority in 2000 and has undertaken research related to the Hong Kong and mainland Chinese economies. She currently leads a team monitoring and researching into macroeconomic, monetary and financial issues on Mainland China. Prior to this, she worked for the Bank of England. She obtained her PhD degree in finance from the University of Birmingham, UK.

Part I International Experiences

1
Global Roles of Currencies

Christian Thimann

1.1 Introduction

Policy discussions and academic contributions on the international role of currencies abound. They come in two strands. The first strand deals with the general importance of a given currency in the world economy, and its standing and significance in the international monetary system. These are the contributions that occasionally make media headlines, especially when they raise questions such as whether the dollar could lose its leading global status to the euro, why the yen has lost global importance, and if one day the Chinese renminbi could challenge one – or all three – of these currencies. The second strand of contributions focuses more narrowly on the cross-border use of currencies, analysing which currencies are used outside their home constituencies, by what type of economic agents and for what purposes.

One can usefully label the first strand as the 'global role' of currencies, reflecting the standing and importance of a currency in the global economy, while the second strand can be labelled as the somewhat narrower 'international role', reflecting the use of a currency outside its constituency of issuance. Empirically, both concepts can be interrelated: currencies that are used heavily outside their constituencies are more likely to play an important global role and, conversely, currencies that are globally important are likely to be used more heavily outside their own constituencies. Nevertheless, both notions are conceptually distinct; they are not necessarily driven by the same factors and do not necessarily have the same policy implications. Despite the conceptual distinction, however, both strands of the literature have so far largely used the same quantitative basis, namely the use of currencies in the international debt securities market. Although other indicators – such as shares in the foreign exchange reserves of central banks – are sometimes used as well, the respective currency shares of securities outstanding in the international debt market remain the most pertinent quantitative measure used to assess the international role of currencies in global capital markets.[1] The main objective of this chapter is to demonstrate the limitations of this established measure with regard to the first strand of literature and to present a more appropriate measure for the 'global role of currencies', which also gives rise to some new empirical findings and policy implications.

The international debt market represents about one-tenth of the global bond market. It comprises all debt securities issued by non-residents of a certain currency area. The largest issuers in this market are globally operating financial institutions and corporations. They choose internationally used currencies – mainly the US dollar, the euro and the Japanese yen – to finance part of their operations outside their home markets. The international debt market for US dollars is dominated by European banks and corporations, while the market for the euro is dominated by investment banks and corporations from the United States, the United Kingdom and a few other European countries outside the euro area. In the past, sovereign issuers from emerging economies were also important, but given their vastly improved financial position, only a few have been tapping this market on a large scale in recent years.

The relative importance of the international debt market in overall international activities in global capital markets is falling, as other financial markets develop and previously domestic markets open up to – and are used by – foreign investors. Therefore, the international debt market is increasingly less representative of the international importance of certain currencies. The penetration of bond and equity markets by international investors is rising, a development which is by no means driven by private sector agents alone. Both central banks in emerging economies and sovereign wealth funds have become large-scale global investors, and are mostly active in the treasury, corporate bond and equity markets. Yet the international debt market excludes the treasury market and the bulk of the corporate bond market, as these are classified as domestic markets, even if they attract significant international investor interest. Moreover, the international debt market also excludes equity markets, where the number of international activities – cross-listings of global corporations on several stock exchanges and penetration by international investors – has risen considerably in recent years. Today, the equity market makes a significant contribution to international activities and to the international role of underlying currencies.

In addition, activity in the international debt market is strongly driven by the business needs of those banks and corporations that dominate it, as well as conjunctural factors. Hence, short-term variations in the shares of individual currencies in this market hardly capture the more fundamental motives of international currency use that many investors and policy-makers are interested in and that correspond to the first strand of contributions mentioned above. Measuring actual currency use outside the issuing area properly would require a survey based on strictly comparable and comprehensive census data for the currencies of the major advanced and emerging economies. This would imply a significant extension of the IMF portfolio survey in its current form.

This chapter aims at providing a quantitative concept to underpin the first strand of contributions, namely those focusing on the global role of currencies. The global concept developed intends to capture the significance of various currencies in the international financial system. This concept does not, therefore, distinguish between 'domestic' and 'international', but encompasses both dimensions. It provides information about the overall status of a currency and its financial markets in the global economy. More precisely, the chapter will develop a measure of the global role of currencies based on the magnitude and stage of development of various financial market segments that are open to a given currency. The measure is based on 15 size indicators and 16 structural indicators relating to the currency's financial markets and the underlying economy. In relation to financial markets, size indicators include the amount of assets, instruments and turnover; structural indicators focus on the regulatory quality or the absence of barriers. For the underlying economy, size indicators include the share in global GDP and trade; structural indicators relate to macroeconomic stability and the institutional environment. In the case of a number of countries, especially emerging economies, international activity in some financial market segments is constrained through capital account restrictions and other barriers. The chapter, therefore, also suggests an 'adjusted global concept' that takes into account existing restrictions to openness.

The chapter develops these indicators for 22 currencies, including the US dollar, euro, Japanese yen, pound sterling, Swiss franc, and the Australian, Canadian and New Zealand dollars, as well as 14 emerging market currencies of the main economies in Asia, Eastern Europe and Latin America. The intention is to expose currencies in emerging economies that have mostly been excluded so far from international currency concepts because of the very low level of activity in the international debt market in such currencies. The international role of the 14 main emerging market currencies combined – given by their aggregate share in the international debt securities markets – is only 2.9%. Yet, in recent years, many emerging economies have developed their financial systems and sought to give foreign investors greater access to their local currency markets. The global role concept reflects these trends better by taking a more comprehensive approach than the established international concept. At 11.2%, the global roles of these currencies are almost four times their international role. In line with the shift in weight towards emerging market currencies, the global roles of the main currencies are somewhat smaller than their international roles in the international debt market: the weight of the US dollar falls from 44.3% to 38.7% and the euro from 31.3% to 27.0%. By contrast, the weight of the yen rises somewhat, given the considerable size of Japan's domestic markets, from 5.3% to 8.6%.

The global role indicators are then applied to examine empirically international cross-border holdings of debt and equity securities for a sample of advanced and emerging economies. The empirical findings show that in addition to standard gravity variables, the indicators of a currency's global role help to explain cross-border financial integration. Both the global role of the domestic currency and that of the third country are positively related to bilateral cross-border holdings of financial assets. A comparison between the global role and the established international role in the sub-sample of emerging economies shows that the global role outperforms the international role in explaining cross-border holdings. Hence, the empirical findings lend support to the global role concept as being relevant to understand financial integration; from a policy perspective these findings are in line with the intuitive conjecture that financial market development facilitates international financial integration.

The chapter is structured as follows. Section 1.2 reviews the established concept of international currency use, analysing its appeal as well as its shortcomings. Section 1.3 develops a new concept of the global roles of currencies, applying it to 22 currencies of advanced and emerging economies. Section 1.4 presents an empirical application of the global role concept to international cross-border holdings. Section 1.5 discusses policy issues related to international and global currency use and section 1.6 concludes.

1.2   The established concept of international currency use in capital markets

The literature on the international role of currencies in capital markets is based on two key notions. First, a clear distinction between 'domestic' and 'international' is made; with the literature aiming at identifying strictly what is 'international' in terms of currency use, focusing therefore on the degree to which a currency is used 'outside its home country or issuing area' (Chinn and Frankel, 2007; ECB, 2007). Some authors define an international currency as one that is used in 'international transactions' (Kannan, 2007) or, more specifically, that is used 'outside its home country by non-residents for transactions with residents of the home country or with residents of third countries' (Lim, 2006). Other authors differentiate between cross-border transactions and cross-border holdings of international assets and liabilities (McCauley, 1997), but they also aim at strictly separating between international and domestic use.

The second key concept in the literature on the international role of currencies in capital markets is the international debt market, defined as the market of issuances by non-residents of a currency area. The literature focuses on this market because it reflects the clearest delineation of international activity from domestic activity in capital markets. Accordingly, the market for equities, government bonds and non-international corporate debt are seen as domestic.

The focus on the international debt market reflects the aim to capture the international role of a currency as a financing and investment currency, a concept that is derived from the matrix of functions of money. The international version of the matrix is often attributed to Kenen (1983) but can already be found in Cohen (1971) and is reproduced in a large number of contributions, making it the main conceptual framework of intentional currency use in the academic literature (see Portes and Papaionannou, 2006; Hartmann, 1998; Chinn and Frankel, 2007).[2] The international debt market also features prominently in the ECB's official review on the international role of the euro, even though the ECB uses a somewhat modified conceptual framework from the one used in the academic literature and also includes one global measure in overall debt markets (Table 1.1).

The international debt securities market is still the linchpin of international currency use as far as capital markets are concerned, both in official (ECB, 2007) and academic contributions. Detken and Hartmann (2000) provide a detailed review of this market in assessing the international role of the euro. They suggest taking the share of a given currency in the outstanding stock of the international debt securities market as the headline measure of international currency use. This measure is taken up in various proposals, including the official ECB reporting on the international role of the euro. The core measure focuses only on securities issued by non-residents of the respective currency area. In mid-2007, the shares of the main currencies in this market were 44.1% for the US dollar, 31.4% for the euro, and 5.3% for the Japanese yen (Table 1.2). The remaining close to 20% was spread over a large number of currencies, with the pound sterling and Swiss franc having a somewhat larger role than other currencies.

There is also a broader measure of international debt securities. This measure encompasses the narrow measure by adding securities that are issued by

Table 1.1   The matrix of international currency use

A: Theorist's matrix	Private use	Official use
Medium of exchange	Vehicle currency	Intervention currency
Unit of account	Quotation currency	Anchor currency
Store of value	Investment & financing currency	FX reserves currency
B: Practitioner's matrix	Use in financial markets	Use in third countries
	International debt markets	Exchange rate anchor, FX reserves
	Foreign exchange markets	
	International trade invoicing	Cash and parallel currency use

Source: Cohen (1971), Kenen (1983) for upper panel; ECB (2002) and subsequent editions for lower panel.

Table 1.2 The international debt securities market in comparison (amounts outstanding at end-2006, values at current exchange rates)

	Value outstanding in USD billion	of which: US dollar (% share)	of which: Euro (% share)	of which: Japanese yen (% share)
'Narrow' measure of market[a]	7,857	44.1	31.4	5.3
'Broad' measure of market[a]	18,449	36.3	47.0	2.7
Issuers and market share[b] (in %)	Share in total market	Share in USD market	Share in euro market	Share in yen market
Financial Institutions	77.8	77.2	78.6	74.3
Corporations	10.2	13.1	8.1	12.5
Governments	8.8	7.0	11.7	6.8
International Institutions	3.2	2.8	1.5	6.2

[a] The narrow measure accounts for 11.4% of the total global debt market, the broad measure for 26.8%.
[b] Refers to the market in the broad definition.
Source: ECB (2007) and Bank for International Settlements.

residents but that are estimated to end up in portfolios of non-residents. A security is included in the broad measure if it fulfils one of the following three conditions: (i) it is targeted at international investors (as suggested, for example, by the prospectus); (ii) it is placed by a syndicate of financial institutions of which at least one does not share the borrower's nationality; or (iii) it is governed by a law other than the domestic law. This definition is obviously not clear-cut in terms of actually delivering internationally held securities, and there is no assurance that what is targeted at international investors eventually ends up in their portfolios. This is why the literature has focused more on the narrow measure. However, both concepts cover only a fraction of the global bond market, with the narrow international concept covering 11.4% at end-2006 and the broad concept 26.8%.

In addition to size, there are a few structural issues that limit the overall usefulness of this market as a proxy for the international role of currencies.

- First, the international debt market is, to a large extent, a *US/EU phenomenon*, as these two regions together account for almost 80% of the market. In the dollar segment of the market, the EU accounts for about 60% of issuances; in the euro market, the United States and non-euro area EU countries account for close to 70%.
- Second, the international debt market is *relatively narrow in sectoral composition*, as financial institutions account for close to 80% of the market

(Table 1.2). The remaining 20% are split between corporates on the one hand, and governments or international institutions on the other. In 2006, the top international issuers in the euro were Morgan Stanley, HBOS/Bank of Scotland, Citigroup and HSBC in the group of financial institutions (issuing a total of close to EUR 30 billion), and Daimler Chrysler North America and Vodafone in the group of large corporations (issuing a total of over EUR 7 billion). The dollar market is dominated by financial institutions from the euro area and the United Kingdom.

- Third, the pattern of issuers suggests that specific *business motives* (balance sheet management, project financing and tax issues) as well as short-term cyclical factors (exchange rate forecasts and interest differentials) play an important role in international currency choice. ECB (2004) and Siegfried et al. (2007) investigate issuer behaviour and consider that hedging exposure to foreign exchange volatility is a key driver behind issuance activity. They draw this conclusion after combining bond data with balance sheet information and observe that foreign exposures of firms, through foreign subsidiaries or M&A activities, increase the likelihood of issuing in a foreign currency. Cohen (2005) finds that expectations of exchange rate changes and interest rate differentials – hence cyclical variables – play a decisive role in international bond issuance.

In sum, the market for international debt securities, especially in the narrow definition, measures a specific aspect of international currency issuance, but captures only a small share of the respective currency's role in the global capital market. In particular, by excluding the domestic bond market and the equity market, the international debt market does not reflect important motives of international currency use and overlooks key aspects of international financial integration.[3] Such motives are more related to the size and structure of domestic financial markets and the underlying macroeconomy (Bobba et al., 2007).

However, the established concept of the international use of currency is highly imprecise even in measuring cross-border use. This is confirmed by a comparison with available information on cross-border holdings of debt and equity securities (Table 1.3). The IMF's Coordinate Portfolio Investment Survey – although not free from reporting issues[4] – shows that USD 11.2 trillion of bonds are held across borders, far more than the total stock of international debt securities in the narrow definition (USD 7.8 trillion). At the same time, actual holdings fall far short of the broad measure of international debt securities (USD 18.4 trillion), suggesting that this measure is not in line with actual international currency use either.[5] Moreover, the IMF data show that cross-border holdings of equity securities are substantial, at USD 8.8 trillion. Omitting equities makes the results for the yen particularly biased, in which international holdings in equities are almost four times as high as holdings of debt. Hence, the established measure of international

Table 1.3 Cross-border bond and equity holdings (end-2005, USD billions)

Investment from:	United States	Euro area	United Kingdom	Japan	All countries
Investment in:					
Panel A: Bonds					
United States	...	779.6	320.0	55.1	3601.0
Euro area	296.1	...	455.4	529.8	2488.8
United Kingdom	276.9	573.5	...	74.4	1219.9
Japan	26.7	102.3	52.9	...	279.1
China	1.6	2.6	1.5	0.4	15.8
All countries	1273.4	2520.5	1297.9	1706.7	11160.5
Panel B: Equities					
United States	...	668.2	270.0	192.6	1698.3
Euro area	757.4	...	307.2	71.5	1605.4
United Kingdom	537.9	357.3	...	39.5	1217.8
Japan	493.3	207.6	143.0	...	953.8
China	26.9	12.8	8.9	3.6	96.2
All countries	3317.7	1872.8	1076.0	408.6	8802.7

Note: Figures exclude intra-euro area cross-border holdings.
Source: IMF (Coordinated Portfolio Investment Survey).

currency use is precise in accounting for such activity in a very specific and relatively narrow market segment, but does not capture the actual international use, nor the broader standing of individual currencies in the world economy.

1.3 A global concept of currency use

This section presents a global concept of currency use. It starts by addressing two main questions: what contribution does a 'global role of currencies' concept make to understanding international monetary and financial developments and related policy issues; and what should be the main ingredients of such a concept?

1.3.1 Motivation

As we have seen, the established notion of international roles of currencies focuses on the use of currencies outside their issuing area. This notion has often been used in a much wider context, related to the broader standing or recognition of a currency. A rising international role was seen as a rise in the importance of the respective currency in the global economy. However, the linchpin measurement of international currency use in the academic literature, based on the share in the international debt securities market, is an imprecise proxy of actual currency use outside the issuing area. In order to properly measure actual currency use outside the issuing area, a survey based on strictly comparable comprehensive census data for all of the currencies of the major advanced and emerging economies would be required. The United States conducts a census of this sort periodically, but updates it using less satisfactory data in-between updates. A few other countries conduct similar censuses, but do not coordinate the dating and coverage of their benchmark studies.[6]

But even if full information on international investment holdings by currency breakdowns were available globally, doubts would remain with regard to the significance of the distinction between 'domestic' and 'international' in a globalized financial system. Many economic agents in this market – in particular large financial institutions and corporations – are global actors, and it is thus evident that they are cast in a domestic/international scheme. The important role played by financial on-shore and off-shore centres illustrates the residency issue, which is often motivated by tax considerations, arising in international financial statistics even today.

The established international concept of currency use based on the international debt market becomes even less pertinent when used in the wider context of international monetary and financial issues; namely, whenever the global standing of a certain currency in the world economy is discussed. For the latter type of issue, a 'global concept' of the standing of a currency would be more appropriate. Such a concept should reflect the standing in terms of the size and stage of development of the financial markets and the instruments available in this currency, and the size and stage of development of the underlying economy. Investment decisions in global asset allocations closely link the currency choice to the overall size and development of financial markets as well as the underlying economy. Sovereign wealth funds hold equity in a certain currency because they aim to acquire a stake in the underlying firm and indirectly partake in the development of the underlying economy; central banks hold securities in a certain currency because of the liquidity of the foreign exchange markets in this currency; banks hold government paper because of the size and liquidity of the underling bond market; and investors in general hold a certain currency also reflecting confidence in the stability of its intrinsic value. Hence, such a summary measure of the global role could also be a benchmark for currency allocation in the set-up of an international portfolio.

1.3.2 Implementation

This section applies the global concept introduced above to the currencies of eight advanced economies and 14 emerging economies (listed in Table 1.4) and compares the results with the established international currency concept. In line with the earlier presentation, the global role of currencies is based on both the size and the structural characteristics of each currency's capital market and underlying economy (Tables 1.4 and 1.5, respectively).

Table 1.4 Global role of currencies – selected size indicators (2006)

	Advanced Economies										
Indicator	**United States**	**Euro Area**	**Japan**	**United Kingdom**	**Canada**	**Australia**	**Switzerland**	**New Zealand**	**Weight in composite global indicator**	**Total advanced (shares in**	**Total EME world total)**
Size of economy									**0.33**		
Share in world GDP in current prices (in %)	27.30	21.90	9.10	5.00	2.60	1.60	0.80	0.20	(0.5)	68.5	18.9
Share in global trade (imp. + exp) (in %)	15.00	14.30	5.80	6.00	3.70	1.30	1.50	0.30	(0.5)	47.9	29.7
Size of financial markets									**0.67**		
Debt market (in bn USD) – "broad" concept									0.33		
Amounts outstanding of domestic debt									(0.67)		
Governments	6,247	5,598	6,748	835	615	97	111	20		84.0%	11.0%
Financial Institutions	13,812	3,566	986	379	254	215	98	0		91.6%	4.9%
Corporations	2,800	1,323	673	23	116	144	14	0		88.7%	8.5%
Amounts outstanding of international debt											
Governments	468	979	34	18	17	11	23	2	(0.33)	95.4%	0.2%
Financial Institutions	5,160	6,559	373	1,291	147	148	227	31		97.1%	0.9%
Corporations	873	678	63	193	8	6	16	0		97.5%	0.5%
International institutions	187	129	31	96	9	36	8	14		86.7%	3.6%

Total amount of debt securities outstanding	29,547	18,831	8,908	2,835	1,166	658	497	68		90.1%	6.3%
Amounts outstanding of international debt, by type											
Money market instruments	287	354	14	147	3	11	20	5		96.1%	2.9%
Bonds and notes	6,401	7,990	487	1,450	178	191	254	42		96.7%	0.8%
Stock market									0.33		
Market capitalization (in bn USD, end 2006)	19,569	8,354	4,796	3,794	1,701	1,096	1,212	45	(0.5)		
as % of world market capitalization	38.60%	16.50%	9.50%	7.50%	3.40%	2.20%	2.40%	0.10%		80.2%	14.6%
Number of listed companies	6,005	3,114	2,883	3,256	3,842	1,829	348	182	(0.1)	52.8%	23.5%
Share of foreign listed companies[a] in %	14.50	20.60	0.90	10.50	1.40	4.30	26.40	17.00	(0.1)	12.0	8.5
Average daily turnover (in mn USD)	136,252	40,877	24,493	30,046	5,107	3,411	5,564	89	(0.1)	88.4%	7.4%
Average turnover velocity (% of market capitalization)	161.50%	136.00%	123.90%	124.80%	76.40%	88.40%	130.20%	51.60%			

(*Continued*)

Table 1.4   (Continued)

	Advanced Economies										
Indicator	United States	Euro Area	Japan	United Kingdom	Canada	Australia	Switzerland	New Zealand	Weight in composite global indicator	Total advanced	Total EME (shares in world total)
New capital raised in IPOs (in bn USD)	54.5	78.6	na	55.8	9.1	12.9	2.9	0.2	(0.1)	66.0%	24.1%
Number of ETFs listed (end 2006)	340	437	13	na	33	9	61	6	(0.1)	79.3%	10.4%
Dervivates market									0.17		
OTC interest rate derivatives, amounts outstanding (in bn USD)	97,612	112,116	37,954	22,274	2,125	1,042	3,544	26	(0.33)	94.8%	0.2%
OTC interest rate derivatives, daily turnover (in bn USD)	532	656	137	172	na	na	na	na	(0.33)	88.8%	0.0%
OTC FX derivatives, amounts outstanding (in bn USD)	33,775	15,907	9,548	6,128	1,764	1,498	2,307	48	(0.33)	176.6%	1.6%

Foreign exchange (FX) market

									0.17		
Share in global FX market turnover (April 2007)	43.20%	18.50%	8.30%	7.50%	2.10%	3.40%	3.40%	1.00%	(0.5)	87.4%	5.5%
Share in global FX reserves[b]	64.70%	25.80%	3.20%	4.40%	na	na	0.20%	na	(0.5)	98.3%	0.0%

	Emerging Asia								Latin America			Emerging Europe & Africa			
Indicator	Hong Kong	Singapore	China	India	South Korea	Malaysia	Thailand	Indonesia	Brazil	Mexico	Argentina	Russia	Turkey	South Africa	World
Size of economy															
Share in world GDP in current prices (in %)	0.4	0.3	5.5	1.8	1.8	0.3	0.4	0.8	2.2	1.7	0.4	2.0	0.8	0.5	$48,245 bn
Share in global trade (imp. + exp) (in %)	3.1	2.6	7.9	1.8	3.1	1.4	1.2	0.9	1.1	2.2	0.4	2.2	1.1	0.7	$24,337 bn
Size of financial markets															
Debt market (in bn USD) – broad concept															
Amounts outstanding of domestic debt															
Governments	18	56	786	305	460	59	73	69	512	168	45	33	na	70	24,145
Financial Institutions	25	18	328	16	292	34	0	4	178	112	1	0	na	25	21,070
Corporations	8	5	70	5	258	53	36	4	6	27	0	0	na	14	5,744
Amounts outstanding of international debt															
Governments	1	0	0	0	0	0	0	0	3	0	0	0	na	0	1,627

(*Continued*)

Table 1.4   (Continued)

Indicator	Emerging Asia								Latin America			Emerging Europe & Africa			World
	Hong Kong	Singapore	China	India	South Korea	Malaysia	Thailand	Indonesia	Brazil	Mexico	Argentina	Russia	Turkey	South Africa	
Financial Institutions	77	19	1	0	0	0	2	1	6	7	0	2	na	9	14,348
Corporations	2	1	0	0	1	1	0	0	0	2	0	1	na	2	1,884
International institutions	3	0	0	0	0	1	0	0	1	2	0	1	na	13	588
Total amounts outstanding	135	101	1,185	326	1,011	148	112	77	707	319	47	37	na	133	69,405
Amounts outstanding of international debt, by type															
Money market instruments	22	2	0	0	0	0	0	0	0	1	0	0	na	0	875
Bonds and notes	62	19	2	0	1	1	3	1	11	10	1	3	na	23	17,571
Stock market															
Market capitalization (in bn USD, end 2006)	1,715	384	1,145	774	834	236	140	139	710	348	51	na	162	711	50,635
as % of world market capitalization	3.4%	0.8%	2.3%	1.5%	1.6%	0.5%	0.3%	0.3%	1.4%	0.7%	0.1%	na	0.3%	1.4%	
Number of listed companies	1,173	708	1,421	1,156	1,689	1,025	518	344	350	335	106	na	316	389	40,635
Share of foreign listed companies in %	0.7	34.9	0.0	0.0	0.0	0.4	0.0	0.0	0.9	60.6	4.7	na	0.0	7.7%	

Average daily turnover (in mn USD)	3,370	721	4,809	1,694	5,434	306	415	202	1,123	386	21	na	891	1,254	278,252
Average turnover velocity (% of market capitalization)	62.1%	58.2%	173.3%	67.8%	171.4%	36.2%	72.7%	44.8%	45.5%	29.6%	7.2%	na	141.3%	48.9%	
New capital raised in IPOs (in bn USD)	43.0	4.8	13.8	4.5	2.9	0.3	0.5	0.4	6.0	0.9	0.0	na	0.9	0.0	324
Number of ETFs listed (end 2006)	9	13	4	5	12	1	na	na	1	58	na	na	6	9	1,134
Dervivates market															
OTC interest rate derivatives, amounts outstanding (in bn USD)	453	na	na	na	na	na	2	na	na	na	na	na	na	na	291,987
OTC interest rate derivatives, daily turnover (in bn USD)	na	na	na	na	na	na	na	na	na	na	na	na	na	na	1,686
OTC FX derivatives, amounts outstanding (in bn USD)	631	na	na	na	na	na	6	na	na	na	na	na	na	na	40,179

(Continued)

Table 1.4   (Continued)

Indicator	Emerging Asia								Latin America			Emerging Europe & Africa			
	Hong Kong	Singapore	China	India	South Korea	Malaysia	Thailand	Indonesia	Brazil	Mexico	Argentina	Russia	Turkey	South Africa	World
Foreign exchange (FX) market															
Share in global FX market turnover (April 2007)	1.4%	0.6%	0.3	0.4%	0.6%	0.1%	0.1%	0.1%	0.2%	0.7%	na	0.4%	0.1%	0.5%	100.0%
Share in global FX reserves[b]	na	na	0.0%	na	na	na	na	na	na	na	na	na	na	na	

Sources: IMF (World Economic Outlook), World Federation of Exchanges (Annual Report 2006), BIS, ECB.

[a] Including intra-European listings.

[b] The currency shares are based on the reserves of member countries which report the currency composition of their foreign exchange reserves.

Table 1.5 Global role of currencies – selected structural indicators

Indicator	Weights in the composite global indicator	United States	Euro Area	Japan	United Kingdom	Canada	Australia	Switzerland	New Zealand
Financial market regulation	0.25								
Disclosure[a]	(0.20)	100	49	75	83	92	75	67	67
Liability[a]	(0.20)	100	44	66	66	100	66	44	44
Supervision[a]	(0.20)	90	38	0	68	80	90	33	33
Access to equity[a]	(0.20)	67	54	49	63	64	60	61	58
Financial market sophistication[b]	(0.20)	91	83	79	99	91	94	87	97
Size of state	0.25								
Property rights[a]	(0.25)	100	91	100	100	100	100	100	100
Freedom of corruption[a]	(0.25)	79	74	68	90	93	87	91	95
SOE Investment (in % of gross domestic investment)[a]	(0.25)	4	12	8	11	0	16	0	0
Share of government-owned banks (in %)[a]	(0.25)	0	29	0	0	0	12	13	0
Monetary Issues	0.25								
Central bank independence[c]	(0.50)	48	80	38	31	47	29	63	38
Inflation volatility of last 5 years (in %)[d]	(0.25)	0.73	0.07	0.44	0.47	0.34	0.44	0.24	0.63
Inflation absolute in 2006 (in %)[d]	(0.25)	3.24	2.19	0.30	2.30	2.00	3.54	1.05	3.36

(Continued)

Table 1.5.   (Continued)

Indicator	Weights in the composite global indicator	United States	Euro Area	Japan	United Kingdom	Canada	Australia	Switzerland	New Zealand
Trade barriers (Goods and Finance)	0.25								
Freedom of regulatory trade barriers[e]	(0.25)	82	86	69	89	82	90	87	92
International capital market controls[e]	(0.25)	84	82	71	92	83	56	86	91
Capital account openness (Chinn and Ito, 2006, normalised to 0-100)	(0.25)	100	96.6	100	100	100	68.5	93.7	100
Freedom to own foreign currency bank account[e]	(0.25)	100	100	100	100	100	100	100	100

	Emerging Asia								Latin America			Emerging Europe & Africa		
Indicator	Hong Kong	Singapore	China	India	South Korea	Malaysia	Thailand	Indonesia	Brazil	Mexico	Argentina	Russia	Turkey	South Africa
Financial market regulation														
Disclosure[a]	92	100	na	92	75	92	92	50	25	58	50	na	50	83

Liability[a]	66	66	na	66	66	66	22	66	33	11	22	na	22	66
Supervision[a]	87	87	na	67	25	77	72	62	58	35	58	na	63	25
Access to equity[a]	55	55	na	53	50	51	42	45	41	39	32	na	50	59
Financial market sophistication[b]	100	97	54	79	83	88	74	75	66	69	56	58	71	83
Size of state														
Property rights[a]	100	100	na	60	100	80	100	60	60	60	80	na	80	60
Freedom of corruption[a]	70	99	na	25	43	36	21	1	31	20	21	na	22	44
SOE Investment (in % of gross domestic investment)[a]	0	0	na	41	24	16	15	13	22	21	10	na	37	19
Share of government-owned banks (in %)[a]	0	14	na	85	25	10	17	43	32	36	61	na	56	0
Monetary Issues														
Central bank independence[e]	na	17	60	28	37	47	21	84	46	64	79	62	85	48

(*Continued*)

Table 1.5 (Continued)

Indicator	Emerging Asia								Latin America			Emerging Europe & Africa		
	Hong Kong	Singapore	China	India	South Korea	Malaysia	Thailand	Indonesia	Brazil	Mexico	Argentina	Russia	Turkey	South Africa
Inflation volatility of last 5 years (in %)[d]	2.18	0.76	1.67	0.98	0.57	1.08	1.74	3.10	3.99	0.56	7.99	2.38	16.09	2.90
Inflation absolute in 2006 (in %)[d]	2.02	0.97	1.47	6.15	2.24	3.59	4.64	13.10	4.20	3.63	10.90	9.68	9.60	4.69
Trade barriers (Goods and Finance)														
Freedom of regulatory trade barriers[e]	93	93	62	64	74	78	70	60	57	72	60	57	64	77
International capital market controls[e]	92	81	39	43	46	42	44	37	66	57	59	39	50	49

Capital acct.	100	100	15.2	15.2	39.0	39.0	39.0	68.5	45.3	68.5	39.0	39.0	15.2	15.2
openness (Chinn/Ito, 2006, norm. to 0–100)														
Freedom to own foreign currency bank account[e]	100	100	50	0	100	0	0	100	50	50	100	50	100	50

Sources:
[a] La Porta, Lopez-de-Silanes and Shleifer (2006).
[b] World Economic Forum, Global Competitiveness Index.
[c] The Fraser Institute.
[d] Crowe and Meade (2007).
[e] IMF, World Economic Outlook.

1.3.2.1   Size indicators

Starting with size indicators, four main markets are considered: debt securities; equity securities; interest rate derivatives; and foreign exchange markets. All four markets are massive, even when compared with global GDP. At end-2006, the outstanding global volume of debt securities was USD 69.4 trillion; total stock market capitalization amounted to USD 50.6 trillion; and the outstanding amounts of OTC interest rate derivatives amounted to USD 291.9 trillion. As a percentage of world GDP, these figures represent 144%, 105% and 606%, respectively. The size measures in terms of market volume are complemented by specific information relevant for each market segment. For example, in the equity market, the number of listed firms, the number of foreign listed companies, turnover and the recent volume of IPOs are considered (see Table 1.4 for more details). Moreover, the size indicators account for the weight of the economy in the global economy and its share in global trade.

As expected, advanced economy currencies dominate in virtually all size components and their weight in global financial markets is well above their share in global GDP (68.5%) or global trade (47.9%). These economies account for 90% of global debt securities outstanding and 80.2% of the global stock market capitalization. In particular, financial institutions of advanced economies are dominant debt issuers, with US financial institutions alone accounting for one-fifth of the global debt market. In advanced economies, the US dollar weight is particularly important, owing to its share in the global equity market, which is at least twice that of the euro in terms of capitalization, number of listed companies and turnover. The second segment where the dollar stands out relative to the euro is the foreign exchange market, in which US dollar turnover is more than twice that of the euro. In the debt market, the size advantage for the dollar stems mainly from the debt of financial institutions, which is about four times as large as the debt levels outstanding for European financial institutions. The dollar also has the edge in a corporate debt market that is twice that of the euro area. By contrast, the government debt market is much more equal in size for both currencies, and in interest rate derivatives the euro segment actually exceeds that of the US dollar. From the perspective of third-country investors, equity, foreign exchange and private issuers in the bond market are likely to be the most attractive size features of the dollar. A review of the size indicators for the Japanese yen and the pound sterling, two currencies with a considerable global role, shows how uneven the various parameters are distributed among the two. The yen dwarfs the pound in terms of the size of the underlying debt market, but this is mainly due to government debt; with regard to international debt, the pound has the larger market. In equity market terms, both currencies possess a market that is broadly comparable in size; also in FX markets their role is roughly the same.

Emerging market currencies clearly carry a far smaller weight in terms of financial market size than currencies of advanced economies. Interestingly, stock markets are more than twice as important as debt markets, with global shares of 14.6% and 6.4% respectively. Hong Kong and Mainland China combined rank fifth in global stock market capitalization, after the United States, the euro area, Japan and the United Kingdom. Almost one quarter of globally listed firms are listed on EME stock markets, illustrating a strong numerical participation in these markets. EME markets are also relatively important in terms of raising new capital through initial public offerings (about 24%), reflecting a buoyant growth in new access to these markets and IPO activity, especially in Hong Kong but also in Mainland China. Consequently, if EME currencies are to play a greater international role, this is likely to come first through stock markets, where they are a more important player than in global debt markets. The picture could shift somewhat once the renminbi becomes convertible, as outstanding government debt in Mainland China is relatively high in absolute terms and almost stands at the same level as in the United Kingdom.

Emerging market currencies play only a limited role in global derivatives markets, but they are beginning to play a more visible role in global foreign exchange markets. Together, they currently account for about 6% of global FX market turnover. Although this share appears small, the absolute amounts are often quite significant in relation to other financial markets, considering also the particularly high total turnover in the global FX market of close to USD 2 trillion per day. Moreover, it should be noted that whereas FX turnover was negligible in most EMEs until a few years ago, turnover is rising, especially in countries such as Hong Kong, Mexico and South Korea.

1.3.2.2 Structural indicators

Structural indicators may shed further light on the relatively limited role of EME currencies so far. These indicators aim at gauging the development of markets from a more regulatory point of view (Table 1.5). They need to be interpreted with caution, however, since they involve a significant amount of judgement, and only a few indicators are available across the sample of eight advanced and 14 emerging economies considered here.

These indicators, which are based on La Porta, Lopez-de-Silanes and Shleifer (2006), the World Economic Forum's Global Competitiveness Report, the IMF and the Fraser Institute, show that the United States is seen as being particularly advanced in terms of financial market regulation (based on data available until end-2006). The US achieves higher scores than many other advanced economies in terms of disclosure, supervision and financial market sophistication. With the notable exception of Hong Kong and Singapore, most emerging market economies achieve lower scores than the United States, and the gap is generally somewhat wider in the financial market sphere than in barriers to trade in goods and financial services.

These indicators may reveal why the amount of cross-border holdings of financial securities does not exactly mirror the relative size of financial markets, as international access to financial markets may be either fostered or hampered by structural factors. Another way to capture international access is through capital account openness, which reveals another large gap between advanced economies and emerging markets (Chinn and Ito, 2006). Structural indicators mostly reflect the result of direct policy choices. This is the case for many indicators relevant for the regulation and supervision of financial markets, but also for the degree of state involvement in financial markets – for example, through government-owned or government-sponsored financial institutions. Structural indicators are important policy variables that are likely to have an impact not only on domestic financial market development but also on the role of international actors. Hence, they are the bridge to a policy approach to international currency use, which will be dealt with in Section 1.5.

1.3.3   A composite indicator of the global roles of currencies: Main findings

Combining the various size and structural indicators into one single indicator would yield an approximation for one measure of the global role of currencies. Of course, there is no a priori and robust weighting scheme for the various components, and the aggregation is potentially even more problematic for structural indicators than for size indicators. Therefore, we develop a very crude approach, which is necessarily ad hoc, but may serve to illustrate some magnitude of comparison between countries. In order to do so, we construct a composite global indicator that is made up of 15 individual size indicators and 16 individual structural indicators (the individual categories and weights are listed in Tables 1.4 and 1.5). The final global roles indicator is then given by the global size indicator adjusted for the structural indicators relative to a benchmark, for which the United States is used. For example, if a currency receives a rating in the structural indicator of half compared with that of the United States, its global indicator is only half of what its size indicator alone would have suggested. The results of this exercise are summarized in Table 1.6 and are also compared with the traditional structural measure. What are the main findings?

- First, emerging market currencies play a more significant global role than the international concept would suggest. Whereas in the established international concept they jointly carry a weight of only 2.9%, the global role indicator assigns them a share of 11.2%, i.e. almost four times as much. The reason is that these currencies are hardly represented in the international debt market, but nevertheless dispose of considerable overall financial markets in terms of assets, breadth and turnover, and they see their shares rising also in areas such as the global foreign exchange market. The

Table 1.6   The Global roles of currencies based on size and structural indicators (percentages)

	Global role measure	Adjusted global role measure	Established international role measure	Global role measure by country groups	Size indicator US = 100	Structural indicator US = 100	Capital account openness
Advanced economy currencies	*88.8*	*93.5*	*97.1*	*100.0*		*96.2*	*99.6*
1 US dollar	38.7	41.2	44.3	43.7	100.0	100.0	100.0
2 Euro	27.0	27.7	31.3	30.4	66.8	104.2	96.6
3 Japanese yen	8.6	9.2	5.3	9.9	25.3	89.5	100.0
4 Pound sterling	7.1	7.5	9.3	7.9	18.8	96.0	100.0
5 Canadian dollar	2.7	2.9	1.1	3.1	7.1	100.7	100.0
6 Swiss franc	2.3	2.4	3.3	2.5	5.9	97.3	100.0
7 Australian dollar	1.8	1.9	1.9	1.8	4.6	92.4	100.0
8 New Zealand dollar	0.7	0.7	0.6	0.6	1.6	89.9	100.0
Emerging market currencies	*11.2*	*6.5*	*2.9*	*100.0*		*70.5*	*45.6*
1 Mexican peso	1.9	1.4	0.1	15.7	6.7	68.6	68.5
2 Singapore dollar	1.5	1.6	0.2	14.0	4.3	96.4	100.0
3 Hong Kong dollar	1.4	1.4	0.6	13.4	4.5	87.8	100.0
4 South Korean won	1.3	0.5	0.0	12.0	4.3	81.5	39.0
5 Chinese renminbi	1.3	0.2	0.0	11.4	8.6	38.4	15.2
6 Indian rupee	0.8	0.1	0.0	6.8	2.8	70.1	15.2
7 Brazilian real	0.8	0.4	0.1	6.4	2.9	64.8	45.3
8 South African rand	0.5	0.1	0.4	4.4	1.8	70.8	15.2
9 Turkish lira	0.3	0.1	0.2	3.4	1.2	85.0	15.2
10 Malaysian ringgit	0.3	0.1	0.0	3.0	1.3	70.4	39.0
11 Russian rouble	0.3	0.1	0.0	2.6	2.1	36.5	39.0
12 Indonesian rupiah	0.3	0.2	0.0	2.6	1.0	78.1	68.5
13 Thai baht	0.3	0.1	0.0	2.2	1.1	59.3	39.0
14 Argentinan peso	0.2	0.1	0.0	2.1	0.8	79.2	39.0

Note: The global role measure comprises 15 size and 16 structural indicators of a currency's financial markets and the underlying economy (provided in Tables 1.4 and 1.5 and summarized in columns 5 and 6 of this table). The adjusted global role measure takes account of financial markets' openness (which is shown in the last column, based on Chinn and Ito (2006), normalized to 0–100). The established international role measure is based on the currency's share in the international debt market.
Source: Author's compilation.

fact that the global role of these currencies is still relatively limited is due to the lower stage of financial development, reflected in a smaller size of their markets vis-à-vis advanced economies, and the fact that some of them are still lagging in terms of structural development and openness.

- Second, the weight of the dollar and euro both shrink compared with their pure 'international role', but their relationship – whereby the euro reaches about 70% of the dollar's value – remains unchanged. This illustrates that the international measure used so far is heavily concentrated on these two currencies. The US dollar is clearly the leading global currency, with a global share of 38.7%, well above the share of the US economy, which reflects the size and structural stage of development of US financial markets.
- Third, the Japanese yen and pound sterling switch places from an international to a global concept, as, for the latter, the larger domestic financial market in Japan plays a role, and the same holds true for the Canadian dollar and the Swiss franc. Similarly to the pound sterling, the Swiss franc is used much more internationally than its domestic markets would suggest.
- Fourth, among emerging market currencies, the Mexican peso, the Singapore and Hong Kong dollars and the Korean and Chinese renminbi stand out with a relatively significant global role. Singapore and Hong Kong benefit from the fact that in terms of financial market regulation, governance and openness, their markets are virtually as developed as those of the United States as a benchmark. The inverse holds true for the renminbi, which scores highly in size but lower in structural factors.

1.3.3.1   An adjusted global role

Not all financial markets are equally open to international investors. Restrictions exist in particular in several emerging economies, which retain capital account restrictions or other barriers to foreign participation in financial markets. To address this aspect, one can adjust the global role for the degree of openness. To keep matters relatively straightforward, we take a single index – the one developed by Chinn and Ito (2006) – but one can in theory also construct composite indices of financial market openness from various sources.

Adjusting the global role measure for the degree of openness shows that the share of emerging market currencies drops by roughly half, from 11.2% to 6.5%, which is due to the fact that, on average, the emerging markets achieve a reading on the openness index of only 45.6% of the most open markets. Nevertheless, their share remains double the share in the established concept. The drop in the global role owing to actual openness is particularly significant for countries such as China, which maintain broad capital account restrictions. By contrast, for financial centres such as

Hong Kong and Singapore the result remains largely unchanged, given their openness and full integration into the international financial system.

1.4   Empirical application of the global role concept to cross-border holdings

We can now apply the global role measure of currency use to an empirical issue to see whether it provides value added in the context of international finance. We choose the issue of cross-border holdings of financial assets to see whether the global role measure helps to explain some of the phenomena linked to such holdings, especially the home bias puzzle. Home bias in international portfolio allocation, reflecting the fact that cross-border portfolio holdings fall short of benchmarks derived from portfolio models, is a well-established puzzle in international finance. It is attributed to a wide range of factors, including transaction and information costs (Portes and Rey, 2005; Cai and Warnock, 2006), the quality of institutions (Burger and Warnock, 2003; Gelos and Wei, 2005), or exchange rate volatility (Fidora, Fratzscher and Thimann, 2008).

We can test whether the global role of a country's currency is linked to cross-border holdings of financial assets. We use the IMF Coordinate Portfolio Investment Survey (CPIS) database and focus on the 22 currencies of the eight advanced and 14 emerging economies for which the global role indicator has been developed in this chapter. Since we use bilateral cross-border holdings, we arrive at 440 observations for the whole sample and 164 observations for the emerging market currency sample. As a further robustness check we take the whole sample excluding the two most dominant currencies, the dollar and the euro.

Let cb_{ij} be the total cross-border holdings of debt and equity securities from country i in country j for end-2006 (in USD million) as derived from the CPIS database. We then estimate standard gravity-type models to explain such cross-border holdings, including the global role of the country's currency. The four estimated equations, standardized and expressed as logarithms, are shown below. We start with the narrow model that includes only the global role of the currency of the origin country, gr_i, and that of the destination country, gr_j, in addition to a constant:

$$cb_{i,j} = \alpha + \beta_1 \cdot gr_i + \beta_2 \cdot gr_j + \varepsilon \tag{1}$$

The results show both variables to be significant; the global role of the origin country is significant at the 1% level in all samples; that of the destination country is significant at this level for all except the emerging market sample. Comparing the size of the coefficient suggests that the global role of the origin country's currency is about twice as important as that of the destination country in explaining bilateral cross-border holdings (Table 1.7).

Table 1.7 Determinants of cross-border portfolio holdings across advanced and emerging market economies
(Dependent variable: total bilateral cross-border portfolio holdings according to IMF CPIS)

Regressors	Total sample				Emerging markets				Total sample without dollar and euro			
	(1)	(2)	(3)	(4)	(1)	(2)	(3)	(4)	(1)	(2)	(3)	(4)
Global role i	0.504***	0.482***	0.423***		0.385***	0.397***	0.455***		0.487***	0.490***	0.643***	
Global role j	0.308***	0.284***	0.188***		0.128*	0.131*	0.143*		0.199***	0.200***	0.196***	
Distance		−0.158***	−0.156***	−0.1333***		−0.318***	−0.288***	−0.274***		−0.144***	−0.135***	−0.1777***
Common border		−0.022	−0.036	0.095		0.196	0.3	0.153		0.256	0.34	−0.133
Common language		0.296***	0.340***	0.526***		0.043	−0.037	0.287		0.398***	0.340***	0.482***
GDP i			0.076	0.393***			−0.187**	−0.044			−0.233***	0.198***
GDP j			0.125**	0.263***			−0.014	0.034			0.01	0.142***
Constant	−0.016	−0.113**	−0.128***	−0.194***	−0.042	−0.083	−0.073	0.087	−0.024	−0.144***	−0.133***	−0.139**
Number of Obs.	440	440	440	440	164	164	164	164	359	359	359	359
Adj. R squared	0.341	0.383	0.389	0.306	0.144	0.251	0.274	0.097	0.267	0.323	0.351	0.104
F (df)	114.66	55.60	40.96	39.82	14.67	11.95	9.77	4.48	66.21	35.13	28.62	9.27
Prob > F	0.000	0.000	0.000	0.000	0.000	0.000	0.000	0.001	0.000	0.000	0.000	0.000
Log-Likeli-hood			−511.84	−540.77			−202.40	−221.33			−427.84	−486.75
LR-test value (df)			57.855 (2)				37.852 (2)				117.822 (2)	

Note: The dependent variable is CBij, cross-border holdings of bonds and equity securities from country i into country j at end 2006.
Source: IMF Coordinated Portfolio Investment Survey.
The total country sample includes currencies of eight advanced and 14 emerging market economies.
All variables are standardised and expressed in logs; estimation is OLS; significance levels are indicated as follows: * = 10%; ** = 5%; *** = 1%.

As a second step, we add standard gravity variables such as distance and dummies for common border and common language to the equation; and we add proxies for the size of both economies through GDP for countries i and j to yield further estimation equations:

$$cb_{i,j} = \alpha + \beta_1 \cdot gr_i + \beta_2 \cdot gr_j + \beta_3 \cdot dist_{ij} + \beta_4 \cdot border_{ij} + \beta_5 \cdot lang_{ij} + \varepsilon \qquad (2)$$

$$cb_{i,j} = \alpha + \beta_1 \cdot gr_i + \beta_2 \cdot gr_j + \beta_3 \cdot dist_{ij} + \beta_4 \cdot border_{ij} + \beta_5 \cdot lang_{ij}$$
$$+ \beta_6 \cdot gdp_i + \beta_7 \cdot gdp_j + \varepsilon \qquad (3)$$

The results show that the global role estimators remain broadly similar in magnitude and significance across approaches and samples, while the gravity variables carry the expected sign and are significant overall as well. The possible set of gravity variables in the literature is, of course, wider, but most are more pertinent for international trade models rather than finance.

To check robustness, we also estimate cross-border holdings in the three samples without the global role indicators. It turns out that this approach works less well for all samples, and works particularly poorly for the emerging market sample. As discussed above, these findings suggest that the global role indicators carry explanatory power for advanced economies and their international financial integration, and are particularly relevant in the context of emerging markets, where other gravity-type indicators carry limited explanatory value.

How does the global role indicator fare directly against the established measure? We compare both concepts, each combined with the standard gravity variables in Table 1.8. As expected, the largest difference is shown in the emerging market sample, where the global role concept is significant to explain cross-border holdings, whereas the established international measure is not. This is not surprising, given that the international role measure focuses on the international debt market only, while emerging economy currencies play virtually no role. However, based on standard information criteria, there is positive support for the global role compared with the international role, as well as for the full sample, and even very strong support for the sample without the dominating currencies of the euro and the dollar. Again, this is in line with the hypothesis that for the main established currencies the international concept is not far off the global concept, whereas for other currencies the results are significantly different. The general finding that financial development fosters international financial integration and therefore a falling home bias seems to be reasonably robust.

1.5 Policies

While the previous sections have provided a positive analysis of a country's global or international role, this section takes a normative perspective,

Table 1.8.   Determinants of cross-border portfolio holdings: Comparison of "global role" and "international role" measures
(Dependent variable: total bilateral cross-border portfolio holdings according to IMF CPIS)

	Total sample		Emerging markets		Total sample w/o dollar, euro	
	(1)	(2)	(1)	(2)	(1)	(2)
Regressor						
Distance	−0.156***	−0.157***	−0.288***	−0.293***	−0.135***	−0.167***
Common border	−0.036	−0.052	0.300	0.153	0.340	0.200
Common language	0.340***	0.343***	−0.037	0.222	0.340***	0.342***
GDP i	0.076	0.116**	−0.187**	−0.009	−0.233***	−0.059
GDP j	0.125**	0.138**	−0.014	0.054	0.010	0.054
Global role i	0.423***		0.455***		0.643***	
Global role j	0.188***		0.143*		0.196***	
International role i		0.385***		0.088		0.497***
International role j		0.178***		0.053		0.165***
Constant	−0.128***	−0.128***	−0.073	−0.079	−0.133***	−0.122**
Number of Obs.	440	440	164	164	359	359
Adj. R squared	0.389	0.382	0.274	0.093	0.351	0.304
F (df)	40.96	39.8	9.77	3.39	28.62	23.3
Prob > F	0.000	0.000	0.000	0.002	0.000	0.000
Log-Likelihood	−511.84	−514.30	−202.40	−220.58	−427.84	−440.405
LR-test value (df)	223.9 (7)	218.9 (7)	59.61 (7)	23.2 (7)	162.13 (7)	136.99 (7)
BIC'	−181.37	−176.36	−23.91	12.46	−120.94	−95.802
Difference of BIC'		5.00		36.35		25.14
Support for global model		positive		very strong		very strong

Note: The dependent variable is CBij, cross-border holdings of bonds and equity securities from country i into country j at end -2006.
(*source*: IMF). The total country sample includes currencies of eight advanced and 14 emerging market economies.
All variable are standardised and expressed in logs; estimation is OLS; significance levels are indicated as follows; * = 10%; ** = 5%; *** = 1%.
BIC refers to the Bayesian Information Criterion (aka Schwarz criterion), which can be used to compare non-nested models.

reviewing the positions of key economies towards a greater global or international role of their currency, for example through financial market development and opening.

There are a number of benefits for a country if its currency is used internationally. It enlarges the scope of issuers and investors and may thus lower borrowing costs and ultimately facilitate balance of payment financing. The additional demand for money creates seigniorage revenues, and is likely to imply more business for the country's banks and other financial institutions.[7] International use of the currency will foster economic and financial integration with the rest of the world, which can boost trade and potential growth. Currency use in key markets for commodities or trade invoicing will shift exchange rate risk to third countries and insulate the economy against exchange rate fluctuations. There are even arguments that international currency use will improve a country's terms of trade through externalities and lead to an increase in the purchasing power of the currency (Kannan, 2007).[8] Finally, non-pecuniary benefits include political power and prestige.[9]

However, international currency use also entails costs. The additional demand for money is likely to raise volatility in money demand, especially if foreign shocks are unknown and different from those affecting the home country. With the advancing of statistical reporting, most central banks are able to separate out foreign demand for money, but with regard to some components, such as cash, uncertainty remains. International currency use can also have an impact on financing conditions in a way that is, at times, undesired. During his last years in office, former Federal Reserve Chairman Alan Greenspan said it was a 'conundrum' that long-term interest rates were so low; after his retirement he stated that the Fed 'failed' to get long-term rates to rise sufficiently, largely due to foreign demand for long-term bonds (Greenspan, 2007).

Benefits and costs are not equally distributed within an economy. International currency use is likely to be of particular benefit to the financial industry, the real economy and the fiscal authority. By contrast, the costs, which can arise if the extent of international currency use relative to the size of the home country is high, are mainly concentrated at the central bank; they include issues such as a potentially lower control over monetary and financial aggregates, and a possible blurring of responsibilities. Therefore, it is no surprise that a central bank will, in general, be more reserved towards an international use of its currency than political authorities. All over the world central banks have a strictly domestic mandate and are accountable to a domestic constituency. No international role can compensate for missing domestic objectives and, apart from a blurry reputational gain, international currency use gives little additional gain on top of achieved domestic objectives.

What is the policy stance of authorities issuing a currency that is used internationally, and what, if any, are the structural measures adopted to support or foster its international role?

1. The European Central Bank has explicitly formulated its policy stance towards the international role of the euro, which it neither fosters nor hinders and considers purely as reflecting decisions of markets and economic agents (ECB, 2001 and 2002). The ECB has not launched any technical measure to support international currency use abroad. It has amended its statistical framework to the extent possible so as to net out impacts on money demand from non-residents.[10,11]
2. The US authorities have not established an explicit policy vis-à-vis the international role of the dollar, but from actual developments and policy declarations on specific issues, one can infer that this role is appreciated. The benefits for the US economy are, in particular, the privilege of issuing securities in a currency that is globally accepted, the insulation from exchange rate fluctuations given the dollar's role as an invoicing and quotation currency, and the business opportunities for the US financial system. So it is not surprising that although the authorities do not explicitly state that they are fostering the role of the dollar, they are supporting it through technical means. One example is the worldwide network of the extended custodial inventory system of cash-handling centres that facilitate the use of the US dollar abroad.[12]

The debate on dollarization in parts of Latin America in the late 1990s showed a pragmatic policy stance, based on a cost-benefit analysis.[13] At the time, US Treasury official Lawrence Summers said that 'to the extent that dollarization helped to expand our large role in Latin American markets, it might help to ensure that we continued to benefit disproportionately from their future growth' (Summers, 1999). US Treasury Secretary Rubin was also open to dollarization, provided that the 'Three No's' are respected (no inclusion of a dollarized economy in monetary policy considerations; no extension of bank supervision; and no access to the Fed discount window; Rubin, 1999).

- For several years the Japanese authorities pursued structural measures to foster the international role of the yen. In 1999, the Ministry of Finance called on the Council on Foreign Exchange to develop recommendations regarding the internationalization of the yen. The starting observation was that the international role of the yen had fallen far short of Japan's weight in the global economy and that a stronger role of the yen would create new financial service business and vitalize Tokyo's financial markets. The Council recommended a number of structural policies to open financial markets, strengthen their infrastructure and improve the regulatory environment. These matters were taken up by a 'Study Group for the Promotion of the Internationalisation of the Yen', chaired by Toyoo Gyothen, President of the Institute for International Monetary Affairs in 1999/2000, again under the auspices of the Ministry of Finance.

The study group focused on a comprehensive list of structural measures, which it hoped would 'lead to an increase in the procurement and management of yen funds by non-residents'.[14] The measures included a broad spectrum of liberalization, transparency and infrastructure strengthening. The study group has continued to issue reports, the latest one of which was published in June 2007.

- Finally, the UK and Swiss authorities do not pursue the international role of their currencies, but actively foster the international role of their financial centres.[15] For the United Kingdom, the international role of the sterling is only secondary, as financial institutions in London are heavily engaged in foreign currency use. In fact, the international role of the euro is more significant for London than the international role of the sterling.[16] The situation is similar in Switzerland, where the authorities focus more on the development of Zurich, Geneva and Basel as international financial centres rather than on the internationalization of the Swiss franc. Macroeconomic and monetary stability as well as a very open financial environment are seen as the essential ingredients in this regard.[17]

1.6 Conclusions

For centuries, currencies have been seen – beyond their economic functions – as symbols of sovereignty. Today, in an environment of globalization, they are often seen as symbols of the economic and financial strength of economic areas in an international context. Indeed, for international investors who are considering exposure in foreign currencies, the economic, institutional and financial foundations of currencies are important variables in their decision-making as regards the international allocation of portfolios. This chapter has argued that the size of the underlying economy, as well as the size and stage of development of its financial markets, together with the soundness of the respective governance structure, are the relevant variables in this context. The indicators used to measure size and structural developments contain information that is also relevant from a policy point of view. Policy variables included in the concept are the opening of an economy to international trade and capital flows, the development of the domestic financial market in terms of instruments, regulation and oversight, and the credibility of the overall policy framework. Therefore, the respective shares of the global role of currencies are useful indicators for global investors and the underlying components of this concept are useful indicators for policymakers.

The approach taken in this chapter is different from the established approach vis-à-vis the international roles of currencies, which focuses on cross-border use. This chapter has illustrated the appeal of the most widely established measure based on the international debt securities market, which is the relatively precise accounting of cross-border use in this specific market. However, it has also made the point that, given the global decline in financial home bias, this specific market accounts for a decreasing share of overall cross-border financial activity. Markets for government debt, corporate debt and equities are experiencing a far greater penetration by international investors. Hence, even for cross-border use, the international debt securities market is increasingly narrow. Moreover, it is a market dominated by EU and US financial corporations, and developments in currency shares are in turn influenced by short-term considerations, including firm-specific balance sheet management and cyclical developments. Only a few of the motives underlying currency use in this market are relevant for a policy-oriented debate on the international role or international standing of currencies. Therefore, currency shares in the market of international debt securities provide some (albeit limited) insight from a policy perspective.

This chapter has addressed the more policy-oriented angle relating to the international role of currencies, namely the general importance of individual currencies in the global economy. The chapter has developed a measure of the global roles of currencies based on the size and structural characteristics of the underlying economy and on the size, stage of development and quality of the regulatory framework of the underlying financial markets. Such a measure is important for three reasons: first, it can serve as a benchmark for currency shares in portfolios that are globally diversified; second, it gives an unbiased treatment of currencies from advanced and emerging economies and can therefore put the increasing global role of emerging economies into perspective; and third, it can, over time, help to detect shifts in the international monetary and financial system, for example through financial development and opening. The chapter has also shown that the indicators of global currency use can play a useful role in understanding cross-border financial holdings, providing support to the notion that financial development fosters international financial integration.

The concept of the global role of currencies can enhance the policy discussion on the general importance of certain currencies in the global economy. For example, as far as the US dollar is concerned, the global role concept underscores its attractiveness as the leading global currency, resulting from the economic strength and governance framework of the underlying economy and the size and stage of development of its financial markets (based on data available until end-2006). More specifically, it has been shown that key pillars of the global role of the dollar are the size and liquidity of US equity markets, the amount of debt instruments issued by financial institutions and corporations, and the leading role of the US dollar in global foreign exchange markets and reserves.

As far as the euro is concerned, the concept developed in this chapter suggests that the role of the euro will continue to rise as a result of enlargement – which will gradually add to the global economic weight of the euro area – and, more importantly, through financial development and integration within Europe. In recent years, the growing corporate bond market, the increasing role of equities in external financing and the development of the money market have been important steps in this process. The difference between the underlying financial markets available to the US dollar and the euro is particularly pronounced in the equity market and the foreign exchange market; within the debt market, the government segment is broadly comparable, but the difference is large in terms of debt issued by financial institutions. Moreover, the euro has some segments in the derivatives markets that are larger, reflecting a very advanced stage of financial development, especially with regard to derivatives on government securities that are heavily used by foreign investors.

Finally, the global role indicator sheds light on the relative standing of the currencies of emerging economies. These currencies have been largely neglected in the established analysis of the international role of currencies since they play virtually no role in global foreign exchange reserves and are not used in the international debt securities market, which is dominated by European and US financial institutions and corporations. However, owing to domestic financial market development, a strengthening of the policy and regulatory frameworks and the opening up of markets, they are beginning to play a more significant role in the global economy than in the past.

The quantitative results of this chapter show that the dollar is still the dominant global currency, followed by the euro. However, the yen and pound sterling switch ranks compared with the measure based on the international debt market and a slightly larger global role is attributed to the yen. Additionally, the Canadian dollar looks different from a global perspective: its weight in this concept is more than twice its weight in the international debt securities market. Most importantly, the group of emerging economy currencies receives a weight almost four times as high as in the international debt market, led by Mexico, Brazil and the main emerging economies in South-East Asia. The weights are still well below the trade and economic weights of the respective economies because financial development is ongoing, but even today they suggest a non-negligible role for these currencies in internationally diversified portfolios, as well as in the international monetary and financial system more broadly.

Notes

Article reproduced with kind permission from *International Finance*.
* The chapter has been published in *International Finance* (12/2008). Author affiliation: European Central Bank, 60311 Frankfurt am Main, Germany, e-mail: christian.thimann@ecb.europa.eu. In writing this chapter, I have benefited from many helpful suggestions by Michael Fidora and from excellent research assistance by Benjamin Klaus and Emilia Pérez. The chapter benefited substantially from comments by Benn

Steil and two anonymous referees, as well as by Roland Beck, Thierry Bracke, Menzie Chinn, Alexander Chudik, Marcel Fratzscher, Maurizio Habib, Frank Warnock and Adalbert Winkler. I am also grateful to participants at the HKMA conference on 'The International Role of Currencies and the Renminbi' (Hong Kong, October 2007), where an early version was presented. The usual disclaimer applies.

1. Two measures are usually considered: a 'narrow' concept, comprising only securities issued by non-residents of a certain currency area (e.g. a British bank issuing a bond denominated in euro), and a 'broad' concept, which includes issuances by residents of the currency area that are considered to be 'targeted' at investors abroad, whereby the 'targeting' is inferred from the prospectus, the nature of the syndicate or the type of financial law applied. The narrow measure is more widely used as a benchmark since it is seen as more precise.
2. Within this matrix, or sometimes instead of it, other concepts are used. The most frequent is the distinction between areas in which *diversification* plays a role, pointing towards two or more currencies having an international status, and areas in which *standardization* plays a role, pointing to a single internationally used currency (see Hartmann 1998; Lim 2006).
3. For example, Curcuru et al. (2007), find that key policy puzzles, such as the return differential between US foreign assets and US external liabilities that has often been postulated, vanishes when returns in equity and bond markets are considered jointly and are properly accounted for.
4. See Thomas et al. (2006) for a detailed study on cross-border equity holdings.
5. For a discussion of the reporting challenges and the resulting imprecisions see Warnock (2007).
6. This important point has been raised by one referee.
7. It is interesting to note that most business using the euro – for example, foreign exchange trading – takes place outside the euro area, specifically in London. In 2001, the volume of euro trading in London's FX markets was 125% of trading in the euro area (see the article entitled 'The City of London and the international role of the euro' in the 'Review of the international role of the euro', ECB, December 2003).
8. Kannan (2007) estimates that for the euro area the benefit is 1.7%–2.1% of GDP, of which seignorage is 0.5%–0.7% of GDP.
9. See Portes and Rey (1997) for an overview of the costs and benefits, including political considerations.
10. In general, the reporting by monetary and financial institutions in the euro area distinguishes between residents and non-residents, and the ECB also amended the reporting of money market fund shares to allow for this distinction in 2001 (see ECB Monthly Bulletin May 2001, page 9f.). Hence, the main uncertainty which remains with regard to non-resident components affecting M3 stems from currency in circulation, which – at about 8% of M3 – is not likely to have a significant impact.
11. The policy position of the Deutsche Bundesbank was explicitly critical towards an internationalization of the Deutsche Mark (DM). It stated that 'the Deutsche Mark has acquired an international role *somewhat against the will of the Bundesbank*' (Deutsche Bundesbank, Monthly Bulletin, May 1988, p. 22; see also Mayer (1996) and Frenkel and Goldstein (1999) on this matter). The reasons for the critical attitude lay in perceived risks related to the DM being a reserve currency, including interference with money demand and limited room for manoeuvre.
12. See Baxter (2004) and Botta (2003).

13. See, for example, Altig (2002) 'Dollarization: What's in It for US?' Federal Reserve Bank of Cleveland. For a Fed perspective, see Lambert and Stanton (2001).
14. See www.mof.go.jp/english/if/if025a.htm for the 30 June 2000 interim report and /if043a and /if043b for subsequent reports.
15. See, for example, Clementi (2001).
16. A few years after the launch of the euro, 34% of UK banks' business with non-residents was in euro (compared with only 11% in sterling), and the euro accounted for 23% of the total business of UK banks. Bank of England, *Practical issues arising from the euro*, November 2002, p. 9.
17. See, for example, Roth (1998) and Blattner (2002).

References

Altig, D. (2002). 'Dollarization: What's in It for US?', *Economic Commentary*, Federal Reserve Bank of Cleveland, 15 October 2002.
Baxter, T. (2004). 'Testimony before the Committee on Banking, Housing and Urban Affairs, US, Senate – Oversight of the Extended Custodial Inventory Program', US Congress, 20 May 2004.
BIS (1997). *Quarterly Review*, February, pp. 21–35.
Blattner, N. (2002). 'Swiss Capital Market, Current Topics', Annual General meeting of the Pfandbriefbank Schweizerischer Hypothekarinstitute, St Gallen, 15 May 2002.
Bobba, M., G. Della Corte and A. Powell (2007). 'On the Determinants of International Currency Choice: Will the Euro Dominate the World?', Inter-American Development Bank, Washington, DC, June.
Botta, J. (2003). 'The Federal Reserve Bank of New York's experience of managing cross-border migration of US dollar banknotes', in *China's Capital Account Liberalisation: International Perspective*, BIS Papers No 15, April 2003, pp. 152–62.
Cai, F., and F. Warnock (2006). 'International Diversification at Home and Abroad', NBER Working Paper no. 12220.
Chinn, M. and J. Frankel (2007). 'Will the Euro Eventually Surpass the Dollar as Leading International Reserve Currency?' in R. Clarida (ed.), *G7 Current Account Imbalances: Sustainability and Adjustment*, NBER Report, University of Chicago Press, pp. 283–321.
Chinn, M. and J. Frankel (2008). 'Why the Euro Will Rival the Dollar', *International Finance*, vol. 11, pp. 49–73.
Chinn, M. and H. Ito (2006). 'What Matters for Financial Development? Capital Controls, Institutions, and Interactions', *Journal of Development Economics*, vol. 81, pp. 163–92.
Clementi, D. (2001). 'The City and the Euro: Innovation and Excellence' at City Seminar on 'London into the 21st Century' at Palace Hotel, Tokyo on 13 February 2001, Bank of England.
Cohen, B. H. (2005). 'Currency Choice in International Bond Issuance', BIS Quarterly Review, June 2005, pp. 53–66.
Cohen, B. J. (1971). *The Future of Sterling as an International Currency*, St Martin's Press.
Council on Customs, Tariff, Foreign Exchange and Other Transactions, Ministry of Finance, Japan 'Internationalization of the Yen for the 21st Century – Japans Response to Changes in Global Economic and Financial Environments', 20 April, 1999.
Curcuru, S., T. Dvorak, and F. Warnock (2008). 'Cross-Border Returns Differentials', *Quarterly Journal of Economics*, Vol. 123, No. 4, pp. 1495–1530.

Detken, C. and P. Hartmann (2000). 'The Euro and International Capital Markets', *International Finance*, Blackwell Publishing Vol. 3(1), pp. 53–94.

Deutsche Bundesbank (1984). 'The Deutsche Mark as an International Investment Currency', Monthly Report (January).

—— (1988). Monthly Report (May).

—— (1998). 'Forty Years of the Deutsche Mark', Monthly Report (May).

ECB (2001, 2002, 2003, 2007). Review of the International Role of the Euro (annual editions).

Fidora, M., M. Fratzscher and C. Thimann (2007). 'Home Bias in Global Bond and Equity Markets: The Role of Real Exchange Rate Volatility', *Journal of International Money and Finance*, vol. 26, pp. 631–55

Frenkel, J. A. and M. Goldstein (1999). 'International Role of the Deutsche Mark', in *Fifty Years of Deutsche Mark–Germany's Central Bank and Currency since 1948*, Oxford University Press.

Fujiwara, S., Deputy Governor of the Bank of Japan (1999). Remarks at the Third Financial Forum of Europlace, 29 November.

Gelos, R. and S.-J. Wei (2005). 'Transparency and International Portfolio Holdings', *Journal of Finance*, vol. 60, pp. 2987–3020.

Greenspan, A. (2007). *The Age of Turbulence*. Allen Lane publishers.

Hartmann, P. (1998). *Currency Competition and Foreign Exchange Markets: The Dollar, the Yen and the Euro*, Cambridge University Press.

Kannan, P. (2007). 'On the Welfare Benefits of an International Currency', IMF Working Paper no. 07/49, March.

Kenen, P. (1983). 'The Role of the Dollar as an International Reserve Currency', Occasional Papers no. 13, Group of Thirty.

Lambert, M. and K. Stanton (2001). 'Opportunities and Challenges of the US Dollar as an Increasingly Global Currency: A Federal Reserve Perspective', Federal Reserve Bulletin, September, pp. 567–75.

Lim, E.-G. (2006). 'The Euro's Challenge to the Dollar: Different Views from Economists and Evidence from COFER (Currency Composition of Foreign Exchange Reserves) and other Data', IMF Working Paper no. 06/153, June.

La Porta, R., F. Lopez-de-Silanes and A. Shleifer (2006). 'What Works in Securities Laws?', *Journal of Finance*, vol. 61, pp. 1–32.

Mayer, G. (1996). *Die D-Mark als Leitwährung in Europa? Eine Untersuchung über die Sonderstellungen der Bundesbank und der D-Mark in Europa*, Peter Lang, Frankfurt.

McCauley, R. (1997). 'The Euro and the Dollar', *Essays in International Finance*, Princeton University, no. 205.

Portes, R. and I. Papaionannou (2006). 'The Euro as an International Currency vis-à-vis the Dollar', mimeo, Dartmouth College and London Business School.

Portes, R. and H. Rey (1998). 'Euro vs. Dollar: Will the Euro Replace the Dollar as the World Currency?', *Economic Policy*, April.

Portes, R. and H. Rey (2005). 'The Determinants of Cross-Border Equity Flows', *Journal of International Economics*, vol. 65, pp. 269–96.

Roth, J.-P. (1998). 'The Swiss Frank within an Euro Environment', 12th European Finance Convention and the Euro Week, Vienna, 23 November.

Rubin, R., Treasury Secretary (1999). Press Release of 21 April 1999 – Remarks on Reform of the International Financial Architecture to the School of Advance International Studies.

Siegfried, N., E. Simenova and C. Vespro (2007). 'Choice of currency in bond issuance and the international role of currencies', ECB Working Paper no. 813, September.

Summers, L., Deputy Treasury Secretary (1999). Press Release of 22 April 1999 – Senate Banking Committee, Subcommittees on Economic Policy and on International Trade and Finance.
Summers, L., Deputy Treasury Secretary (1999). Press Release of 21 October 1999 – Senate Budget Committee.
Thomas C., F. Warnock and J. Wongswan (2006). 'The performance of international equity portfolios', NBER Working Paper 12346.
Warnock, F. (2007). 'New Features of the International Monetary System, New Challenges for Global Monetary Governance', Darden Graduate School of Business, University of Virginia, mimeo.

2

External Use of the South African Rand

Johan van den Heever

2.1   Introduction

The rand is the currency of the Republic of South Africa and co-circulates with other currencies in a number of Southern African countries. A formal currency union – the Common Monetary Area or CMA – has been in existence for many years and provides the framework for such co-circulation in three of South Africa's neighbours. The rand also circulates informally in a number of other countries.

It should be noted that inside the borders of South Africa the rand is the only legal tender, and that there is very little use of other currencies inside this area (Van Zyl 2003, p. 134). In South African hotels and shops that are frequented by tourists there are some instances of partial 'dollarization' – with prices possibly quoted in US dollar, euro and rand, and the foreign currencies easily accepted by the hotel or vendor, who would then usually exchange it for rand at an authorized dealer in foreign exchange such as a bank. But both legally and *de facto*, the rand serves as generally accepted means of payment in South Africa. This status has been reinforced by exchange controls which apply to residents, and also by the relatively low inflation which has been experienced in South Africa since the early 1990s, which has helped to support confidence in the rand. Money's ability to function as a means of payment is closely linked to its ability to retain its purchasing power.

The aim of this chapter is to briefly reflect on South Africa's experience with co-circulation of the rand, both in the Common Monetary Area and beyond, focusing principally on the CMA. After a brief introduction to the CMA, attention turns to its history. Key elements of the working of the CMA arrangements are then discussed, and this is followed by some observations regarding the use of the rand currency beyond the CMA, an assessment of the impact of external use of the rand, future prospects for monetary union and a common currency in Southern African Development Community (SADC) countries, and some concluding remarks.

Readers interested in a much more detailed analysis of the CMA will find the paper by Wang et al. (2007) useful.

However, before turning to the CMA and to questions related to physical rand notes and coin, it may be helpful to briefly outline a number of dimensions of the broader international use of rand – including rand deposits and other financial instruments.

It may be noted that the international foreign exchange market in South African rand (ZAR) is relatively liquid. The net turnover in the market in which rand trades against other currencies, as reported by South African banks and South African branches of foreign banks, came to approximately US$12 billion per day in the first nine months of 2007. This implies that in this market it takes less than 25 days to trade an amount equal to South Africa's annual gross domestic product (GDP). Approximately 67 per cent of transactions are with non-residents. Swap transactions nowadays typically constitute around 68 per cent of total transactions, spot transactions 25 per cent and outright forward transactions 7 per cent, although there can be significant variations from day to day and month to month. It may also be noted that apart from this business which is recorded in South Africa, some trading in the rand is conducted fully offshore (outside South Africa), for example in New York.

Underlying the significant international interest in the South African rand are a number of factors. These include the extremely liquid investment opportunities in South Africa, which attract strong non-resident interest. Turnover on the formalized bond exchange in South Africa for instance amounted to approximately R1.3 trillion or US$200 billion per month in the first nine months of 2007. Over the same period, share market turnover amounted to roughly R200 billion or US$30 billion per month. Activity in the derivatives market was also very brisk. There is a strong non-resident interest in all of these markets, in some instances motivated by a desire to have exposure to commodities or to instruments which yield an attractive interest rate. It should also not be forgotten that South Africa has a relatively 'open' economy, with imports and exports of goods and services together exceeding 65 per cent of GDP. The country also has significant foreign direct investment and other financial linkages with the rest of the world.

International interest in the rand is bolstered by a number of important features of the financial system. Solid, well-capitalized and well-supervised banks that are technologically advanced and that maintain strong international linkages are helpful. So is a sophisticated payment system which provides features such as real-time gross settlement and delivery-versus-payment. The rand is also a continuous linked settlement (CLS) currency. A sound legal framework is important, as is having anti-money laundering mechanisms and business continuity plans in place. A considerable benefit is the absence of exchange controls as far as non-residents are concerned.

(Some foreign exchange restrictions still apply to residents, but these have been relaxed considerably since 1995.)

However, as stated previously the focus in this chapter is on the physical demand for cash and the CMA arrangements, to which the discussion now returns.

2.2   A brief overview of the CMA of Southern Africa

The CMA is a formal currency union consisting of South Africa, Lesotho, Namibia and Swaziland (Figure 2.1). South Africa has by far the largest population and economy within the region. Each of the four participating countries has its own currency, issued by its own central bank, which is legal tender within its own borders. However, the South African rand also has legal tender status in Lesotho, Namibia and Swaziland, and co-circulates with the currencies of these three countries within their borders. Furthermore, the currencies of these three countries have a one-to-one exchange rate with the South African rand.

The four CMA countries plus Botswana are also joined in a customs union – the Southern African Customs Union – which is almost a hundred years old.

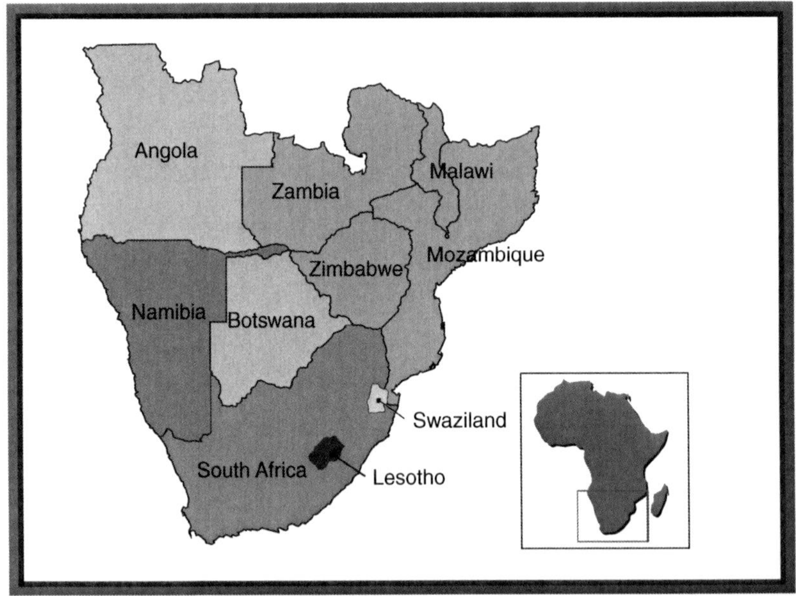

Figure 2.1   Geographical location of the CMA
Source: Clip art line drawing from licensed Corel Draw package; author's compilation.

Table 2.1   The Common Monetary Area: key indicators for 2006

	Population		Gross domestic product		
	Million	**% of total**	**US$ billion**	**R billion**	**% of total**
Lesotho	2.41	4.5	1.63	10.62	0.6
Namibia	2.05	3.9	6.32	42.76	2.4
South Africa	47.39	89.4	255.16	1726.69	96.0
Swaziland	1.15	2.2	2.64	17.93	1.0
Total	53.00	100.0	265.75	1794.00	100.0

Note: R = rand. At the time of writing, roughly R7 equaled US$1.
Source: IMF, 2007; Statistics South Africa, 2007; author's calculations.

Table 2.1 summarizes salient features of the CMA countries.

2.3   History of the CMA

The brief exposition below relies to a considerable extent on the September 2007 report on the SADC's financial systems by the Committee of Central Bank Governors in SADC (2007).

The CMA is a currency arrangement which started with a single common currency – the currency issued by South Africa, which for a long time was the only country of the four with a central bank. Over time, the smaller countries started their own central banks and issued their own currencies, while remaining in the currency union. The CMA started in a fairly spontaneous way and at no stage required individual countries to give up their own currencies and adopt a new one.

After World War I, South Africa was known as the Union of South Africa and was a member of the British Empire. Lesotho at that stage was known as Basutoland, and Basutoland, Swaziland and Betchuanaland (later to become Botswana) were under British administration. Namibia at that stage was known as South West Africa; this former German territory had been assigned to South Africa under mandate in 1920.

The British pound sterling was used in South Africa prior to 10 August 1920, at which point the South African authorities introduced the South African pound at par with the pound sterling. In 1921, the South African Reserve Bank started operations, and the South African pound became the principal currency not only in South Africa but also in Basutoland, Betchuanaland, South West Africa and Swaziland. This regional use of the South African pound continued for 40 years, and did not change appreciably when South Africa abandoned the gold standard on 28 December 1932 – just more than a year after Great Britain had done so on 20 September 1931.

On 14 February 1961, the South African coinage was decimalised. The rand became the new monetary unit, equal to the former South African half-pound, and replaced the South African pound as the principal currency in the region, which then consisted of the later CMA plus Betchuanaland. On 31 May of the same year, the Union of South Africa became the Republic of South Africa.

During the following decade, Bechuanaland gained independence as the Republic of Botswana on 30 September 1966, Basutoland became independent as the Kingdom of Lesotho on 4 October 1966, and Swaziland gained its independence as the Kingdom of Swaziland on 6 September 1968. Initially this did not change these countries' use of the rand as currency, and an informal monetary union continued.

In 1972, Botswana, Lesotho and Swaziland jointly initiated negotiations with South Africa (Selialia 1998, p. 41), which eventually led to a treaty – the Rand Monetary Area Agreement – being signed by South Africa, Botswana, Lesotho and Swaziland on 5 December 1974. This provided a formal framework for monetary cooperation and created the Rand Monetary Area. The agreement included a provision giving the smaller member countries the right to issue their own national currencies.

Swaziland set up a monetary authority and issued its own currency, the lilangeni (plural emalangeni), at a one-to-one exchange rate with the rand from September 1974.

Botswana withdrew from the Rand Monetary Area in 1975 and started issuing its own currency, the pula, from 23 August 1976 (Global Financial Data 2007). Although Botswana initially introduced the pula at par with the South African rand, the external value of the pula was later allowed to move away from parity with the rand.

Lesotho set up a central bank and from January 1980 issued its own currency, the loti (plural maloti), at a one-to-one exchange rate with the rand.

In 1986, Swaziland suspended the legal tender status of the rand in Swaziland but continued to maintain its own currency at par with the rand. Also in 1986, the Rand Monetary Area Agreement was replaced by the Common Monetary Area agreement. This was in fact a set of three agreements: a trilateral agreement between South Africa, Lesotho and Swaziland, and two bilateral agreements, a South Africa-Lesotho agreement and a South Africa-Swaziland agreement (Selialia, 1998).

Namibia became independent in 1990. It joined the CMA in 1992, at which time the CMA Multilateral Agreement replaced the CMA Trilateral Agreement. Namibia set up a central bank and from 1993 issued its own currency, the Namibian dollar, at a one-to-one exchange rate with the rand.

On 19 September 2003, after 17 years, Swaziland restored the legal tender status of the rand.

2.4   Key arrangements in the CMA

The Common Monetary Area agreement and its accompanying bilateral agreements create institutional arrangements which ensure strong monetary cooperation between the CMA countries. The most important provisions are discussed below.

2.4.1   Rand as legal tender

The CMA agreement provides for use of the South African rand as legal tender not only in South Africa but also in Lesotho, Namibia and Swaziland. However, it does not provide for the Lesotho loti, the Namibian dollar or the Swaziland lilangeni to circulate as legal tender in any of the CMA countries other than the country of issue.

2.4.2   Restrictions on issue of local currency

The central banks of Lesotho and Namibia are required to keep foreign reserve holdings to an amount equal to or exceeding the amount of local currency which they issue, under the South Africa-Lesotho and South Africa-Namibia bilateral agreements. This does not apply to Swaziland, although in practice the central bank of Swaziland has maintained foreign reserves in excess of its emalangeni issue throughout the past two decades (Wang et al., 2007).

2.4.3   Compensation payments

For the smaller members of the CMA, accepting the rand as legal tender causes the rand to displace their own currencies and reduces the seigniorage from issuance of their own banknotes and coin accruing to the authorities. Recognizing this, the agreement provides for annual compensation payments by the South African government to the governments of Lesotho, Namibia and Swaziland.

These payments are based on estimates of the value of the rand in circulation in each of the three countries. The payments made are equal to two-thirds of the long-term bond rate multiplied by the estimated amount of rand in circulation in the country involved.

In this equation, the long-term bond rate used is the market yield on long-term bonds issued by the South African government. The ratio of two-thirds was established on the assumption that it approximated the return on a portfolio of reserve assets comprising both long-term and short-term maturities, assuming that the average yield would be less than the full long-term yield (Wang et al., 2007). It should also be kept in mind that significant costs are incurred in the production and distribution of notes and coin.

The amount of the rand in circulation in each of the three countries is estimated; it is never directly measured. In 1974, the base amounts of rand notes and coin in circulation in Lesotho and in Swaziland were estimated using information on variables such as the income level in each of these two countries and the ratio of currency in circulation to income in other broadly similar countries which were issuing their own national currencies. A broadly similar approach was used 18 years later when Namibia joined the currency union and a base amount of the rand in circulation in that country had to be established.

With the base estimates agreed, the next question was how to adjust the estimates of currency in circulation in each country each year. It was argued that the smaller CMA countries had a lower level of economic development and monetization than South Africa, and would gradually catch up in terms of development and monetization. It was therefore agreed that the amount of currency in those countries was likely to grow more rapidly than in South Africa. The formula used to estimate the total amount of currency in circulation in the smaller CMA countries provides for growth in the outstanding balance of notes and coin in those countries to be one-fifth higher than the growth in the amount of rand notes and coin outstanding on the balance sheet of the South African monetary authorities. In other words, if the amount of notes and coin outstanding on the balance sheet of the South African Reserve Bank increases by 10 per cent, the estimated amount of notes and coin in the smaller CMA members rises by 12 per cent. (Conversely, if the amount of notes and coin outstanding on the balance sheet of the South African Reserve Bank were to contract, the estimated amount of notes and coin in the smaller CMA countries would be deemed to contract by only four-fifths of the percentage contraction measured on the balance sheet of the South African Reserve Bank.)

Finally, when each country introduced its own national currency – which earns its own seigniorage – it was provided for by deducting from the estimated *total* currency in circulation in the country (as calculated in the way described above) the amount in circulation of *national* currency issued by that country's central bank, as obtained from the central bank's balance sheet. The remaining amount is the estimated amount of South African rand in circulation in that country, for which a compensation payment is made by the South African government using the formula described earlier.

Table 2.2 illustrates the calculation of the compensation payments in recent years.

Table 2.2   Calculation of compensation payments (in R million) to Lesotho, Namibia and Swaziland (LNS), 2003/4–2006/7

Year	Estimated total notes and coin in circulation in LNS	*Minus*: LNS national currencies in circulation	*Equals*: Rand currency in circulation in LNS	*Times*: Interest rate applied	*Equals*: Compensation payments
2003/04	4,549.5	1,252.8	3,296.7	9.19% × 2/3	202.0
2004/05	5,360.3	1,377.0	3,983.3	8.83% × 2/3	234.5
2005/06	6,112.9	1,466.7	4,646.2	7.89% × 2/3	244.4
2006/07	6,896.3	1,613.4	5,282.9	8.02% × 2/3	282.5

Source: South African Reserve Bank and LNS central banks, unpublished information; Van Rensburg, 2007; South African National Treasury, 2007; author's calculations.

2.4.4   Exchange control

The CMA agreement provides for freedom of movement of funds within the CMA, but for the maintenance of exchange control on transactions between residents and non-residents of the CMA. Exchange controls in Lesotho, Namibia and Swaziland are not allowed to be less restrictive than in South Africa. However, since 1995 exchange controls have been gradually relaxed in South Africa and the rest of the CMA. Current-account transactions are generally free of exchange control, although monitoring provisions apply. Limits on capital-account transactions for residents are nowadays fairly liberal. Non-residents of the CMA are generally not subject to exchange control.

2.4.5   Access to financial markets

The CMA agreement makes provision for Lesotho, Namibia and Swaziland to have access to the South African money and capital markets. For instance, the authorities in these countries may issue securities that can be held by South African financial institutions. The terms of such issues have to be agreed with the South African government.

2.4.6   Repatriation of currencies

Measurement of the stock (outstanding balance) of rand notes and coin in circulation outside the South African Reserve Bank is quite exact – to the cent, as with most central banks' currency liability.

As indicated before, however, the *stock* of rand currency in circulation in Lesotho, Namibia and Swaziland is not measured but is estimated using an agreed formula. Furthermore, the *flows* of the rand between South Africa and its neighbours are generally not measured. With rand being legal tender not only in South Africa but also in the other three CMA countries, there is no need to exchange currencies at any point. Tourists, importers and exporters, cross-border workers and investors alike can simply utilize rand currency in their transactions. For instance, should a South African tourist spend rand notes in one of the other CMA countries, and should those notes be used in several further transactions in that country and then be brought back to South Africa and spent by a tourist from that other country, the authorities would not be able to track those flows. Some rand flows are, however, measured. The central banks of Lesotho, Namibia and Swaziland repatriate rand notes and coin to the South African Reserve Bank – in other words, they return it to the South African Reserve Bank. These central banks have current accounts in the books of the South African Reserve Bank which are then credited by the amount of rand returned. The amounts repatriated by the central banks of Lesotho, Namibia and Swaziland in recent years are shown in Table 2.3.

The rapid escalation in repatriations over the past few years are probably partly related to the strong increases in nominal national income in these

Table 2.3   Repatriations of rand notes and coins by central banks of South Africa's neighbouring countries (in R million), 2004–6

Central bank of	2004	2005	2006	Jan–Aug 2007
Lesotho	218.5	339.2	362.6	305.1
Namibia	316.7	512.4	749.7	674.9
Swaziland	98.4	63.6	122.8	169.4
Total	633.8	915.2	1,235.1	1,149.4

Source: South African Reserve Bank, Currency and Protection Services Department, unpublished information; author's compilation.

Table 2.4   Amount of rand notes and coins repatriated to South African Reserve Bank by LNS central banks in 2006

	Amount deposited R million	Gross domestic product R million	Deposits/GDP percentage
Lesotho	363	10,622	3.4
Namibia	750	42,759	1.8
Swaziland	123	17,931	0.7

Source: South African Reserve Bank, Currency and Protection Services Department, unpublished information; Statistics South Africa (2007); author's calculations.

countries as their governments' revenue from customs and excise duties rose very briskly, and as the prices of their export commodities increased substantially. To some extent, Namibia and Swaziland may also be conduits for returning some rand currency which at some stage circulated in their neighbours, such as Angola and Mozambique, both of which have been experiencing buoyant economic conditions.

To put the amounts of repatriations into perspective in a very basic way, Table 2.4 expresses the amounts of the rand repatriated to the South African Reserve Bank as a percentage of nominal gross domestic product in each of the respective countries of origin (Table 2.4).

One should be careful in interpreting the data in Table 2.4. It is clear that the amounts of the rand repatriated are not insignificant in relation to the gross domestic product in the respective countries of origin. However, the value of rand notes and coins taken across the border in both directions between South Africa and each of the other three countries by individuals and firms in their ordinary conduct of business is unknown. Furthermore, some banks in Lesotho, Namibia and Swaziland are part of a group headed by a bank in South Africa and may choose to move rand notes and coins cross-border between the various banks in the group rather than to deposit it with the central bank. It may therefore escape being officially repatriated from central bank to central bank. Other banks in Lesotho, Namibia and Swaziland have correspondent banking linkages with South African banks and may also prefer to move the rand between the correspondent banking entities rather than to work through the central banks.

Not unexpectedly, rand notes repatriated from Lesotho, Namibia and Swaziland generally seem to have been used a lot in transactions. A fair proportion is soiled to the point where, once deposited with the South African Reserve Bank, they are destroyed rather than re-issued. Generally, a somewhat lower proportion of soiled notes applies to the rand notes deposited with the South African Reserve Bank by South African banks in the private sector.

2.5   Rand circulating beyond the CMA

Beyond the repatriation of rand notes and coin through central banks, there are also repatriation activities taking place through private-sector banks. For instance, a bank in another country which has received rand notes may send such money back to its South African affiliate or correspondent bank and receive credit for it. Such note repatriations are recorded by the South African authorized dealers or banks. The total amounts involved are relatively small and are summarized in Table 2.5. The amount originating in the Southern African Development Community (which consists of 14 countries) shown in the table comes from non-CMA countries in the SADC. Beyond the SADC, the amounts involved are almost negligible.

It may furthermore be noted that rand is readily accepted in bureaux de change throughout the SADC, with the exception of Madagascar where it is legally possible to do so but where the volume of rand business is insufficient to the extent that exchange rates for the rand are rarely quoted. This partly reflects the fact that Madagascar has only recently joined the SADC and that its trade, tourism and financial linkages with South Africa have started off from a low base.

2.6   Assessing the impact of external use of the rand

In a CMA context, the CMA arrangements have helped to maintain and strengthen financial linkages, tourism and trade between the participating countries. The CMA countries plus Botswana have also been in a customs union since 1910, and trade linkages between the Southern African Customs Union countries have been extensive. More than 80 per cent of Lesotho, Namibia and Swaziland imports are from South Africa. It should be noted that CMA countries' trade and financial linkages with Botswana, which is not in the CMA, are also extensive and successful. Table 2.6 gives an indication of the importance of foreign trade within the CMA.

Table 2.5   Rand notes repatriated in 2006 through South African authorized dealers

	Amount repatriated (R million)	Number of countries involved
Originating in SADC	288.9	6
Rest of Africa	1.4	1
Rest of world	0.4	1

Source: South African Reserve Bank, Exchange Control Department, unpublished information; author's compilation.

Table 2.6   Imports from and exports to South Africa of the smaller CMA countries plus Botswana, 2003

	Percentage of total imports originating from South Africa	Percentage of total exports destined for South Africa
Lesotho	86.0	19.4
Namibia	81.5	28.6
Swaziland	89.0	68.2
Botswana	72.5	10.4

Source: Wang et al., 2007, Table 3.1; author's compilation.

While a monetary union clearly strengthens economic ties between participating countries, factors such as proximity, well-functioning markets in foreign currency and the absence of import duties also play an important and sometimes overriding role in strengthening trade ties.

However, within the CMA the use of the rand as legal tender and the maintenance of one-to-one exchange rates with the rand for the national currencies of Lesotho, Namibia and Swaziland have led to a significant degree of convergence in inflation rates, as shown in Table 2.7. Partly this is a function of the high proportion of imports which the smaller CMA countries source from South Africa – with a one-to-one exchange rate, price developments in South Africa are quickly transmitted across the border. But moreover, the CMA dispensation has also ensured that Lesotho, Namibia and Swaziland have had to follow monetary policies quite similar to that of South Africa. Short-term interest rates within the CMA follow the movements of the South African Reserve Bank key lending rate, the repurchase rate, quite closely.

The CMA dispensation implies that the smaller CMA countries have had to sacrifice their own, independent monetary policy. At the same time, the advantages of being linked to a comparatively large economy and to have access to well-developed financial institutions cannot be denied. The compensation

Table 2.7   Consumer price inflation (%) in the CMA countries

Year	Lesotho	Namibia	Swaziland	South Africa
1991	17.3	11.9	8.9	15.6
1992	18.1	17.7	7.6	13.7
1993	10.7	8.5	12.0	9.9
1994	8.3	10.8	13.8	8.8
1995	9.7	10.0	12.3	8.7
1996	8.9	8.0	6.4	7.3
1997	8.4	8.8	7.9	8.6
1998	8.2	6.2	7.5	6.9
1999	7.8	8.6	5.9	5.2
2000	4.5	9.3	7.2	5.4
2001	6.9	9.3	7.5	5.7
2002	12.5	11.3	11.7	9.2
2003	7.3	7.2	7.4	5.8
2004	5.0	4.1	3.4	1.4
2005	3.4	2.3	4.8	3.4
2006	6.1	5.1	5.1	4.7
Aug 2007	8.7	6.8	8.6	6.7

Source: National central banks; author's compilation.

payments for the rand circulating as legal tender in the other CMA countries have also acted as an incentive for continued participation in the currency union.

With the smaller CMA countries having a large proportion of their foreign trade with South Africa, the one-to-one exchange rate between the CMA currencies has contributed towards stability, at least as far as trade within the CMA is concerned. However, trade with countries beyond the CMA has on occasions been influenced by quite substantial changes in the exchange rate of the rand – and with it the other three CMA currencies. The graph below (Figure 2.2) depicts the movements of the exchange value of the rand since 1990. As South Africa generally experienced higher inflation than its main trading partner countries, the decline of the nominal effective exchange value of the rand during the 1990s is not surprising. The volatility of the rand has been a factor complicating the competitiveness of all CMA producers of tradable commodities competing with producers from elsewhere. Although the foreign-currency market in the CMA – in particular in South Africa – is quite sophisticated and offers mechanisms such as forward cover to manage currency risk, currency volatility probably inhibits long-term planning and investment decisions. Greater stability in recent times has been helpful; the South African authorities have *inter alia* accumulated foreign reserves, contributing to a more robust environment and reduced currency volatility.

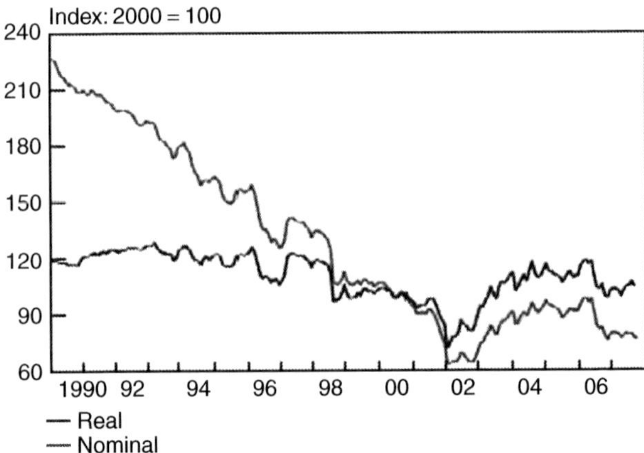

Figure 2.2   Effective exchange rates of the rand
Source: South African Reserve Bank, author's compilation.

2.7   Future prospects

Initiatives are in progress to further economic integration in Southern Africa and in Africa. Part of this process relates to monetary integration. For instance, the SADC has set a goal to achieve a SADC monetary union by 2016 and to adopt a common currency by 2018. Continental initiatives are also being developed. As individual countries increasingly pursue sound and sustainable economic policies, the expansion of monetary unions becomes increasingly feasible.

2.8   Conclusion

South Africa's experience with external use of the rand has been positive. External use of the rand – in particular through the CMA arrangements – has contributed to international trade and regional stability. However, the quantification of 'how much rand is out there in other countries' will remain imperfect, to say the least. Measurement issues and hurdles regarding key balances and flows related to the external use of the rand have been and will continue to be a frustration.

In having a national currency accepted in an external role, the size of the issuing economy clearly counts. Stability-oriented and consistent monetary policies also count. Arrangements to divide seigniorage on a fair basis between the participants in the currency union also reinforce participation, as do provisions which enable participants to issue their own national currencies, However, certain tensions are likely to remain – in particular for the smaller participants on account of not being able to pursue an independent monetary policy of their own.

The CMA arrangement has a long history. The single common currency which served the entire CMA area up to the mid-1970s certainly contributed to the establishment of a successful currency union. Building on this history, and retaining momentum in the pursuit of regional economic integration and growth, are likely to further advance the external use of the rand.

Notes

Johan van den Heever is head of the Research Department in the South African Reserve Bank. This chapter is drawn from the paper presented at the conference on 'External Use of Currency: International Experience and Implications for Renminbi' arranged by the Hong Kong Institute for Monetary Research and held in Hong Kong on 15–16 October 2007. The views expressed are those of the author and are not necessarily in agreement with those of his employer.

References

Committee of Central Bank Governors in SADC (2007). *SADC Financial Systems: Structures, Policies and Markets, September 2007*. Pretoria: Secretariat of the Committee of Central Bank Governors in SADC.

Global Financial Data (2007). *The Global History of Currencies: Botswana*. Available at www.globalfinancialdata.com, accessed on 1 October 2007.

IMF (International Monetary Fund) (2007). *IMF World Economic Outlook Database, April 2007*. Available at www.imf.org, accessed on 1 October 2007.

South African National Treasury (2007). *2007 Estimates of National Expenditure*. Pretoria: National Treasury.

Selialia, F.L. (1998). *The Purchasing Power Parity (PPP) Theory, Fixed Exchange Rate Regime and the Rate of Inflation: The Case of the Common Monetary Area (CMA) of Southern Africa*. Research Bulletin special issue 1998: Inflation in Southern Africa. Gaborone: Bank of Botswana.

South African Reserve Bank (2007). *South African Reserve Bank Quarterly Bulletin, September 2007*. Pretoria: South African Reserve Bank.

Statistics South Africa (2007). *Bulletin of Statistics, September 2007*. Pretoria: Statistics South Africa.

Van Rensburg, D.J. (2007). Personal Communication, 11 October 2007. Pretoria: National Treasury Director: International Economics.

Van Zyl, L. (2003). *South Africa's Experience of Regional Currency Areas and the Use of Foreign Currencies*. BIS Papers No. 17, May 2003. Basel: Bank for International Settlements.

Wang, J., I. Masha, K. Shirono & L. Harris (2007). 'The Common Monetary Area in Southern Africa: Shocks, Adjustment, and Policy Challenges'. IMF Working Paper No. 07/158. Washington, DC: International Monetary Fund.

3
Internationalizing the Australian Dollar

Robert N. McCauley

> *Asian policymakers are giving consideration to allowing their currencies to be used by non-residents. If policy allows this and a robust fixed income market provides support, the Australian experience indicates that a currency can internationalize fairly quickly, particularly if it offers a yield pickup.*

Asian policymakers combine ongoing or episodic resistance to financial globalization with a keen interest in the potential for their currencies to be used by non-residents. Despite attempts to stave off capital inflows as these mounted in 2006 and early 2007, the authorities of Korea, India and China have all paid attention to the potential for more extensive international use of their currencies. In May 2006, the Korean Ministry of Finance and the Economy (2006) described its acceleration of the schedule to liberalize the won and capital flows as 'facilitating the internationalization of the won'. In July 2006, the Tarapore Committee of the Reserve Bank of India (2006) devoted several paragraphs to the internationalization of the Indian rupee. In August 2008, the People's Bank of China created a new unit to analyse the exchange rate of the renminbi and its internationalization. As the papers in this volume attest, Chinese scholars are not waiting for the full liberalization of the Chinese capital account to consider the potential of the renminbi as an international currency.[1]

Currency internationalization can serve as a means to an end or constitute part of an end, but it can also pose risks to other ends. Asian policymakers seek to develop their financial markets, and internationalization of their currencies is seen as potentially making an important contribution. The aforementioned authorities all have some vision of Seoul, Mumbai or Shanghai as international financial centres. An internationalized currency can seem to be a defining feature of such a centre, despite London's interval from 1947 to 1979 as an international financial centre operating more with the US dollar than with sterling. Still, the global financial turmoil that hit the major financial centres in August 2007 has highlighted the risk to exchange rates, bond yields and financial stability of international capital flows. This experience has no doubt reinforced the caution already evident among policymakers in the big Asian economies with the greatest latent demand by non-residents to use their currencies.[2]

The Australian dollar offers a useful case for study. Its internationalization occurred within the last 30 years, rather than over a century ago as in the case of sterling or the dollar (Flandreau and Jobst, 2006). Policy tended to be neutral rather than discouraging, as in the case of the Deutsche mark or Swiss franc. It is a simpler story than that of the euro, which must treat the euro's predecessor currencies. Finally, it has been argued that the initial conditions shared some of the features of today's Asian economies (Debelle and Plumb, 2006; Debelle et al., 2006).

Updating and extending earlier work (McCauley, 2006), this chapter first defines an internationalized currency in terms of the domain of its use as a means of exchange and as a store of wealth. Then the path of the Australian dollar is traced from insular to internationalized currency. Policy permitted rather than discouraged or encouraged this process. In addition, both domestic financial development and relatively high interest rates played important roles. The chapter concludes by briefly considering the effects of internationalization on bond yields and the exchange rate. If the Australian experience is any guide, Asian bond yields can be expected to move more in line with those in major bond markets once currencies are internationalized. As for the impact of internationalization on the exchange rate, the long-term effect depends on whether a currency attracts both global borrowers and lenders, or attracts one rather than the other.

3.1   Defining and measuring an internationalized currency

An internationalized currency can be defined as one that is freely traded against other currencies and used to denominate contracts, including bank accounts and bonds, outside its country of issue. In the bond market, internationalization requires more than non-residents becoming important holders of domestically issued bonds: that is, the domestic bond market is taken to be fully internationalized only when non-residents figure as important issuers of bonds denominated in the domestic currency. In addition, an internationalized currency is used to denominate bonds sold outside its domestic financial markets, in offshore markets, by both domestic and foreign issuers who choose to tap non-resident investors. A telling sign of internationalization is a non-resident issuer of a bond denominated in the domestic currency that is sold offshore to non-resident investors.

3.1.1   Australian dollar trading in the global foreign exchange market

Australian dollars are actively traded by non-residents. Like most major currencies, the Australian dollar trades more outside the home economy

Table 3.1   The geography of global foreign exchange trading (in billions of US dollars per day in April 2007)

	Global trading	Domestic trading[1]	Offshore trading	Memo: Offshore percentage
US dollar	2660.3	548.3	2111.9	79%
Euro	1139.4	264.5	874.9	77%
Yen	509.7	169.6	340.2	67%
Sterling	460.8	297.3	163.5	35%
Swiss franc	208.8	69.3	139.5	67%
Canadian dollar	129.8	40.4	89.3	69%
Australian dollar	205.2	84.6	120.6	59%
New Zealand dollar	58.7	7.3	51.5	88%
Chinese renminbi	14.6	9.1	5.6	38%
Hong Kong dollar	85.6	73.4	12.2	14%
Indian rupee	21.1	16.4	4.7	22%
Indonesian rupiah	3.3	1.8	1.5	44%
Korean won	34.0	27.1	6.9	20%
Malaysian ringgit	4.3	2.7	1.6	37%
Philippine peso	3.5	2.2	1.3	37%
Singapore dollar	37.7	24.2	13.4	36%
New Taiwan dollar	11.6	6.6	5.1	44%
Thai baht	6.4	4.7	1.6	26%

[1]Domestic trading includes both onshore-onshore and onshore-offshore trading.
Source: BIS (2007), Tables E1 and E7.

than within (Table 3.1). That is, if one defines offshore trading in a currency as that between two non-residents, then such trades represent the major part of global transactions for major currencies. On this measure, the Australian dollar is as much an internationalized currency as the yen, although somewhat less so than the US dollar, euro or New Zealand dollar. Among the major currencies, sterling stands out as trading mostly in the home market, which is also the largest centre for trading foreign exchange.

In contrast to most of the major currencies and the Australian dollar, Asian currencies other than the Japanese yen trade mostly in the domestic market (Tsuyuguchi and Wooldridge, 2008). As a share of total trading, strictly offshore trading in Asian currencies ranges from 14% and 20% for Hong Kong and Korea, respectively, to 44% for the Indonesian rupiah and the New Taiwan dollar.[3]

Currency internationalization tends to rise with economic development. This regularity is evident when the offshore trading percentage in April 2007 is plotted against gross domestic product per capita at market prices (Figure 3.1). On this view, offshore trading is light not only for sterling but also for the Hong Kong and Singapore dollars, suggesting the financial

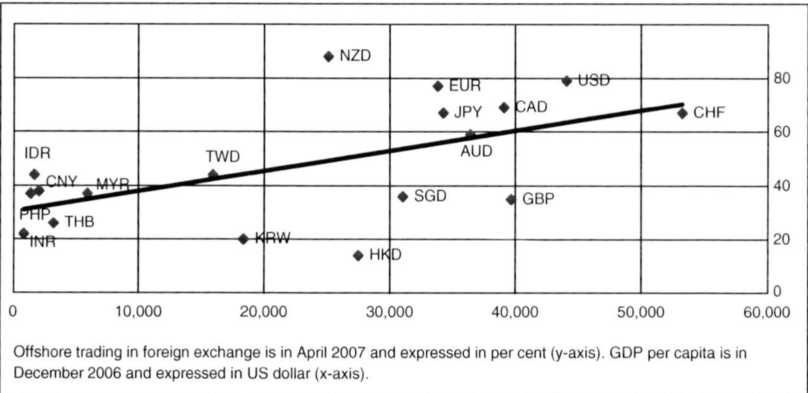

Offshore trading in foreign exchange is in April 2007 and expressed in per cent (y-axis). GDP per capita is in December 2006 and expressed in US dollar (x-axis).

Figure 3.1 Offshore foreign exchange trading share in relation to GDP per capita (in per capita)
Sources: IMF, *World Economic Outlook*; BIS, *Triennial Central Bank Survey (2007)*.

centres concentrate trading in their own currencies (see Box 3.1 for regression analysis). The Korean won's low rate of offshore trading is noteworthy. On the other side, the New Zealand dollar stands out with the highest fraction of offshore trading.

Box 3.1 Regression analysis of currency internationalization in the forex market

This box reports the results of cross-sectional regression analysis of two measures of currency internationalization in the foreign exchange market. In the body of this chapter, the fraction of strictly offshore trading has been used to measure internationalization. A second, broader measure adds cross-border trading to such strictly offshore trading. This measure closes much of the gap between the international financial centres of London, Hong Kong and Singapore and economies of like GDP per capita (Figure 3.2).

For either measure, GDP per capita has a strong positive association with currency internationalization in the foreign exchange market (Table A). This association is even stronger for the broader measure than for strictly offshore trading. In the case of strictly offshore trading, financial centres have systematically lower (by 28–38%) offshore trading. This effect is much weaker for the sum of offshore and cross-border trading, and is generally not statistically significant.

Box 3.1 (Continued)

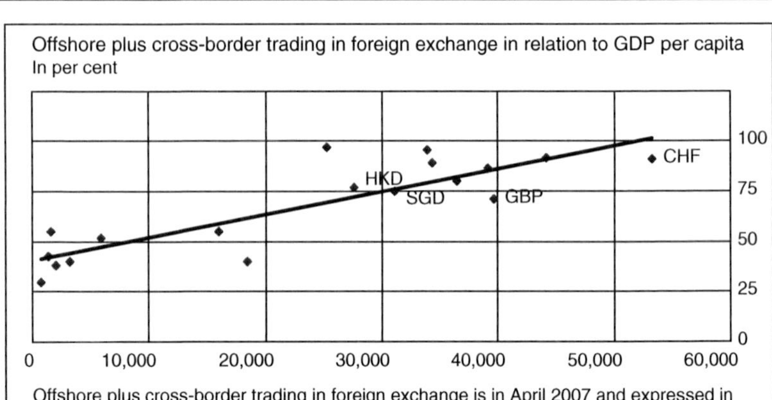

Offshore plus cross-border trading in foreign exchange is in April 2007 and expressed in per cent (y-axis). GDP per capita is in December 2006 and expressed in US dollar (x-axis).

Sources: IMF, *World Economic Outlook*; BIS, *Triennial Central Bank Survey (2007)*.

Table A: Impact of macroeconomic variables on location of foreign exchange trading April 2007

	Offshore trading			Offshore + cross-border trading		
	(1)	(2)	(3)	(4)	(5)	(6)
Intercept	−55.731*	−30.338	−32.911	−65.608**	−38.491	−39.923
	(0.074)	(0.347)	(0.329)	(0.012)	(0.108)	(0.112)
GDP per capita (log)	11.627***	8.221**	7.412*	14.170***	10.533***	10.083***
	(0.002)	(0.037)	(0.088)	(0.000)	(0.001)	(0.004)
Financial centre	−28.456**	−38.072***	−36.268**	−4.803	−15.071*	−14.067
	(0.015)	(0.005)	(0.011)	(0.567)	(0.085)	(0.133)
International bonds	– –	0.368 (0.112)	0.378 (0.115)	– –	0.393** (0.024)	0.399** (0.028)
Nominal GDP (log)	– –	– –	1.462 (0.626)	– –	– –	0.813 (0.706)
Adjusted R^2	0.442	0.505	0.476	0.671	0.757	0.742

Note: GDP per capita is expressed in US dollars. Financial centre is a dummy variable. Nominal GDP is expressed in billions of US dollars. Bonds are international bonds and notes outstanding expressed as a percentage of total bonds and notes outstanding. The financial centres are Hong Kong, Singapore, Switzerland and the United Kingdom. P-values are in parenthesis. *** indicates 1% significance, ** indicates 5% significance, * indicates 10% significance.

Source: IMF, *World Economic Outlook*; BIS, *Triennial Central Bank Survey (2007)*; author's estimates.

Box 3.1 (Continued)

The share of international bonds in the stock of bonds in a given currency was entered to see whether internationalization of the bond market internationalization affects that of the foreign exchange market. The influence from the bond market to the forex market seems significant only when the broader measure is analysed.

Nominal GDP was entered with the expectation that it might attract a negative coefficient, with New Zealand as the archetype of a small economy with an extremely internationalized currency. However, the estimated parameter had a positive sign with either measure and in any case did not attain conventional levels of significance.

Overall, the fraction of variance accounted for by this cross-sectional Kuznets curve is quite high. In particular, income per capita and either the financial centre status or the international bond share jointly account for two-fifths to one-half for strictly offshore trading, and two-thirds to three-quarters for the sum of offshore and cross-border trading.

The Australian dollar's internationalization is mature. This maturity can be illustrated by plotting the offshore trading percentage in April 2004 and April 2007 and drawing an arrow between them (Figure 3.2). The vector is flat for the Australian dollar, indicating that the degree of

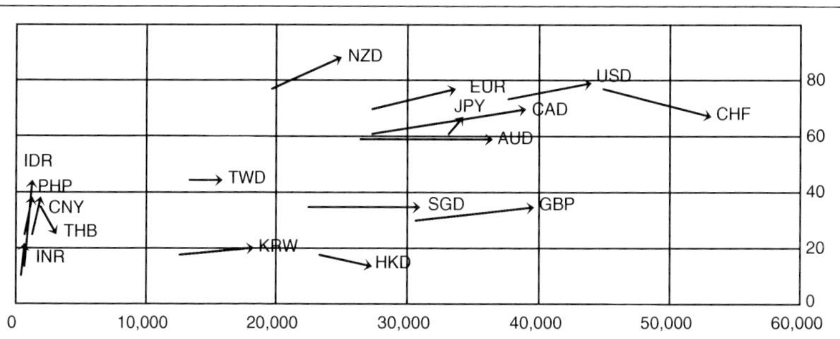

Offshore trading in foreign exchange is in April 2004 and 2007 and expressed in per cent (y-axis). GDP per capita is in December 2003 and 2006 and expressed in US dollar (x-axis). The arrows trace the shift from 2004 to 2007. The 2004 survey captured only Shanghai interbank trading of the Chinese renminbi, leaving onshore trading not comparable to that of the other currencies. Ho et al. (2005, p. 53), estimate the domestic trading as at least USD 2.7 billion, and this estimate is used here.

Figure 3.2 Offshore trading in foreign exchange in relation to GDP per capita (change from April 2004 to April 2007)
Sources: IMF, *World Economic Outlook*; BIS, *Triennial Central Bank Survey (2005, 2007)*.

internationalization did not change with the rise in incomes in Australia (including that from the appreciation of the Australian dollar). At lower levels of income, the arrows tend to point to the northeast, indicating that an increase in GDP per capita is associated with a more internationalized currency.

3.1.2   The Australian dollar in the global bond market

An internationalized currency also serves non-residents as a store of value whenever they buy or sell deposits or bonds denominated in the currency.[4] For the Australian dollar, this goes well beyond non-resident investment in the domestic bond market, where about half of the Australian Commonwealth bonds issued domestically in Australian dollars are held by non-residents. Non-resident investors have also enjoyed the convenience of Australian issuers selling Australian dollar bonds offshore (Table 3.2). A larger sum still has been raised by non-resident borrowers issuing Australian dollar bonds in the domestic market (foreign bonds known as 'kangaroo bonds'). A similar sum has been raised by non-resident issuers of Australian bonds marketed to offshore investors. The balance between these two has shifted over the last several years, with more non-resident paper being marketed (at least in part) in Australia. All told, Australian dollar bonds marketed offshore and kangaroo bonds amount to about 40% of Australian dollar bonds outstanding globally. (Taking account of non-resident holdings of domestic bonds issued by Australians would raise the international share to more than one-half.)

In an international comparison, the Australian bond market is more internationalized than most, but by no means the most internationalized (Figure 3.3, upper panel). After a generation of internationalization, the yen bond market remains overwhelmingly domestic (Nishi and Vergus, 2006).

Table 3.2   The Australian dollar in the global bond market (in billions of US dollars, at end 2007)

Australian dollar bond issuers	Location of market		Total
	Australia	Offshore	
Australian	326	73	399
Others	82	82	164
Total	408	155	563

Note: According to BIS data, issuers of Australian nationality had $447 billion in outstanding international bonds and notes at end 2007, leaving $374 billion outstanding in other currencies, presumably mostly swapped. The Australian Bureau of Statistics (2008) reports foreign holdings of Australian bonds of A$513 billion ($449 billion), including general government bonds of A$39 billion ($34 billion).
Source: Dealogic; Euroclear; International Capital Market Association (ICMA); Thomson Financial Securities Data; national authorities; BIS.

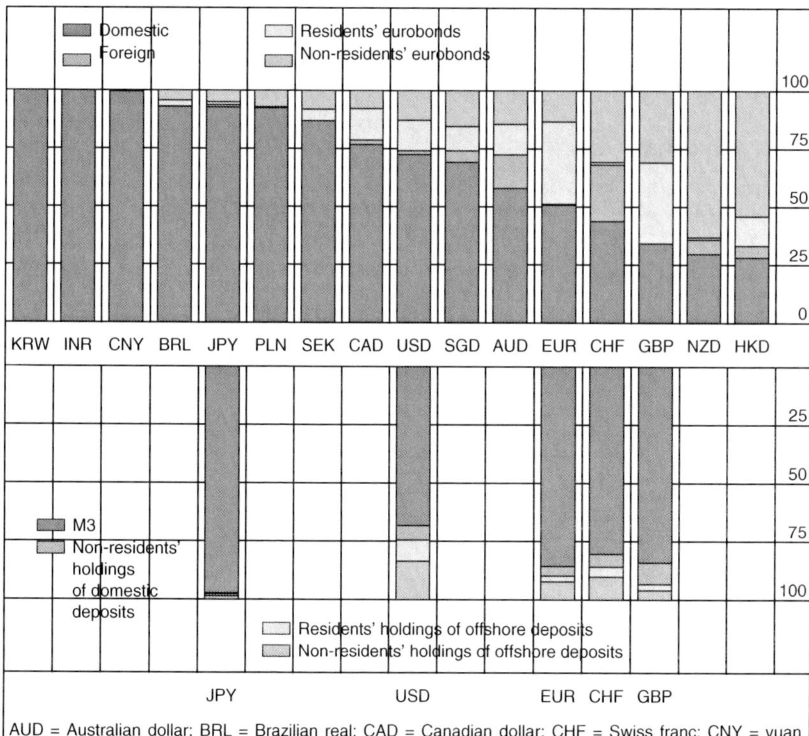

Figure 3.3 Selected currencies in the global bond and deposit market (at end 2007, in per cent)

Note: The currency breakdown in the international banking statistics is limited to the currencies shown in the lower panel. M3 for United States at end 2007 estimated using ration of M3/M2 in March 2006. Euro denominated non-residents' holdings of domestic deposites exclude cross-border holdings within the euro area.

Sources: Dealogic; Euroclear; ISMA; Thomson Financial Securities Data; national authorities; BIS.

The US dollar bond market likewise remains heavily domestic, albeit with non-residents holding a substantial fraction of domestic bonds. Only the euro and sterling bond markets, among major currencies, and the Swiss franc, New Zealand dollar and Hong Kong dollar bond markets, among smaller currencies, have a relatively larger offshore and foreign component than the Australian bond market.

For other Asian bond markets, however, things look much different. The large Korean won bond market, for instance, remains very local.

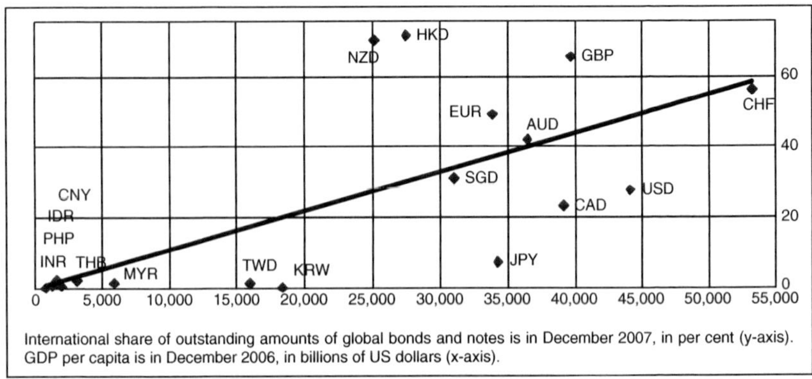

Figure 3.4 International share of global bonds and notes in relation to GDP per capita
Sources: *World Economic Outlook*; BIS.

There have been at most scattered offshore issuances and a few foreign bond issues by international financial institutions and multinational corporations.

Like the internationalization of the foreign exchange market, the internationalization of bond markets tends to rise with economic development. This regularity is evident when the offshore and foreign fraction of bond markets by currency is plotted against gross domestic product per capita at market prices (Figure 3.4). On this view, the purely domestic bond markets of many Asian currencies are associated with their low incomes, while the Australian bond market's considerable internationalization (and the still higher internationalization of the Swiss franc market) reflects the country's higher income.

The internationalization of foreign exchange markets and bond markets is mutually reinforcing. This is evident when the offshore trading in foreign exchange is plotted against the offshore and foreign share of bond markets (Figure 3.5). If bonds in a given currency are sold and traded offshore, then a demand for transactions offshore is generated. At the same time, if non-residents hold bank deposits in a given currency, they will look to place some of the funds in fixed-income instruments, giving rise to demand for offshore bond issues.

While no data are available on offshore deposits in Australian dollars, the evidence for the major currencies in the lower panel of Figure 3.3 suggests that only a small proportion of Australian dollar deposits are held offshore. Only the US dollar deposit market shows a ratio of cross-border or offshore deposits of over one-quarter.[5] Thus, for major currencies and the Australian dollar, measured internationalization tends to be high for currency trading, moderately high for bond markets, and low for deposits.

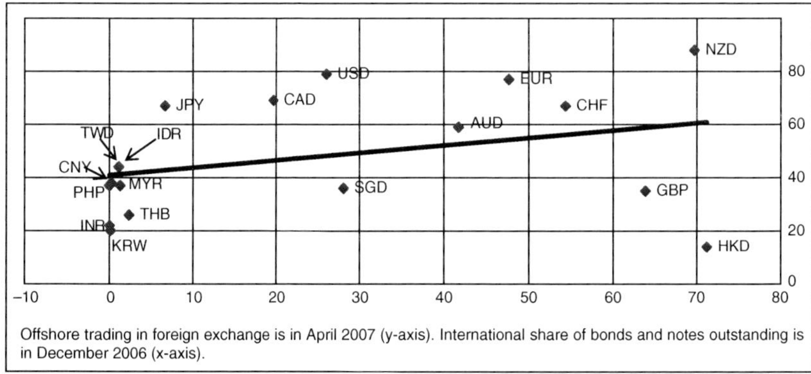

Figure 3.5   Offshore trading in foreign exchange in relation to international share of bonds and notes outstanding (in per cent)
Sources: IMF, *World Economic Outlook;* BIS.

3.2   From insular to international currency

The Australian dollar's transition from an initial insularity to the current state of internationalization took about a decade. The development of derivatives markets, and in particular the currency swap market, played an important role against the background of the Australian dollar's yield advantage over the US dollar. In addition, whereas a withholding tax was levied on coupon interest paid by domestic bonds, a broad exemption applicable to offshore issues gave the latter an extra source of support.

3.2.1   Insularity

Australia's foreign exchange, money and bond markets in the 1970s and early 1980s remained quite insular. This was a policy choice in service of a succession of exchange rate regimes from bilateral peg through basket peg to basket crawl (Debelle and Plumb, 2006). In general, the Australian dollar was not used outside the country. Capital controls required exporters to surrender foreign exchange and generally restricted Australian portfolio investment abroad. The Reserve Bank of Australia limited forward cover to trade transactions. Banks were prohibited from paying interest on deposits of non-residents, and non-resident banks and governments were restricted to minimum working balances in order 'to discourage the development of a reserve currency role for the Australian dollar' (Campbell Committee, 1981, p. 147). Withholding taxes deterred investment in domestic bonds.

Even in this period, however, there were practices and policies that looked forward to a less insular future. First, between 1976 and 1980, there were

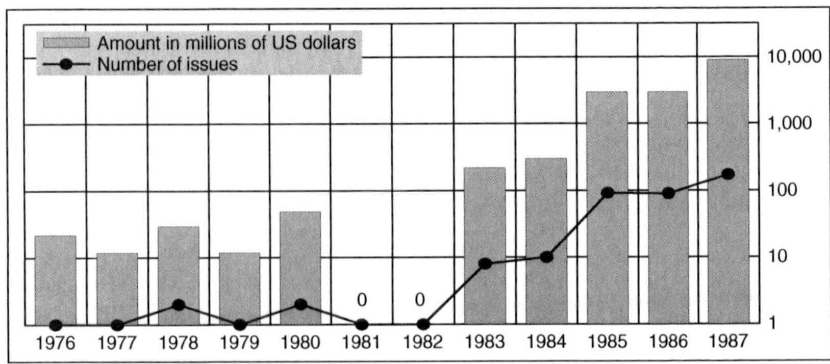

Figure 3.6   Issuance of Australian dollar eurobonds
Note: Semi-logarithmic scale.
Sources: Burnett and kerr (1984, p 115): Gallant (1988. p 100).

seven small Australian dollar issues offshore, in amounts between A$10 million and A$15 million (Figure 3.6). Sold to Benelux and Middle East investors, these resembled private placements. Dealers could not readily hold and fund inventory given the above restrictions and the consequently limited supply of offshore Australian dollar funding (Burnett and Kerr, 1984). Second, when the Australian dollar was under upward pressure the authorities did permit selected portfolio outflows. And third, the authorities permitted an onshore non-deliverable forward market to develop. Settled in Australian dollars, this market was in some ways the mirror image of the non-deliverable markets in Asia, where offshore players settle their side bets in dollars (Ma et al., 2004; Debelle et al., 2006).

3.2.2   Opening

The Australian dollar was floated in 1983 and the capital controls that had buttressed the former regime were dismantled. Subsequently, an Australian dollar deposit market, integrated with the spot and forward foreign exchange markets, developed in London, Hong Kong and Singapore.[6] After a depreciation of the Australian dollar in early 1983, the Australian dollar eurobond market reopened with a A$20 million five-year offering from the Primary Industry Bank of Australia. The issue yielded some three percentage points more than US dollar bonds but a full one percentage point less than did the Commonwealth of Australia's domestic five-year bond. Withholding taxes on sovereign bonds onshore left offshore investors willing to accept lower yields from inferior credits that were marketed offshore.

During the mid-1980s, the representative issuers in the Australian dollar sector of the eurobond market shifted. Issuers in the 1970s and early 1980s were Australian names. As late as 1985, the top four issuers were two Australian

Table 3.3 Top five issuers of Australian dollar eurobonds (in millions of US dollars)

1985		1986		1987		2005	
Issuer	**Amount**	**Issuer**	**Amount**	**Issuer**	**Amount**	**Issuer**	**Amount**
ANZ Banking	142	IBM Australia	143	Deutsche Bank	491	New South Wales Treasury	2,792
Common-wealth Bank	100	Deutsche Bank	102	IBJ Australia	321	IBRD (World Bank)	2,652
GJ Coles	84	Common-wealth Bank	100	Westlb Finance	246	Bank Nederlandse Gemeenten	1,673
Austr Ind Dev Co	82	GMAC Australia	80	IBRD	242	Crusade Global Trust	1,425
Security Pacific	74	Hamburg Landes-bank	72	SEK	218	Rabo Bank	1,112

Source: Gallant (1988, p. 100) for 1985–87; BIS (2005) for 2005.

banks, an Australian retailer and an Australian agency (Table 3.3). The following year, however, demand shifted from Benelux retail buyers to Swiss and German buyers (Beard, 1985). As a result, German banks took the opportunity to capitalize on their name recognition to become two of the top five issuers. By 1987, most large Australian dollar eurobonds were issued by high-quality issuers with little or no intrinsic need for Australian dollar funding.

The pattern set in 1987 essentially holds to this day. While the largest state in Australia, New South Wales, a home-grown top credit, topped the list of issuers in 2005, the top five issuers included the World Bank and two Dutch banks. Issuance by a vehicle backed by Australian residential mortgages, namely the Crusade Global Trust, highlighted the development of asset securitization. Instead of a bond issued by an Australian bank, offshore institutional investors bought a bond backed by the obligations of Australian households to an Australian bank. In 2007, offshore demand for securitized Australian mortgages dropped off, and stand-alone quality borrowers regained their ascendancy.

The development of the cross-currency swap market played a key role in the internationalization of the Australian dollar bond market. Without such swaps, the high demand for credit quality on the part of the buyers of Australian dollar bonds would have run up against the limited roster of top-quality Australian borrowers. Instead, top global issuers have been induced by favourable all-in costs of US dollar funding to issue and to swap. As Box 3.2 illustrates, the cross-currency swap market caters to the preference of the end investor in offshore Australian dollar bond issues for top-quality names. In effect, a chain of banks and swaps links the saver and the ultimate borrower.

Box 3.2 An example of a swapped offshore Australian dollar bond

1. AAA-rated German agency KfW sells an Australian dollar bond that is heavily marketed to Japanese households (under so-called *uridashi* rules).

2. KfW swaps the proceeds, namely a fixed-rate obligation in Australian dollars, with an underwriter for floating rate US dollars; KfW meets its funding target at an attractively low yield below dollar Libid.

3. An Australian bank borrows floating rate US dollars from a bank or by selling a US dollar bond and swapping the proceeds for floating rate US dollars (see figure below).

4. The Australian bank swaps its liability in floating rate US dollars with the underwriter for a fixed-rate obligation in Australian dollars.

5. The Australian bank lends to an Australian firm in fixed-rate Australian dollars.

6. In sum, AAA-rated KfW has sourced Australian dollar funding from Japan for a second-tier Australian firm.

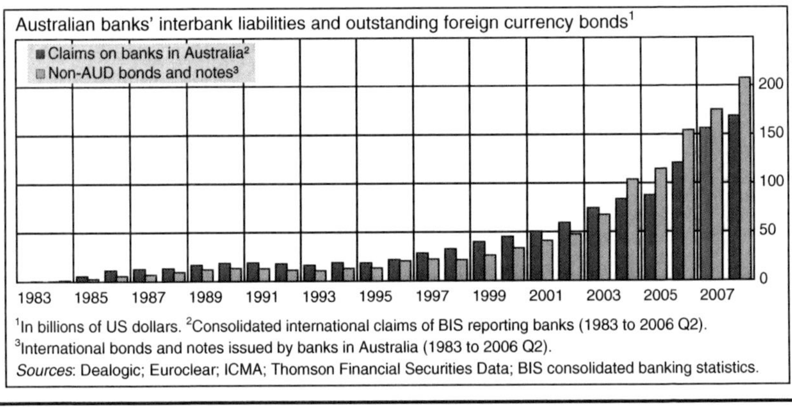

[1] In billions of US dollars. [2] Consolidated international claims of BIS reporting banks (1983 to 2006 Q2).
[3] International bonds and notes issued by banks in Australia (1983 to 2006 Q2).
Sources: Dealogic; Euroclear; ICMA; Thomson Financial Securities Data; BIS consolidated banking statistics.

Against this background, the nascent offshore market for Korean won issues seems to be taking a different path. Prime Australian names opened the offshore Australian dollar market before the days of currency swaps and to this day Australian names figure prominently. At the outset, the Korean won market instead features foreign financial issuers seeking cheap US dollar funding. As the market for Korean won issues widens, the investor preference for top quality may become more important. Given Korea's single-A rating, foreign issuers may come to dominate the offshore won market, much as they do in smaller markets like New Zealand's (Drage et al., 2005; Ólafsson, 2005).

3.2.3 An international Australian dollar market

By the end of the 1980s, the Australian dollar had made the transition to an internationalized currency. Four characteristics mark what is now a thoroughly internationalized Australian dollar bond market: (i) its grounding in the domestic fixed income market; (ii) the demand for quality among international investors in Australian dollar paper; (iii) the importance of the cross-currency swap market; and (iv) the importance of yield to international investors. Consider each in turn.

The internationalized Australian dollar bond market depends on a well-functioning set of domestic markets. In the early 1980s, government bond issuance through taps gave way to auctions, and the government ceased to have recourse to the central bank. Even as the offshore market developed, the domestic government bond market attracted international investment.[7] Though not large, the cash government bond market still supports a ten-year government bond futures contract that performs a critical role in price discovery. In addition, well-developed interest rate swap and currency swap markets link domestic and international markets (see below). While withholding tax remains on most foreign investment in most domestically issued bonds, whereas offshore issues of bonds are exempt, this impediment to foreign investment in the domestic market may actually have encouraged resident issuers to issue offshore.

As noted, foreign investors in Australian dollar bonds can avoid credit risk even as they accept currency risk. In fact, the issuers who have chosen to sell Australian dollar bonds offshore have been of the highest quality. This can be confirmed by a comparison of ratings (Figure 3.7) assigned to eurobonds sold by either non-Australians or Australians (targeted to foreign investors) and the foreign and domestic bonds sold in Australia (targeted to domestic investors). This comparison is apt because both sets of issuers are drawn from the same universe. The bias towards quality in the offshore issues is very clear. In the case of the Australian dollar issues, this bias stands in sharp contrast to a general finding that lower-quality Australian names issue bonds outside Australia (Battellino, 2002). This reflects the greater openness of the global US dollar bond market to low-rated paper.

As a result of the strong demand for credit quality by offshore investors, the currency swap market plays a crucial role. Most observers judge that the entirety of Australian dollar bond issues by non-residents, $164 billion (Table 3.2), is swapped and is thereby ultimately serviced by the Australian

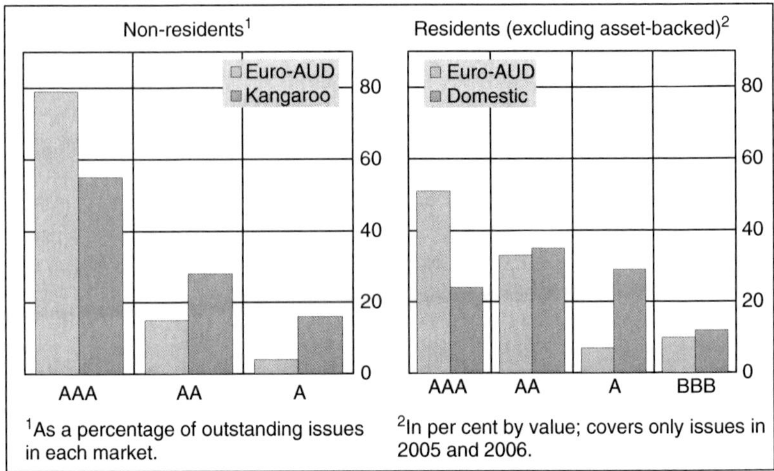

Figure 3.7   Onshore and offshore issuance by Australian residents and non-residents, by rating
Sources: Reserve Bank of Australia; BIS.

private sector (Australian Bureau of Statistics, 2001). On this supposition, at least 30% of the Australian bond market depends on currency swaps.

Finally, overseas demand for Australian dollar paper, as for bonds denominated in other currencies (Cohen, 2005), responds positively to the interest rate premium offered. Australian dollar issuance dried up in 1981–2, when US interest rates rose sharply against a backdrop of relatively stable Australian rates (Figure 3.6). Gallant (1988, p. 99) suggests that 'investors look for good quality credits issuing paper with coupons around 5 per cent more than a comparable issue in US dollars'. Of course, such spreads reflected inflation differentials that have since disappeared, leaving the Australian yield premium subject to cyclical developments. Thus, offshore issuance by both non-residents and residents weakened in 1997–2000 as yields converged. After US interest rates fell to extraordinarily low levels in 2001–2003, the issuance of higher-yielding Australian dollar bonds rebounded once more (Figure 3.8).

3.3   Implications for the currency and interest rates

By making capital more mobile, the internationalization of the Australian dollar (Blundell-Wignall et al., 1993) affected the currency and long-term yields. The discussion takes up first the level, then the volatility of each.

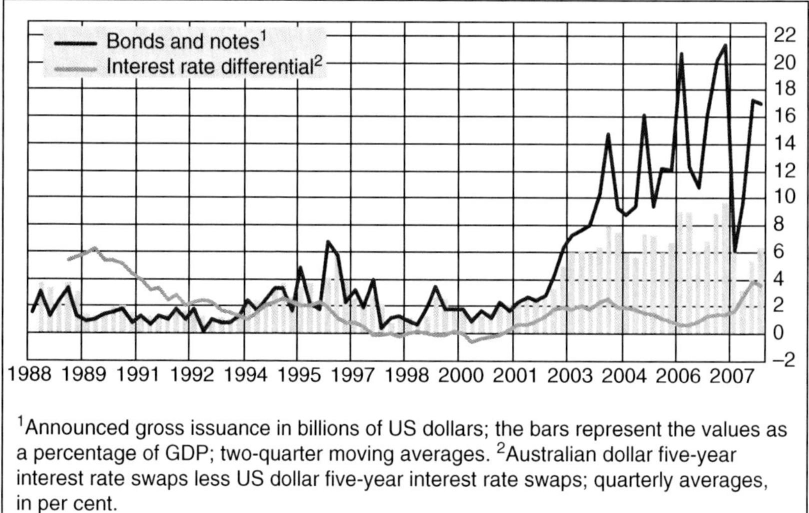

[1]Announced gross issuance in billions of US dollars; the bars represent the values as a percentage of GDP; two-quarter moving averages. [2]Australian dollar five-year interest rate swaps less US dollar five-year interest rate swaps; quarterly averages, in per cent.

Figure 3.8   Onshore issuance of Australian dollar bonds and notes
Sources: Bloomberg; Datastream; Dealogic; Euroclear; ISMA; Thomson Financial Securities Data; national data; BIS.

The internationalization of the Australian dollar has, on balance, probably strengthened its exchange rate over the years. This conjecture is based on the idea that the Australian dollar's internationalization is asymmetric, in that it has drawn international investment, but rarely international borrowing, to the currency. This is a case of 'lopsided internationalization', which Sakakibara and Kondoh (1984) feared might characterize the yen. In contrast, the US dollar and the euro attract not only outside investors, but also borrowers who do not hedge their liability positions. This leaves ambiguous the effect of these currencies being used internationally (McCauley, 1997). Most observers consider that the Australian dollar, with exceptions such as in early 1998 (FSF, 2000), has primarily attracted long positions (even if some of them, such as those held by Japanese life insurers, may be variably hedged).

On this same reasoning, the internationalization of the Australian dollar may, on balance, have reduced Australian dollar long-term interest rates over the years. In fact, the internationalization of the Australian dollar was associated with a shift in the composition of capital inflows from direct investment to bonds (Tease, 1990). Since most home mortgages in Australia are at floating interest rates, the stimulative effect of this development may have been largest in the corporate sector. Indeed, Gallant (1988, p. 98) reported that Australian firms had then to look offshore for 'most medium-term funding'. Onshore funding opportunities have improved since then, but the offshore bid may still weigh on Australian bond yields to the benefit of the corporate sector.[8] Of course, to the extent that the Australian dollar has been stronger, policy rates have been lower, making mortgages more affordable. In New Zealand, by contrast, because of the recent shift to mortgages priced off two- or three-year interest rate swaps, the housing sector has benefited directly from the offshore demand for New Zealand paper (Drage et al., 2005).

Regarding volatility, observers worry that a waning of international demand can lead to periods of currency instability. A particular concern focuses on downward pressure during periods when Australian dollar yields have converged to US dollar yields. In such circumstances, offshore investors can be less inclined to roll the funds from maturing offshore Australian dollar issues into new ones. Of course, offshore issues can be bought by Australian investors before maturity, and by the same token non-residents can sell holdings of domestic bonds. Still, the Statement on Monetary Policy of the Reserve Bank of Australia (RBA, 2006) gives attention not only to the pace of sales of Australian dollar bonds offshore, but also to the schedule of upcoming maturities of such bonds outstanding, as providing a clue to the near-term currency volatility.[9] That said, any effect of internationalization on volatility is likely to be minimal compared to the effect of the policy stability conditioned by the structure of the economy (Simon, 2001).

With the onset of financial turbulence in late 2007, the reliance of the Australian banks on offshore local-currency funding was subjected to a real-world stress-test. Demand for Australian bonds offshore dried up for a month starting in August (Figure 3.8 and McCauley, 2008, p. 16), and short-term 'carry' trades in the Australian dollar were unwound in Tokyo and Chicago (RBA, 2007, p. 31). The Australian dollar moved very sharply, particularly against the Japanese yen.[10] 'In response to the thin and disorderly conditions in foreign exchange markets at the time, the Reserve Bank dealt in the market to add liquidity by selling foreign exchange and purchasing Australian dollars. This was the first time that the Bank has bought Australian dollars in the market since 2001' (RBA, 2007, p. 29).

As for the volatility of bond yields, internationalization may heighten common movements at the expense of country-specific movements. Today, the Australian bond market moves closely with major bond markets (Figure 3.9, upper panel). Price discovery in the Australian bond market takes place to a considerable extent outside Australian trading hours. As reviewed by Kearns (2006), US news, arriving in the overnight gap between Sydney close on one day and Sydney opening on the following day, has more effect on bond yields than Australian news. Not even the substantial cyclical differences between the Australian and the US economies that emerged in the early years of the century, the disconnect between a US economy in recession, and an Australian economy enjoying growth

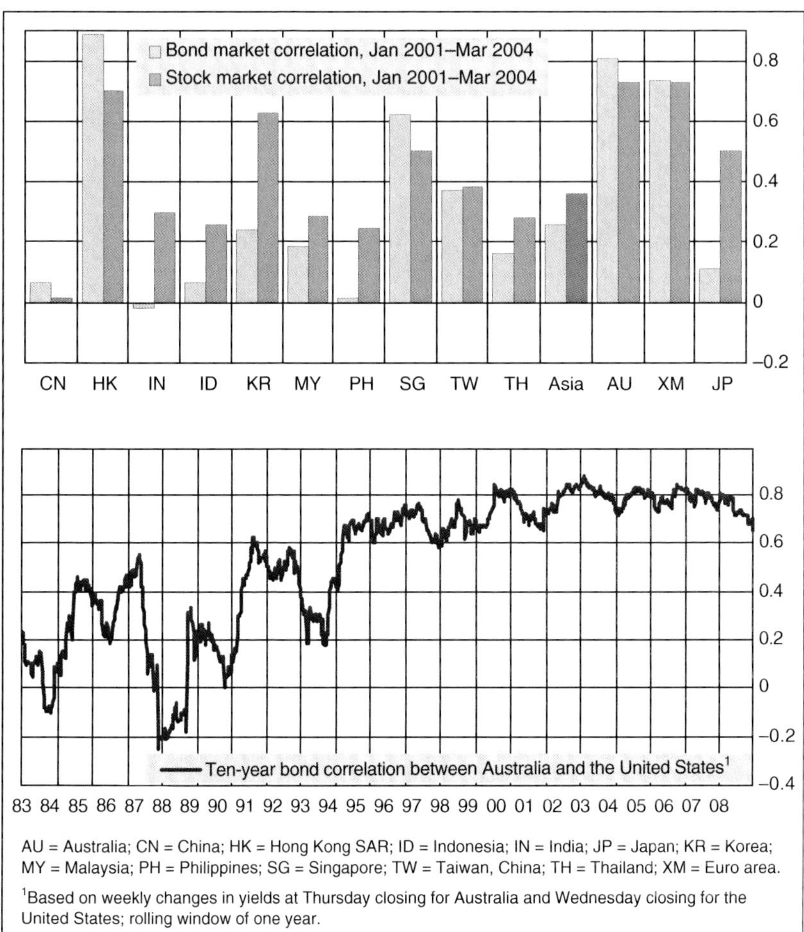

Figure 3.9   Bond and stock market correlations
Note: Based on weekly changes in benchmark yields (stock price indices) at Thursday closing for
Asia and the Pacific and Wednesday closing for US Treasuries (S&P 500).
Sources: McCauley and Jiang (2004); Bloomberg.

seriously disturbed the coupling of long-term interest rates. Updating
Kortian and O'Regan (1996), the lower panel of Figure 3.9 shows that the
Australian bond market had at the time of its opening no more connection
to the US bond market than a number of Asian bond markets have today.
Asian policymakers already have some experience with openness to global
factors in their equity markets. The internationalization of their currencies
could similarly increase the correlation of their bond markets with the US
Treasury market.

3.4 Conclusion

Judging from the Australian experience, a currency can make the transition from extensive controls designed to restrict its use to domestic residents to the status of an internationalized currency in a relatively few years. The process is permitted by a removal of various restrictions but can also be encouraged by a vibrant domestic fixed-income market on which a range of derivatives markets can be based. Indeed, the potential for development of these latter markets (Hohensee and Lee, 2006) probably means that internationalization of a currency can happen more quickly now than in the 1980s.

The relevance of Australia's experience may also depend on the prospective interest rates on any Asian currencies that are opened up to the world. Non-resident demand for Australian dollar bonds has waxed and waned with the interest rate differential. On balance, the rest of the world has been attracted by relatively high interest rates and has accumulated a long position in Australian dollar fixed-income instruments. This position may be modest from a global point of view but has permitted Australia to run up a significant international indebtedness basically in its own currency. So, too, Asian currencies with higher coupons might internationalize more rapidly than currencies with relatively low coupons.

Notes

The author thanks Paola Gallardo, Philippe Hainaut, Denis Pêtre, Swapan-Kumar Pradhan and Michela Scatigna for research assistance, and Robert Aliber, Claudio Borio, Michael Davies, Guy Debelle, Anella Munro, Frank Packer, Yung Chul Park, Philip Wooldridge, James Yetman and participants in seminars at the Reserve Bank of Australia, the Hong Kong Institute for Monetary Research, the International Finance Bureau, the Korean Ministry of Finance and the Economy, the Bank of Korea, Bank Negara Malaysia and the Bank of Thailand for discussion. All errors remain the responsibility of the author. The views expressed are those of the author and not necessarily those of the BIS.

1. Implicitly, Gao and Yu (this volume) and Li and Liu (this volume) challenge the judgement of Cohen (2000, p. 6): 'Among currencies in circulation today, there seems to be no candidate with even the remotest chance in the foreseeable future of challenging the top rank currently enjoyed by the dollar, euro and yen.'
2. See McCauley and Ma (2008), 'Resisting financial globalization in Asia'.
3. Tsuyuguchi and Wooldridge (2008) report higher turnover in the Hong Kong and Singapore dollars as a result of differences in aggregation procedures. Since the additional turnover is thought to take place offshore, the concentration of trading of the domestic currency in these two centres may be overstated to some extent.
4. Data on Australian dollar bank accounts held offshore are lacking, although some central bank holdings of Australian dollars are likely to be in this form. For example, the Riksbank (Sveriges Riksbank, 2006) targets a 5% share of foreign exchange reserves in the Australian dollar. For an indication that a portion of

such holdings are invested in offshore bank deposits, see the rising liabilities of BIS reporting banks to official monetary authorities denominated in 'other' foreign currencies in Table 5C of the BIS *Quarterly Review*.
5. Here we estimate M3 for the United States at end 2007 and ignore the double-counting that arises when some cross-border deposits are included in M3.
6. As late as 1983, settlement in the Australian dollar eurobond secondary market still tended to be made in US dollars (Burnett and Kerr, 1984, p. 116). Manuell (1986, p. 45) alludes to the second-order exchange risk run by Australian borrowers offshore 'because of the necessity for Australian dollar funds to be received or paid via the US dollar'.
7. As early as in Burnett and Kerr (1984), Japanese institutional investors are described as involved in Australia's domestic bond market, in contrast to continental European retail investors who were willing to accept lower yields on Australian dollar eurobonds than on domestic Commonwealth bonds. Gallant (1988, p. 98), by contrast, describes Australian Commonwealth bonds as 'actively traded in London'.
8. In the case of Iceland, Ólafsson (2005, p. 75) holds that demand for domestic currency eurobonds has 'dampened the effectiveness of Central Bank monetary policy across the yield curve' and thus strengthened the exchange rate channel of monetary policy transmission.
9. Efforts to identify the effect of issuance and maturities in the case of the New Zealand dollar have not found statistically significant effects (Drage et al., 2005).
10. See Gyntelberg and Remolona (2007) on the distribution of daily changes of the Australian dollar against the yen.

References

Australian Bureau of Statistics (2001). 'Measuring Australia's Foreign Currency Exposure', *Balance of Payments and International Investment Position, Australia*, December.

Australian Bureau of Statistics (2008). 'Balance of Payments and International Investment Position', Australia, June 2008 (1 September).

Battellino, R. (2002). 'Why Do So Many Australian Borrowers Issue Bonds Offshore?', *Reserve Bank of Australia Bulletin*, December, pp. 19–24.

Beard, P. (1985). 'Why Euro-A\$ Bonds Are Booming', *Euromoney*, August, pp. 95–6.

BIS (Bank for International Settlements) (2005). *Triennial Central Bank Survey: Foreign Exchange and Derivatives Market Activity in 2004.*

——— (2007). *Triennial Central Bank Survey: Foreign Exchange and Derivatives Market Activity in 2007.*

Blundell-Wignall, A., J. Fahrer and A. Heath (1993). 'Major Influences on the Australian Dollar Exchange Rate', in A. Blundell-Wignall (ed.), *The Exchange Rate, International Trade and the Balance of Payments*. Reserve Bank of Australia.

Burnett, D. and J. Kerr (1984). 'The Australian Dollar Sector', in I.M. Kerr (ed.), *A History of the Eurobond Market. The First 21 Years*. London: Euromoney Publications, pp. 115–6.

Campbell Committee (1981). *Final Report of the Committee of Inquiry into the Australian Financial System*. Canberra: Australian Government Publishing Service.

Cohen, B. (2005). 'Currency Choice in International Bond Issuance', *BIS Quarterly Review*, June, pp. 53–66.

Cohen, B.J. (2000). 'Life at the Top: International Currencies in the Twenty-First Century', *Princeton Essays in International Economics*, No. 221 (December).

Debelle, G. and M. Plumb (2006). 'The Evolution of Exchange Rate Policy and Capital Controls in Australia', *Asian Economic Papers*, Vol. 5, No. 2 (Spring–Summer), pp. 7–29.

Debelle, G., J. Gyntelberg and M. Plumb (2006). 'Forward Currency Markets in Asia: Lessons from the Australian Experience', *BIS Quarterly Review*, September, pp. 53–64.

Drage, D., A. Munro and C. Sleeman (2005). 'An Update on Eurokiwi and Uridashi Bonds', *Reserve Bank of New Zealand Bulletin* 61(2), 100–11.

Flandreau, M. and C. Jobst (2006). 'The Empirics of International Currencies. Historical Evidence', Centre for Economic Policy Research, No. 5529 (March).

FSF (Financial Stability Forum), Working Group on Highly Leveraged Institutions (2000). Report, Annex E, Report of the Market Dynamics Study Group, April.

Gallant, P. (1988). *The Eurobond Market*. New York: Woodhead-Faulkner.

Gao, H. (2008). 'Internationalization of the Renminbi and Its Implications for Monetary Policy' (this volume).

Gyntelberg, J. and E.M. Remolona (2007). 'Risk in Carry Trades: A Look at Target Currencies in Asia and the Pacific', *BIS Quarterly Review*, December, pp. 73–82.

Ho, C., G. Ma and R.N. McCauley (2005). 'Trading Asian currencies', *BIS Quarterly Review*, March, pp. 49–58.

Hohensee, M. and K. Lee (2006). 'A Survey on Hedging Markets in Asia: A Description of Asian Derivative Markets from a Practical Perspective', in *Asian Bond Markets. Issues and Prospects, BIS Papers*, No. 30 (November), pp. 261–81.

Kearns, J. (2006). 'Asset Prices and Monetary Policy in Australia: The Contrast of Bonds and Housing', paper submitted to the BIS Autumn Central Bank Economists' Meeting (October).

Korean Ministry of Finance and the Economy (2006). 'The Foreign Exchange Liberalization Plan of the Korean Ministry of Finance and the Economy', 19 May.

Kortian, T. and J. O'Regan (1996). 'Australian Financial Market Volatility: An Exploration of Cross-Country and Cross-Market Linkages'. Reserve Bank of Australia *Research Discussion Paper* No. 9609.

Li, D.D. and L. Liu (2009). 'RMB Internationalization: Empirical and Policy Analysis' (this volume).

Ma, G., C. Ho and R.N. McCauley (2004). 'The Markets for Non-deliverable Forwards in Asia', *BIS Quarterly Review*, June, pp. 81–94.

Manuell, G. (1986). *Floating Down Under: Foreign Exchange in Australia*. Sydney: The Law Book Company.

McCauley, R.N. (1997). 'The Euro and the Dollar', *Princeton University Essays in International Finance*, No. 205, November.

McCauley, R.N. (2006). 'Internationalising a Currency: The Case of the Australian Dollar', *BIS Quarterly Review*, December, pp. 41–54.

McCauley, R.N. (2008). 'Managing Recent Hot Money Capital Inflows in Asia', ADB Institute Discussion Paper No. 99 (March).

McCauley, R.N. and G. Jiang (2004). 'Diversifying with Asian Local Currency Bonds', *BIS Quarterly Review*, September, pp. 51–66.

McCauley, R.N. and G. Ma (2008). 'Resisting Financial Globalisation in Asia', paper presented to Bank of Thailand International Symposium 2008, 'Financial globalization and emerging market economies', 7–8 November 2008 (http://www.bot.or.th/English/EconomicConditions/Semina/Pages/Intersym2008.aspx).

Ólafsson, T.T. (2005). 'Króna-Denominated Eurobond Issues', Central Bank of Iceland *Monetary Bulletin*, no. 4, pp. 55–83.

Nishi, F. and A. Vergus (2006). 'Asian Bond Issues in Tokyo: History, Structure and Prospects', in *Asian Bond Markets: Issues and Prospects*, BIS Papers, No. 30 (November), pp. 143–67.

RBA (Reserve Bank of Australia) (2006). 'Statement on Monetary Policy', section on 'International and Foreign Exchange Markets', May.

——— (2007). 'Statement on Monetary Policy', section on 'International and Foreign Exchange Markets', November.

Reserve Bank of India (2006). *Report of the Committee on Fuller Capital Account Convertibility*, 31 July.

Sakakibara, E. and A. Kondoh (1984). 'Study on the Internationalisation of Tokyo's Money Markets', *Japan Center for International Finance Policy Study Series*, No. 1, June.

Simon, J. (2001). 'The Decline in Australian Output Volatility', Reserve Bank of Australia, *Research Discussion Paper,* 2001–01.

Sveriges Riksbank (2006). 'Riksbank Changes Currency Allocation', press release, 21 April.

Tease, W. (1990). 'The Balance of Payments', in S. Grenville (ed.), *The Australian Macroeconomy in the 1980s*, Reserve Bank of Australia.

Tsuyuguchi, Y. and P. Wooldridge (2008). 'The Evolution of Trading Activity in Asian Foreign Exchange Markets', BIS Working Paper No. 252 (May).

4
Foreign Exchange Liberalization and Its Implications: The case of the Korean Won

Kyungsoo Kim[1] and Chi-Young Song[2]

4.1 Introduction

After the East Asian financial crisis of 1997–8, the South Korean government enthusiastically pursued capital account liberalization. In April 1999, the *bona fide* principle of foreign exchange transactions was abolished. Most regulations on capital account transactions by domestic firms were lifted, such that corporations and financial institutions are now able to borrow overseas and issue short-term foreign currency-denominated bonds. Further, non-residents are allowed to make deposits and open trust accounts denominated in Korean won (KRW). In January 2001, over-the-counter (OTC) securities transactions between residents and non-residents were liberalized, and multi-netting between a corporate headquarters and its branches was allowed. More details are summarized in Appendix 2.

Foreign exchange liberalization has spurred foreign exchange transactions. According to BIS (2007), daily average foreign exchange market turnover, which in 1998 was only US$4 billion, increased to US$10 billion in 2001, US$20 billion in 2004 and US$33 billion in 2007 – roughly two-thirds that of Belgium's but still less than one-fifth that of Australia's. The volume of derivatives has exploded, although it remains far less than in mature economies. The daily average OTC foreign exchange derivative turnover increased from almost nil in 1998 to US$7 billion in 2007.

In fact, the Korean won may be exchanged freely abroad and, under certain conditions, it can be used as a settlement instrument in foreign export and import transactions. As of December 2004, the won joined the Continuous Linked Settlement, an industry-led initiative to eliminate settlement risk in foreign exchange transactions. In September 2006, won-dollar futures and options were listed on the Chicago Mercantile Exchange.

Most regulations on capital outflows by domestic residents were lifted in May 2006, including the acquisition of overseas real estate, the raising of ceilings on individual overseas investment and the easing of regulations on foreign exchange position. Currently, regulations remain in force on the offshore issue of won-denominated securities. The remaining regulations are expected to be removed by 2009, with just a few exceptions including won-denominated fundraising by non-residents.[3]

However, won-denominated financial transactions by non-residents remain restricted while won-denominated assets may be freely purchased through an exclusive account. Won settlement between non-residents in real and financial transactions is also regulated. Won funding intermediated through capital markets and banks is subject to *de facto* regulation.[4] This is because the issue of won-denominated securities by non-residents, which could be a very effective device in times of currency crisis, is considered to have the potential to harm the stability and soundness of the foreign exchange market. Consequently, non-residents' holdings in the Korean bonds market are trivial in comparison to the size of the market;[5] their share has never exceeded 2%.[6] In this sense, internationalization of the won may be very low in the case of the bonds market since a telling sign of the depth of internationalization is the existence of non-resident issuers of bonds denominated in the domestic currency that are sold offshore to non-resident investors (McCauley, 2006).

By way of offshore Non-Deliverable Forwards (NDF) foreign exchange markets and other derivatives markets, however, foreign investors circumvent rules and regulations. Furthermore, branches of overseas banks equipped with advanced financial technology play a pivotal role in linking domestic financial markets to the international market. Arbitrage activity is one notable feature. Once the return on won-denominated securities diverges from that on foreign securities, the foreign bank branches play a central role in capturing the potential profits. In doing so, they have a deep impact on the domestic financial market. Above all, thanks to foreign exchange liberalization, onshore and offshore foreign exchange markets have become closely interlinked and the domestic market has deepened.

Using daily data, this chapter finds that foreign exchange market efficiency holds in the long run, although significant inefficiency remains in the short run. While exchange rates tend to move along the path of familiar covered interest rate parity, this takes time. In other words, exchange rate movements are autoregressive and, therefore, the foreign exchange market is inefficient in the short run. Moreover, domestic forward rates take much more time than NDF rates to reach the long-run equilibrium, and the two markets also have different implications on the interaction between spot foreign exchange markets and money markets. Thus, in spite of the current phase of foreign exchange liberalization, onshore and offshore foreign exchange markets have not been fully integrated.

Deploying financial derivatives, the foreign exchange market is able to draw some arbitrage profits. While foreign exchange swaps, Currency Swaps and Interest Rate Swaps (IRS) are popular instruments, other hybrids such as Total Return Swaps (TRS), Index swaps, and structured notes are also traded.

Branches of overseas banks have led the arbitrage activity because their funding cost is low enough to take advantage of arbitrage opportunities, even taking into account transaction costs. In fact, the profits from financial derivatives transactions were astronomical in 2005, the most recent year for which data are available. Other domestic financial institutions, such as pension funds and insurance companies, have also engaged in this activity. Furthermore, using derivatives such as the Korean Treasury Bond (TB) futures and TRS, foreign investors who are restricted in their access to won funding have an increasing influence on the TB market even though they are only minor players.

The chapter goes on to examine the macro aspects of foreign exchange liberalization (section 4.2), where we explore how foreign exchange liberalization has influenced the way financial market variables such as foreign exchange rates, money market interest rates and yields on TBs behave. In section 4.3, we discuss the micro aspects of foreign exchange liberalization. The arbitrage activities of financial corporations are highlighted as one way of reacting to foreign exchange liberalization. In particular, we focus on the role of Branches of Overseas Banks (BOB) at the center of arbitrage operations. Section 4.4 rounds off the chapter with some concluding remarks.

4.2 Macro aspects of foreign exchange liberalization: Financial market

Foreign exchange liberalization has spurred the transaction volume of foreign exchange and other derivative products. The daily foreign exchange market turnover of the Korean won in 2007 has increased about eightfold compared to that in 1998. Above all, OTC derivatives have grown more than 34 times during the same period. But when compared to other countries, the numbers are still low. According to the BIS (2007), the market turnover of traditional foreign exchange transactions in South Korea in April 2007 was comparable to two-thirds that of Belgium, and even lower when OTC derivatives are included (See Table 4.1).

These low numbers by international standards notwithstanding, the market for OTC derivatives appears to influence the domestic financial sector significantly. This is because derivatives transactions themselves involve leverage whereby market A should be more closely linked to market B. In assessing the impact of foreign exchange liberalization in South Korea, however, one should take into account the offshore NDF market rather than the onshore domestic forward market. As in other Asian countries where foreign investors are restricted from access to the domestic market, NDF market participation is less regulated and onshore players such as domestic banks are also important participants.

Table 4.1 Geographical distribution of reported foreign exchange market turnover (Daily average in April, billion USD)

	Traditional foreign exchange market				OTC derivatives			
	1998	2001	2004	2007	1998	2001	2004	2007
Australia	47	52	81	170	32	51	84	155
Belgium	27	10	20	48	25	22	45	57
Canada	37	42	54	60	34	43	53	71
HK	79	67	102	175	51	52	82	160
Japan	136	147	199	238	121	132	185	226
Korea	4	10	20	33	1	4	11	23
Singapore	139	101	125	231	91	73	100	210
Switzerland	82	71	79	242	63	63	74	206
UK	637	504	753	1,359	591	628	1176	2,105
US	351	254	461	664	294	285	599	959
Total	1,958	1,612	2,406	3,989	1,303	1,353	2,409	4,172

Note: Traditional foreign exchange transactions = Spot + outright forwards + foreign exchange swaps; OTC derivatives = Foreign exchange + interest rate.
Source: Triennial Central Bank Survey, various issues, Bank for International Settlements.

Table 4.2 Volume of NDF and spot transaction (billion USD)

	2000	2001	2002	2003	2004	2005	2006
NDF (A)[†]	0.4	0.5	0.7	1.3	1.7	2.6	4.2
Spot (B)[‡]	2.4	2.7	2.5	2.6	3.9	4.5	6.3
A/B(%)	16.8	18.7	26.4	51.3	43.6	57.7	66.2

Note: [†]transaction between foreign exchange banks and non-residents; [‡]inter-bank transaction.
Source: "Foreign Exchange Market Trends," Press Releases (Quarterly), Bank of Korea.

Previous studies suggest that while NDF transactions by non-residents enhance the liquidity in the foreign exchange market, it raises the volatility of the spot rate (Lee, 2003). Moreover, arbitrage transactions through the NDF market lead to capital inflows, depress long-term interest rates and build up external debts (Cho and Suh, 2005; Shin and Jang, 2006). Unlike in Japan and Singapore, the covered parity in the NDF market holds only in the long run (Suh, 2005).

The faster growth of NDF transactions than spot transactions indicates that non-residents are increasingly participating in the domestic financial market (Table 4.2). This trend is likely to continue as long as current regulations on non-residents remain.

While foreign investors participate only in the NDF market, the hedging activity of market-making foreign exchange banks has the effect of integrating the onshore and offshore foreign exchange markets. As foreign exchange liberalization continues, the difference between domestic and NDF rates

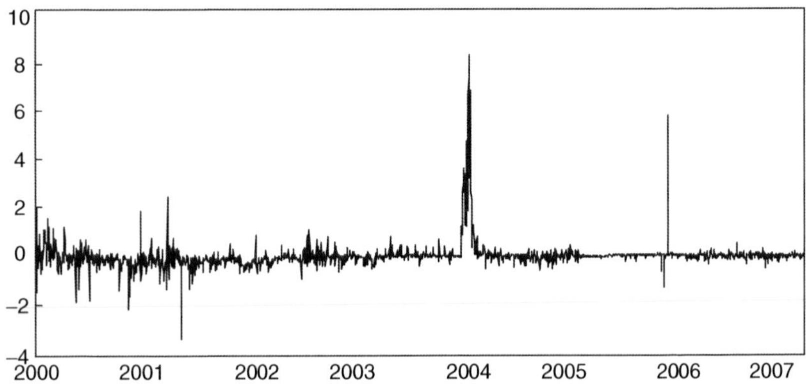

Figure 4.1   Difference between domestic forward and NDF rates
Source: Bloomberg.

tends to diminish (Figure 4.1). Occasionally, however, big discrepancies are found. For example, early in 2004 the South Korean government imposed regulations on the positions of foreign exchange banks participating in the NDF market, which more strictly restrict the domestic banks' purchase of US dollars in the NDF market. These regulations aimed at curbing the spillover effect of non-residents' speculative selling of US dollars in the NDF market into the onshore foreign exchange market. They had an immediate impact on the NDF rate, which diverged sharply from the domestic rate.

Liberalizing foreign exchange transactions enables potential arbitrage opportunities to be captured and causes the covered parity to hold. The equation for the covered interest rate differential (CID) is defined as follows:

$$CID_t = i_t - i_t^* - \frac{F_t - S_t}{S_t} \times 400$$

In the equation, i_t is the three-month CD interest rate, i_t^* is three-month Libor, F_t is the three-month KRW per US\$ forward exchange rate and S_t is the spot rate. Figures 4.2 and 4.3 plot the CID based on domestic forward and NDF rates using daily data for the sample period 1/3/2000–4/30/2007, respectively.

When the covered interest rate parity holds, the CID should be mean reverting and therefore should follow a stationary process. In order to detect the stationarity, an augmented Dickey-Fuller (ADF) unit root test was performed, and the presence of stationarity confirmed (Table 4.3). This indicates that the CID temporarily diverges from the mean but is eventually mean reverting.

Table 4.4 reports the estimated value of the mean and its standard deviation. For the whole period the mean is 10bp and the standard deviation 30–35bp.

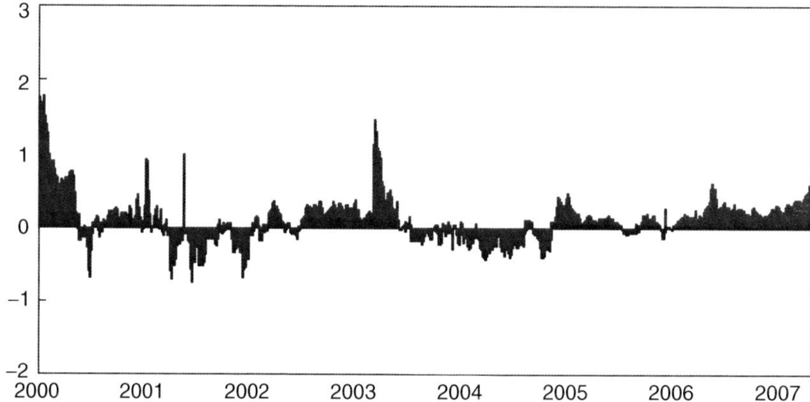

Figure 4.2 Covered interest rate differential (%): Domestic forward rate
Source: Bloomberg.

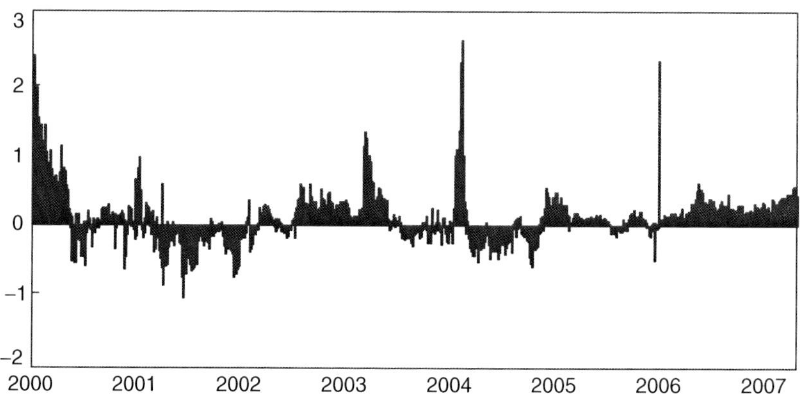

Figure 4.3 Covered interest rate differential (%): NDF rate
Source: Bloomberg.

With a 95% confidence interval, the mean ranges between 8 and 11bp for domestic forward rates and between 9 and 12bp for NDF rates. Therefore, in the long run, the CID returns to a positive value, reflecting the constraint on capital mobility and the non-exchange rate risk premium against political risk, credit risk and liquidity risk, transaction costs etc. The mean varies from year to year and it is not necessarily positive. In fact, it was negative in 2001 and 2004.

While both the interest rate differential $(i_t - i_t^*)$ and the swap rate $\left(\dfrac{F_t - S_t}{S_t} \times 400 \right)$ do follow a non-stationary process (Table 4.5), it is highly likely that in the long run the two variables have a co-integrating relationship. In order

Table 4.3   ADF unit root test on covered interest rate differential

Lag order (k)	Domestic forward	NDF
k = 1	−5.899* (0.000)	−8.436* (0.000)
k = 2	−6.005* (0.000)	−7.847* (0.000)
k = 3	−6.101* (0.000)	−7.605* (0.000)
k = 4	−6.037* (0.000)	−7.574* (0.000)
k = 6	−6.133* (0.000)	−7.432* (0.000)
k = 8	−6.002* (0.000)	−7.005* (0.000)

Note: Sample period: January 3, 2000–April 30, 2007; Figures in parentheses indicate p-values; *significant at 1% level.

Table 4.4   Mean of covered interest rate differential (%)

Year	Domestic forward		NDF	
	Mean	Standard deviation	Mean	Standard deviation
2000	0.34	0.46	0.33	0.53
2001	−0.14	0.28	−0.19	0.29
2002	0.14	0.14	0.11	0.18
2003	0.12	0.32	0.12	0.31
2004	−0.14	0.19	−0.01	0.44
2005	0.08	0.11	0.08	0.12
2006	0.20	0.10	0.21	0.17
2007	0.34	0.09	0.33	0.10
Whole period	0.10	0.30	0.10	0.31

Note: The year of 2007 includes only the period until April 30, 2007.
Source: authors' calculations.

to confirm this possibility, the Johansen co-integration test (Johansen, 1988) was executed and the results are reported in Table 4.6. As expected, they have one co-integrating vector, implying that in the short run the two variables may deviate from each other, whereas in the long run they have a common trend. The fact that the constant terms of the estimated coefficients are statistically significant assures the long-run non-equality of the interest rate differential and swap rate, as is shown in Table 4.4.

Although the CID is mean-reverting, it is highly positively auto-correlated. Looking at Figures 4.2 and 4.3 closely, the movements of the CID are not erratic. When it deviates from mean, it is persistent. For example, the CID was highly positive between mid-2005 and April 2007 and was persistently negative during August 2003–October 2004. High positive auto-correlation implies that once interest rates and the exchange rate deviate from parity (plus alpha), it takes a long time to return to parity. Therefore, the foreign exchange market is inefficient in the sense that the CID is predictable.

Table 4.5 ADF unit root test on interest rate differential and swap rate

Lag order (k)	Interest differential $(i_t - i_t^*)$	Swap Rate $\left(\dfrac{F_t - S_t}{S_t} \times 400\right)$	
		Domestic forward	NDF
k = 1	−0.062 (0.963)	−0.680 (0.850)	−1.626 (0.469)
k = 2	−0.120 (0.946)	−0.689 (0.848)	−1.446 (0.561)
k = 3	−0.180 (0.939)	−0.667 (0.853)	−1.353 (0.607)
k = 4	−0.216 (0.934)	−0.622 (0.863)	−1.340 (0.613)
k = 6	−0.189 (0.937)	−0.673 (0.852)	−1.349 (0.608)
k = 8	−0.299 (0.923)	−0.644 (0.858)	−1.302 (0.631)

Note: Sample period: January 3, 2000–April 30, 2007; Figures in parentheses indicate p-values.
Source: authors' calculations.

Table 4.6 Johansen cointegration test on interest rate differential and swap rate

	Trace statistics		
Null hypothesis	Domestic forward	NDF	Critical values (5%)
N = 0	40.519	60.174	20.262
N ≤ 1	0.563	0.478	9.165

	Estimated coefficients	
	Domestic forward	NDF
Swap rate	−0.959* (0.029)	−0.973* (0.029)
Constant	−0.120* (0.056)	−0.109* (0.055)

Note: Sample period: January 3, 2000–April 30, 2007; N = number of cointegrating vectors; Coefficients are normalized by the interest rate differential; Figures in parentheses are standard errors; * significant at 1 per cent level.
Source: authors' calculations.

Table 4.7 reports the estimated results of the autoregressive model for CID defined as follows:

$$CID_t = \alpha + \sum_{i=1}^{20} \beta_i CID_{t-1} + \varepsilon_t$$

where ε_t is the error term. The estimation result suggests that the CID shows strong positive auto-correlation. Using the domestic forward rate, the movements of CID_{t-1} and CID_{t-2} and CID_{t-15} (in terms of business day 3) has a statistically significant effect on CID_t, with an estimated coefficient of 0.813, 0.182 and 0.079, respectively. In particular, CID_{t-1}, among others, has the largest effect.

Similar results for the NDF rate have been found. The lagged variable CID_{t-1} is the most influential among CID_{t-1}, CID_{t-2}, CID_{t-3}, and CID_{t-13}. The difference,

Table 4.7 Estimation of autoregressive model: Covered interest rate differential

Variables	Domestic forward	NDF	Variables	Domestic forward	NDF
Constant	0.002 (0.002)	0.005 (0.003)			
CID_{t-1}	0.813* (0.023)	0.504* (0.023)	CID_{t-11}	−0.098* (0.030)	0.029 (0.027)
CID_{t-2}	0.182* (0.030)	0.300* (0.026)	CID_{t-12}	−0.009 (0.030)	0.033 (0.027)
CID_{t-3}	0.005 (0.030)	0.075* (0.027)	CID_{t-13}	0.065 (0.030)	0.082* (0.027)
CID_{t-4}	−0.050 (0.030)	0.045 (0.027)	CID_{t-14}	−0.061 (0.030)	−0.064** (0.027)
CID_{t-5}	0.038 (0.030)	0.021 (0.027)	CID_{t-15}	0.079* (0.030)	0.002 (0.027)
CID_{t-6}	−0.005 (0.030)	−0.037 (0.027)	CID_{t-16}	−0.016 (0.030)	0.026 (0.027)
CID_{t-7}	−0.041 (0.030)	−0.002 (0.027)	CID_{t-17}	−0.023 (0.030)	−0.007 (0.027)
CID_{t-8}	−0.028 (0.030)	−0.040 (0.027)	CID_{t-18}	−0.027 (0.030)	−0.052** (0.026)
CID_{t-9}	0.013 (0.030)	0.043 (0.027)	CID_{t-19}	−0.000 (0.030)	−0.002 (0.026)
CID_{t-10}	0.088 (0.030)	−0.032 (0.027)	CID_{t-20}	0.043 (0.023)	0.016 (0.023)
D.W.	1.991	1.999	$\overline{R}^2$	0.934	0.808

Note: Sample period: January 3, 2000–April 30, 2007; Figures in parentheses are standard errors; *, ** significant at 1% and 5% levels, respectively.
Source: authors' calculations.

however, is that the coefficient of the lagged CIDs is lower. Thus, CID_t is less autoregressive. That is, in the NDF market arbitrage opportunities are gone much faster than in the domestic forward market. Using the autoregressive equation, Table 4.8 reports the number of working days spent until the size of the shock, assuming $\varepsilon_t = 1$ diminishes to 1/2, 1/4 and 1/10, respectively.

The numbers in Table 4.8 are working days computed when only significant lagged variables are considered. Numbers in parenthesis are working days when the whole autoregressive equation is used regardless of the significance. In the NDF market, it takes only 14 days until the initial shock shrinks to 1/10. However, in the domestic forward market it takes 138 days.

Table 4.8   Time to diminish

Size of shock	Number of working days (Domestic Forward Market)	Number of working days (NDF market)
1/2	7(7)	1(1)
1/4	49(67)	5(9)
1/10	138(287)	14(24)

Note: Size of initial shock = 1; numbers in the parenthesis are computed based on the whole autoregressive equation regardless of significance.
Source: authors' calculations.

This striking difference dramatically demonstrates what foreign exchange liberalization implies in terms of market efficiency.

The mean reverting property of the covered interest rate differential has important implications. The foreign exchange market is inefficient in the short run. The arbitrage opportunities remain. However, in the long run they are fully exploited and, therefore, the efficiency of foreign exchange market is preserved. Furthermore, the NDF market is more efficient than the domestic forward market since the arbitrage opportunity evaporates faster. In fact, it makes perfect sense considering that the NDF market is less regulated and different types of market players participate. It should be noted, however, that long-run efficiency of the foreign exchange market is obtained in a limited sense since the CID does not disappear entirely even in the long run. The non-zero CID in the long run may be explained by risk premium, transaction costs, market illiquidity and regulations on funding.

While the NDF market is less regulated, it receives and disseminates important information to other markets. Using a vector error correction model, we have performed Granger causality tests on spot and forward exchange rates, swap rates and interest differential. Table 4.9 reports the results.[7] Both NDF and spot rates mutually Granger (G)-cause each other with a lag order of no less than four working days. Similarly, the NDF and domestic forward rate mutually G-cause each other. In contrast, during the sample period no G-causality is observed in any direction between domestic forward and spot rates. The statistical results suggest that the NDF market plays a pivotal role in pricing exchange rates.

However, the swap rate based on NDFs does not G-cause the interest rate differential to as great an extent as swap rate based on domestic forwards; it does so only with a lag order of three and four at the 5% significance level. Reversely, the interest differential G-causes the swap rate based on NDFs with a lag order higher than two. On the other hand, both the swap rate based on the domestic forward rate and interest rate differential G-cause mutually. This implies that in the NDF market it is the interest rate that leads to the long-run covered interest rate parity. Conversely, in the

Table 4.9 Granger causality test on spot, forward, swap rates and interest rate differential

Null hypothesis	k = 1	k = 2	k = 3	k = 4	k = 5	k = 6	k = 7	k = 8
DF $\xrightarrow{X}$ Spot	0.297	0.993	0.767	0.805	0.634	1.141	1.196	1.817
	(0.586)	(0.371)	(0.512)	(0.522)	(0.674)	(0.336)	(0.301)	(0.070)
Spot $\xrightarrow{X}$ DF	0.072	0.850	0.651	0.667	0.530	1.003	1.057	1.697
	(0.788)	(0.428)	(0.583)	(0.615)	(0.754)	(0.421)	(0.389)	(0.094)
NDF $\xrightarrow{X}$ Spot	1.374	0.682	0.595	5.362*	4.658*	3.846*	3.545*	4.205*
	(0.242)	(0.506)	(0.618)	(0.000)	(0.000)	(0.000)	(0.000)	(0.000)
Spot $\xrightarrow{X}$ NDF	0.483	0.805	0.843	5.253*	4.829*	4.037*	3.661*	4.500*
	(0.487)	(0.447)	(0.470)	(0.000)	(0.000)	(0.000)	(0.000)	(0.000)
DF $\xrightarrow{X}$ NDF	0.759	2.481	3.226**	5.649*	5.528*	4.925*	4.013*	3.899*
	(0.384)	(0.084)	(0.022)	(0.000)	(0.000)	(0.000)	(0.000)	(0.000)
NDF $\xrightarrow{X}$ DF	0.426	1.368	2.317	5.539*	5.238*	4.583*	3.704*	3.555*
	(0.514)	(0.255)	(0.074)	(0.000)	(0.000)	(0.000)	(0.000)	(0.000)
ID $\xrightarrow{X}$ Swap Rate (DF)	34.325*	17.248*	12.253*	9.278*	7.966*	6.865*	5.874*	5.165*
	(0.000)	(0.000)	(0.000)	(0.000)	(0.000)	(0.000)	(0.000)	(0.000)
Swap Rate (DF) $\xrightarrow{X}$ ID	15.281*	8.347*	8.291*	6.618*	5.319*	4.473*	3.019*	4.137*
	(0.000)	(0.000)	(0.000)	(0.000)	(0.000)	(0.000)	(0.000)	(0.000)
ID $\xrightarrow{X}$ Swap Rate (NDF)	18.492	12.663*	8.863*	6.724*	5.996*	5.169*	4.462*	3.954*
	(0.001)	(0.000)	(0.000)	(0.000)	(0.000)	(0.000)	(0.000)	(0.000)
Swap Rate (NDF) $\xrightarrow{X}$ ID	0.328	2.186	3.046**	2.609**	2.081	1.806	1.651	1.606
	(0.567)	(0.113)	(0.028)	(0.034)	(0.065)	(0.094)	(0.117)	(0.118)

Note: Sample period: January 3, 2000–April 30, 2007; Spot = won/dollar Spot exchange rate; DF = Domestic forward rate; NDF = Non-deliverable forward rate; ID = Interest rate differential; Figures in the table indicates F-statistics; Numbers in parentheses are p-values; k = lag order; *, ** significant at 1% and 5% levels, respectively; Domestic forward rates, NDF rates and spot exchange rates are all in the natural log form.
Source: authors' calculations.

domestic forward market both the swap rate and interest rate differential jointly equilibrate to the long-run parity. The causality between the NDF rate and interest rate differential, and the observation that in the NDF market arbitrage opportunity evaporates much faster, strongly indicates that arbitrage transactions are a much more important activity in offshore NDF markets than onshore markets.

Foreign exchange liberalization has also caused the currency swap market to thrive. When arbitrage opportunity persists, not only foreign exchange swap but also longer-term currency swaps serve as arbitrage instruments. A positive covered interest differential puts downward pressure on the CRS interest rate, which is defined as KRW (fixed) interest rate in exchange for Libor. Through currency swap, BOB can capitalize arbitrage profits. Furthermore, when the yield on Treasury exceeds the CRS interest rate by any wider margin than the spread on dollar-denominated foreign exchange stabilization bonds (FESB) issued by the South Korean government, then fixed income foreign investors prefer TB to FESB.

Figure 4.4 plots yields on three-year maturity TB subtracted from the three-year term CRS interest rate between April 30, 2002 and August 29, 2007. Unlike CID, it shows only a weak mean reversion behavior, as can be also found in Table 4.10 which reports the results from the unit root test. It may be because the mean may vary along with the period. The mean—the spread on FESB—reflects the financial condition of emerging market economies in general as well as country-specific factors.

The causality between the CRS interest rate and yield on Korean treasury bonds has been tested. Table 4.11 reports the G-causality test between the first differences of the two variables. Since the TB rate has a unit root, as Table 4.10

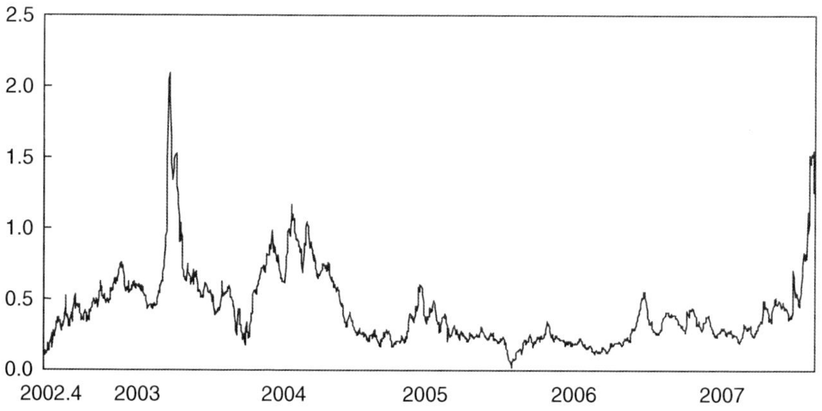

Figure 4.4   TB–CRS (%)
Source: Bloomberg.

Table 4.10   ADF unit root test on TB and CRS rates

Lag order (k)	TB-CRS	TB	CRS
k = 1	−3.634(0.005)[*]	−2.503(0.115)	−3.331(0.014)[**]
k = 2	−3.115(0.026)[**]	−2.491(0.118)	−3.238(0.018)[**]
k = 3	−2.701(0.074)	−2.554(0.103)	−3.251(0.017)[**]
k = 4	−2.704(0.074)	−2.644(0.085)	−3.327(0.014)[**]
k = 6	−2.741(0.067)	−2.480(0.121)	−3.234(0.018)[**]
k = 8	−1.922(0.322)	−2.439(0.131)	−3.138(0.024)[**]

Note: Sample period: 5/1/2002 – 8/29/2007; CRS = Three year currency swap interest rate; TB = Yield on three year Korean treasury note; Figures in parentheses indicate p-values; *, **: significant at 1% and 5% levels, respectively.
Source: authors' calculations.

shows, we used the first difference of the variables which are stationary. While the two variables mutually G-cause each other, CRS causes TB more than vice versa. CRS causes TB regardless of the lag order at the 1% significance level. TB causes CRS only with a lag order higher than five. The statistical result clearly shows the domestic TB market is not isolated. Yields on TBs are already strongly influenced by external factors. Furthermore, considering that in addition to CRS contract foreign investors and BOB purchase TBs either directly in the spot or futures markets, there should be other channels to influence yield on TBs. This will be discussed later.

4.3   Micro aspects of foreign exchange liberalization: Financial corporations

Foreign exchange liberalization has brought about strong linkages between domestic and international financial markets. Whenever the covered interest rate differential widens, various forms of arbitrage activity accompanying derivative instruments are triggered. As Garber (1998) correctly noted, derivatives can boost international capital flows. Derivatives can help diversify portfolios and enhance creditworthiness, and also assist in evading prudential regulations and avoiding capital controls and taxes. South Korea is not exceptional in this. Liberalizing foreign exchange transactions facilitates the use of derivative products. Some anecdotal evidence is found.

In the period of January to April 2004, in response to foreign investors selling off US dollars for speculative purposes, regulations were imposed on the position of domestic banks participating in the NDF market. These regulations led to an excess supply of US dollars and, consequently, the NDF rate fell to a level such that an excellent opportunity for arbitrage was created. Therefore, instead of speculation, arbitrage activity emerged. Foreign investors invested in domestic bonds such as money stabilization bonds (MSB) and treasuries and at the same time hedged their positions through NDFs transactions.

Table 4.11 Granger-Causality test on TB and CRS rates

Null hypothesis	k = 1	k = 2	k = 3	k = 4	k = 5	k = 6	k = 7	k = 8
CRS $\xrightarrow{X}$ TB	16.474*	10.294*	6.995*	5.287*	4.400*	4.677*	4.042*	3.560*
	(0.000)	(0.000)	(0.000)	(0.000)	(0.000)	(0.000)	(0.000)	(0.000)
TB $\xrightarrow{X}$ CRS	1.200	2.149	1.515	1.089	0.828	3.258*	2.783*	2.391*
	(0.294)	(0.117)	(0.209)	(0.360)	(0.053)	(0.000)	(0.007)	(0.017)

Note: Sample period: May 1, 2002–August 29, 2007; CRS = Three year currency swap interest rate, TB = Yield on three year Korean treasury note; First differences of the variables are used for the test; Figures in the table indicate F-statistics; Numbers in parentheses are p-values; k = lag order; *, **: significant at 1% and 5% levels, respectively.
Source: authors' calculations.

In February 2004, foreign investors purchased domestic-listed bonds worth over KRW1.6 trillion—more than ten times the purchase during the whole of 2003.

Recently, a strong incentive for arbitrage has emerged when export firms hedge their export revenues and, as a result, the swap rate has significantly fallen short of the interest rate differential. Since April 2006, the interest rate differential has been greater than the swap rate by a margin of 30–40bp in annual terms. A huge sell-off of US dollars by export firms in the forward exchange market has led domestic banks to buy and sell in the foreign exchange swap market in order to square their positions[8] (see Figure 4A.1). In response to the deviation of the swap rate from the interest rate differential, the BOB have actively engaged in such arbitrage transactions.

This section identifies the major market players and explains the way they operate under the new regime. They include branches of overseas banks, domestic banks and other financial firms such as insurance companies and pension funds, and foreign investors.

4.3.1   Branches of overseas banks

The BOB have been at the center of arbitrage activities. This is because they have the dual advantage of dollar funding costs (and capabilities of making products, of course) over domestic banks, and of Korean won funding costs over non-residents.

Since BOB are unable to issue KRW bonds,[9] they borrow US dollars from their main office and exchange KRW via selling and buying foreign exchange swaps[10] and invest either in certificates of deposit (CD) with a maturity of three months or bonds with a maturity of one year (see Figure 4A.2). Arbitrage transactions have boosted their won-denominated assets, such that, since January 2006, those accumulated by BOB have more than doubled (Figure 4.5). As of January 2008, BOB own 13.8 per cent of TB and MSB issued and outstanding (see Figure 4A.3).

In contrast, when the swap rate is greater than the interest rate differential BOB borrow KRW from the short-term money market at the call rate, and raise US$ via buying and selling foreign exchange swaps and lend to their main office at Libor (see Figure 4A.4).

BOB play a pivotal role in the internationalization of South Korea's financial market. Among the 33 BOB, around ten branches are active.[11] Comparing the March 2007 balance sheet to that of December 1999 when foreign exchange liberalization began, two notable changes are observed (Table 4.12). First, although net worth has changed only somewhat, both assets and liabilities have increased tremendously. On the liability side, borrowings and bonds, both won-denominated and foreign currency-denominated, have increased greatly. Financing won mostly depends on

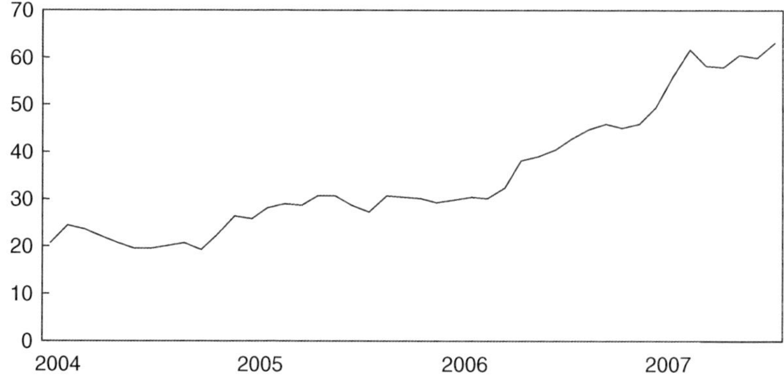

Figure 4.5   Securities holding by BOB (trillion won)
Source: *Monthly Financial Statistics Bulletin*, Various Issues, Financial Supervisory Service.

Table 4.12   Balance sheet of BOB, March 2007 (billion won, %)

Assets		Liabilities	
cash and deposit		depository liabilities	
won 2404.8 (2.0)		won 7033.4 (5.9)	
foreign currency 413 (0.3)		foreign currency 1139.5 (1.0)	
securities 60883.3 (51.2)		borrowings and bonds	
Loan and discount		won 25494.6 (21.5)	
won 12867.1 (10.8)		foreign currency 7260.4 (6.1)	
foreign currency 6326.1 (5.3)		derivatives	15263 (12.8)
derivatives	14105.3 (11.9)	other liabilities	58835.6 (49.5)
other assets	21838.9 (18.4)	**total liabilities**	115026.5 (96.8)
total asset	118838.5 (100)	**NW**	3812 (3.2)

Source: Summarized from Monthly Financial Statistics Bulletin, various issues, Korean Financial Supervisory Service.

the "won call" market, South Korea's inter-bank market. BOB borrow dollars from their main office and offshore inter-bank market. Since 2006, when potential arbitrage profits began to grow, foreign-currency funding has risen dramatically. In addition to borrowing from the main office, BOB now depend more on offshore funding, while funding from other sources, such as domestic foreign call markets, is insignificant.

Second, on the asset side, instead of loans and discounts, security holding increases tremendously and at the same time derivatives become important

Balance sheet of BOB: December 1999 (billion won, %)

Assets		Liabilities	
cash and deposit		depository liabilities	
won 2036.8 (7.1)		won 4857 (17.0)	
foreign currency 418.6 (1.5)		foreign currency 938.2 (3.3)	
securities 8375 (29.3)		borrowings and bonds	
loan and discount		won 2345.8 (8.2)	
won 8646.7 (30.3)		foreign currency 1007 (3.5)	
foreign currency 5114.1 (17.9)		derivatives	1965.4 (6.9)
derivatives	1931.4 (6.8)	other liabilities	14409.6 (50.5)
other assets	2027.4 (7.1)	**total liabilities**	25523 (89.4)
total asset	28550 (100)	**NW**	3027 (10.6)

Source: Summarized from Monthly Financial Statistics Bulletin, various issues, Korean Financial Supervisory Service.

items. This implies that Korean securities, most of which are Treasuries and MSB issued by the Bank of Korea (BOK), are used as underlying assets for derivative trading. As Table 4.11 shows, during the period the proportion of securities and outstanding derivative contracts out of total asset increased by 80%.

Looking at the income statement of BOB in Table 4.13, it is clear that the operation has changed dramatically since foreign exchange liberalization. In 1999, foreign exchange trade was the core business, while activities involving derivatives were only peripheral. However, since 2000, derivatives transactions have become one of the most important operations. The size of the derivatives contract has increased more than 17-fold (Table 4.14). Recently, interest rate-related contracts have become more important than currency-related ones, such that BOB must now be more influential than ever on domestic financial markets.

4.3.2 Non-residents[12]

Non-residents have never owned more than 2% of listed won bonds, which contrasts with their more than 30% ownership of the stock market capitalization (Figure 4.6).[13,14] The reason is that the bond market is not liquid enough to be able to leverage positions. For example, the inter-bank repo market is not active since 14.5% of withholding tax rate is applied to interest income. Therefore, buy and hold is the only viable option.

In spite of the lock-in effect, however, foreign investors began to invest aggressively in bonds when arbitrage opportunity started to grow. Between January 2007 and July 2007, foreign investor holdings of bonds increased by

Table 4.13   Income Statement of BOB (billion won, %)

Year	1999	2000	2001	2002	2003	2004	2005	2006	2007 1Q
Revenue	10131	13974	20563	25166	28049	57501	48534	52598	12299
	(100)	(100)	(100)	(100)	(100)	(100)	(100)	(100)	(100)
interest	730	1006	981	1098	1069	1000	1188	1730	633
	(7.2)	(7.2)	(4.8)	(4.4)	(3.8)	(1.7)	(2.4)	(3.3)	(5.1)
FX	7773	1844	2106	2214	3787	7328	8042	12066	2194
	(76.7)	(13.2)	(10.2)	(8.8)	(13.5)	(12.7)	(16.6)	(22.9)	(17.8)
derivatives	-	9162	15461	20196	21884	47649	38117	37064	8832
	(0.0)	(65.6)	(75.2)	(80.3)	(78.0)	(82.9)	(78.5)	(70.5)	(71.8)
Other	1628	1962	2015	1658	1309	1524	1188	1738	640
	(16.1)	(14.0)	(9.8)	(6.6)	(4.7)	(2.7)	(2.4)	(3.3)	(5.2)
cost	9807	13293	20027	24888	27641	57210	48441	52374	12202
	(100)	(100)	(100)	(100)	(100)	(100)	(100)	(100)	(100)
interest	188	357	474	336	350	612	659	1072	420
	(1.9)	(2.7)	(2.4)	(1.4)	(1.3)	(1.1)	(1.4)	(2.0)	(3.4)
FX	7632	1944	2021	1757	3477	7496	7997	11063	2498
	(77.8)	(14.6)	(10.1)	(7.1)	(12.6)	(13.1)	(16.5)	(21.1)	(20.5)
derivatives	-	8677	15155	20759	21903	47688	37193	37751	8545
	(0.0)	(65.3)	(75.7)	(83.4)	(79.2)	(83.4)	(76.8)	(72.1)	(70.0)
Other	1634	1809	1845	1557	1468	1076	2193	1991	592
	(16.7)	(13.6)	(9.2)	(6.3)	(5.3)	(1.9)	(4.5)	(3.8)	(4.8)

Source: Computed from Monthly Financial Statistics Bulletin, various issues Korean Financial Supervisory Service.

Table 4.14   Derivative Activity of BOB (End of period, trillion won, %)

	1999	2000	2001	2002	2003	2004	2005	2006	2007.3
Derivative contracts	103.6 (100.0)	147.2 (100.0)	229.5 (100.0)	480.9 (100.0)	645.5 (100.0)	714.6 (100.0)	929.4 (100.0)	1434.0 (100.0)	1726.8 (100.0)
Interest rates	18.5 (17.8)	33.5 (22.8)	114.5 (49.9)	320.3 (66.6)	309.1 (47.9)	336.4 (47.1)	512.7 (55.8)	875.6 (61.1)	1082.3 (62.7)
Currency	85.1 (82.2)	113.7 (77.2)	115 (51.1)	160.6 (33.3)	336.4 (52.1)	378.2 (52.9)	416.7 (44.2)	558.4 (38.9)	644.5 (33.3)

Note: Numbers in parentheses indicate percentage ratio of composition.
Source: *Monthly Financial Statistics Bulletin*, Various Issues, Financial Supervisory Service.

KRW5 trillion.[15] Instead of direct investment, total return swap (TRS) is a useful instrument for non-residents looking for arbitrage profits (see Figure 4A.5). This is because in TRS transactions they do not have to follow the won-denominated security investment procedure in order to comply with foreign exchange transaction rules. Recently, TRS transactions between BOB and non-residents have been boosted. In 2005, the volume was KRW994 billion, in 2006 it was KRW 3776 billion and in the first quarter of 2007 it was KRW2538 billion.

Although foreign investors are minor players in the TB spot market, they are very active in the market for TB futures. Their share of transactions in TB futures increased from 5.1% in 2002 to 14.3% in 2006. Through TB futures and TRS, it is believed that foreign investors have gained significant influence on the TB market, which was discussed in section 4.2.

4.3.3   Domestic banks

Domestic banks are not active in arbitrage transactions, mainly due to higher borrowing costs. Instead, they involve themselves in Korean Treasury Bond index swaps with BOB. Korean TB index swaps are standard foreign exchange derivatives combined with credit default swaps[16] and have been traded since 2002. BOB can borrow at Libor and, therefore, capitalize potential arbitrage profits, but they are unwilling to take country risk. Domestic banks and BOB split arbitrage profits through Korean TB index swaps (see Figure 4A.6).

Domestic banks also engage in currency swaps linked to foreign-currency lending. Since regulations on the use of foreign-currency lending were lifted in October 2001, foreign exchange banks now enjoy up to a maximum 42bp profit on foreign-currency lending; unlike won lending, it is not subject to contributions to institutions-related credit guarantee. Domestic banks may also borrow at Libor "plus" from overseas markets and lend to domestic firms at Libor "plus-plus." At the same time, they may enter KRW fixed—US$ float currency swaps with domestic firms after receiving won from another KRW fixed—USD float currency swap contract. In this way, domestic banks are able to eliminate exchange risk and *de facto* lend Korean won to domestic firms (see Figure 4A.7). The size of the profit from foreign-currency lending depends on the credit standing of the banks and won interest rate receipt and payment spread in those swap transactions.

In order to curb borrowing overseas, the BOK has recently permitted foreign-currency loans only for the purposes of overseas spending and facilities investment within South Korea. It is thought that more than half of total loans have been spent on the purchase of property and securities. Dollar-denominated loans totaled US$28.4 billion, about 64% of the total, while yen loans came to US$14.1 billion, 32%.

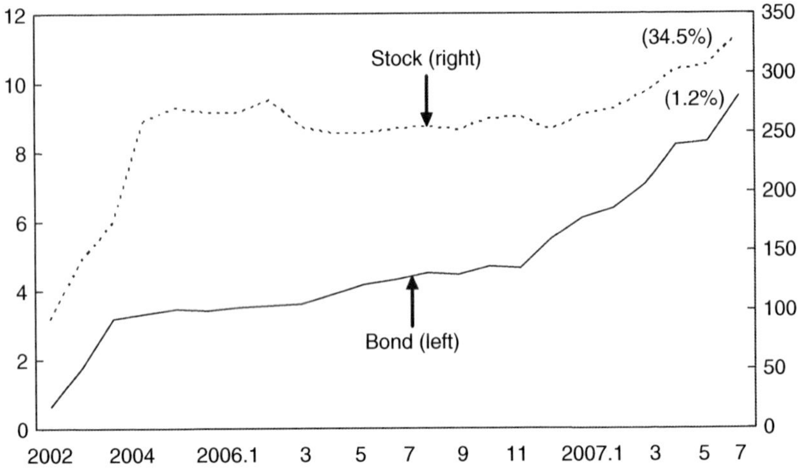

Figure 4.6   Securities owned by non-residents (trillion won)
Source: "Trends in Sales of Securities by Non-residents," Press Releases (Monthly), Financial supervisory Service.

4.3.4   Other financial firms

The longer-term excess of the swap rate over the interest rate differential provides an opportunity for arbitrage transactions for domestic residents such as insurance companies and pension funds, which look for stable long-term overseas financial investment.[17] For example, an insurance company exchanges US dollars for Korean won through a currency swap with BOB and invests in US dollar long-term bonds. Exchange risk is covered by both the interest rate swap and currency swap with BOB. The insurance company and BOB will split the arbitrage profits (see Figure 4A.8).

4.4   Concluding remarks

Foreign exchange liberalization, although not yet full scale, has already had a significant impact on South Korea's financial market. By way of foreign exchange markets, domestic financial markets are linked to international financial markets. Thanks to the linkage, arbitrage opportunities are created and ultimately fade away. Derivative instruments are able to capitalize on arbitrage opportunities. BOB are at the center of foreign exchange liberalization. Foreign investors, domestic banks and financial institutions such as insurance companies and pension funds engage actively in many different forms of derivative contracts, from simple and short-term foreign exchange swaps to longer-term currency swaps and sophisticated total return swaps.

South Korea's financial market definitely takes advantage of these highly developed financial products.

The internationalization of South Korea's financial market, however, is still only at the half way stage. In spite of foreign exchange liberalization onshore and offshore exchange markets are not fully integrated. This imperfect integration makes the foreign exchange market inefficient in the short run. Arbitrage opportunities once created persist. It takes time to equilibrate to the parity. This inefficiency certainly contributes to financial market imbalances. Arbitrage activities when prolonged emerge in many dimensions of the market and invite international capital flows which would otherwise short-lived. The international capital flows too often cause vulnerability and volatility to the domestic financial market (Kaminsky and Reinhart, 2004). As of now it appears that the NDF market will continue to play its present leading role as the path to the internationalization of South Korea's financial market.

Appendix 1: Arbitrage activity (Source: Bank of Korea)

Example 1

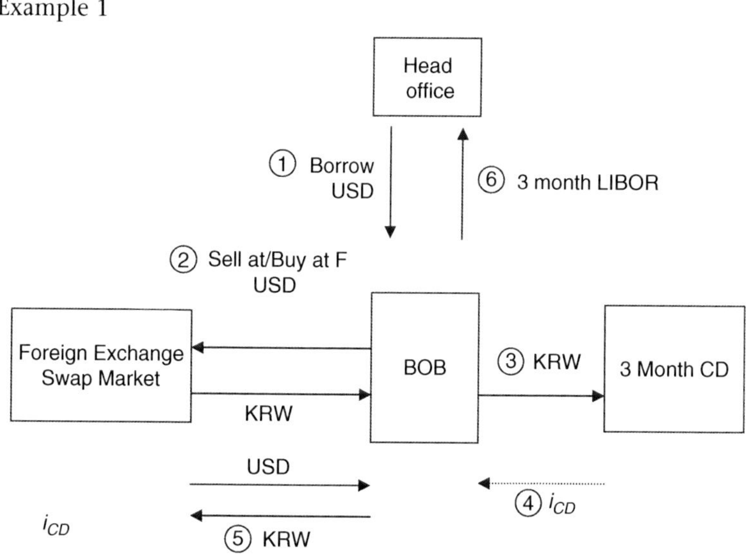

Figure 4A.1   Profit rate $\approx i_{CD} - fp - Libor$

Example 2

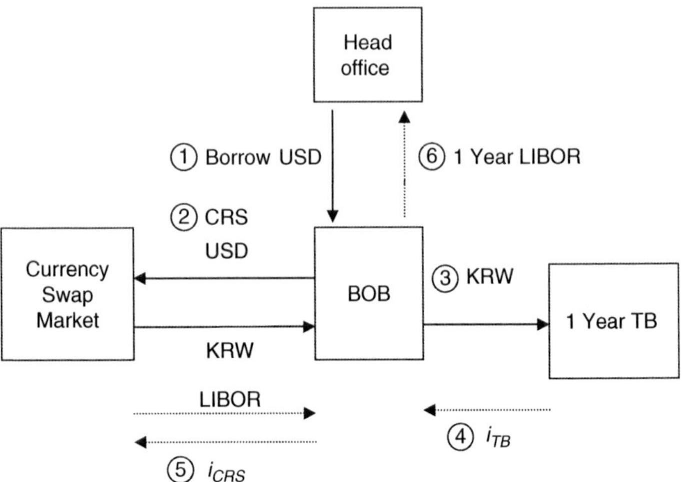

Figure 4A.2 Profit rate $= i_{TB} - i_{CRS}$

Example 3

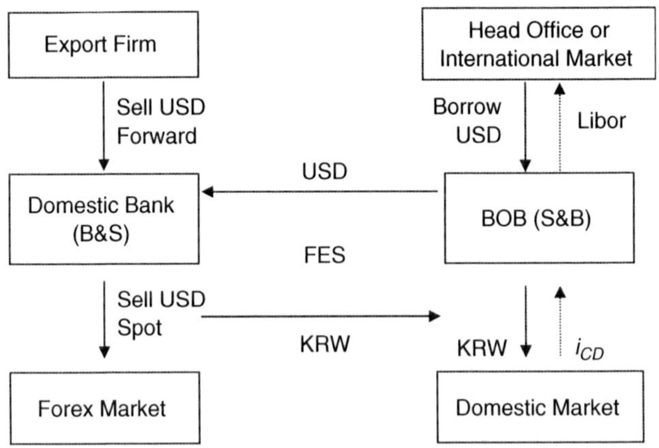

Figure 4A.3 Profit rate $\approx i_{CD} - fp - Libor$

Example 4

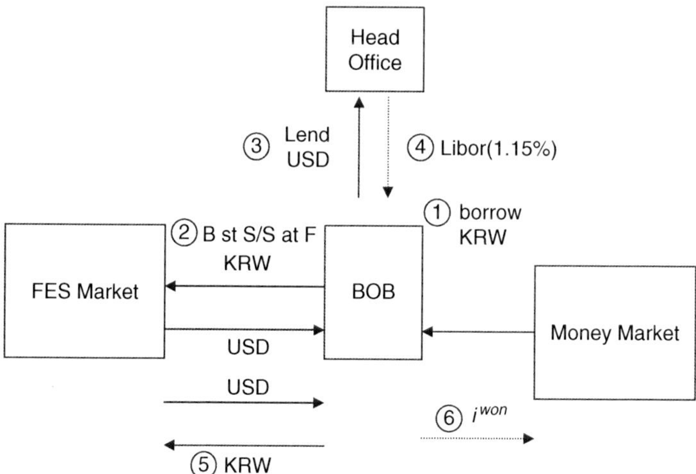

Figure 4A.4   Profit rate $\approx Libor + fp - i^{won}$

Example 5

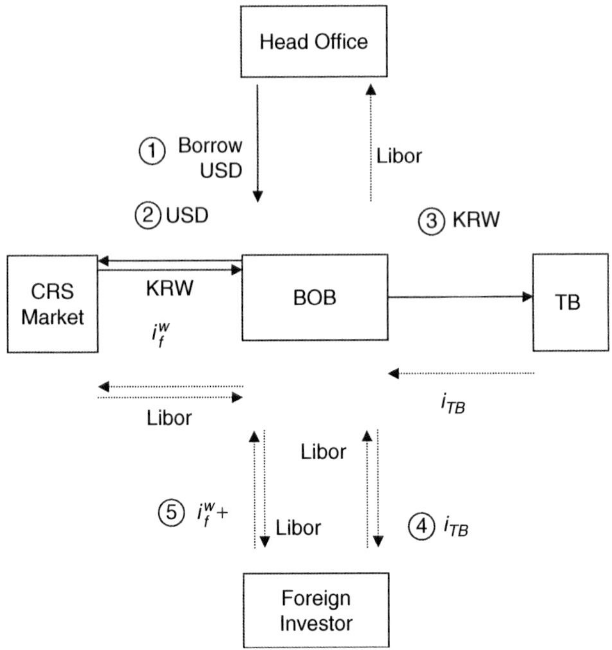

Figure 4A.5   Total Return Swap (TRS)

Foreign investor's profit rate $= i_{TB} - \left(i_f^w +\right)$

BOB's profit rate $= (i_f^w +) - i_f^w$

Joint profit rate $= i_{TB} - i_f^w$

Example 6

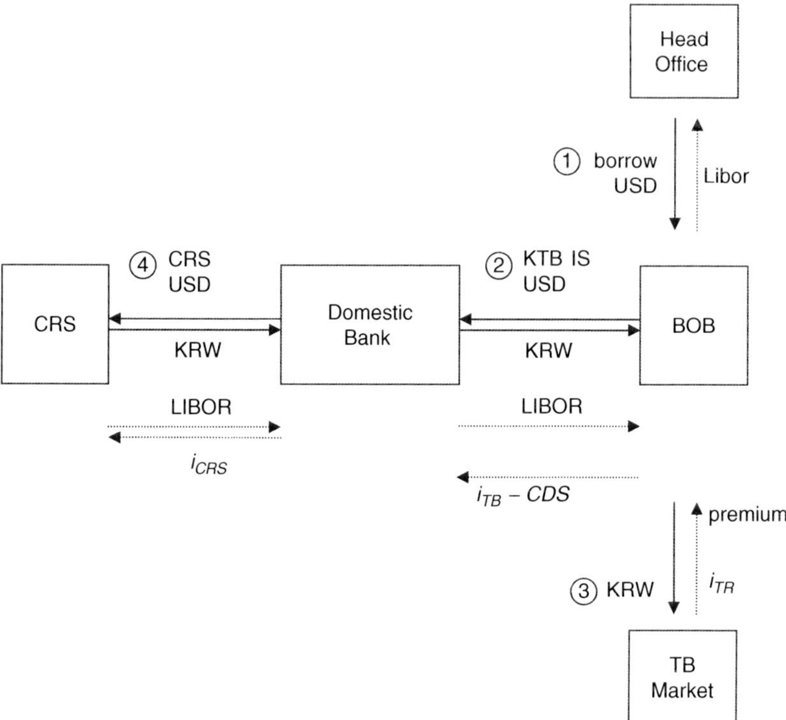

Figure 4A.6   KTB Index Swap

BOB's Profit rate = CDS premium
Domestic bank's profit rate = i_{TB} – CDS premium – i_{CRS}
Joint profit rate = $i_{TB} - i_{CRS}$

Example 7

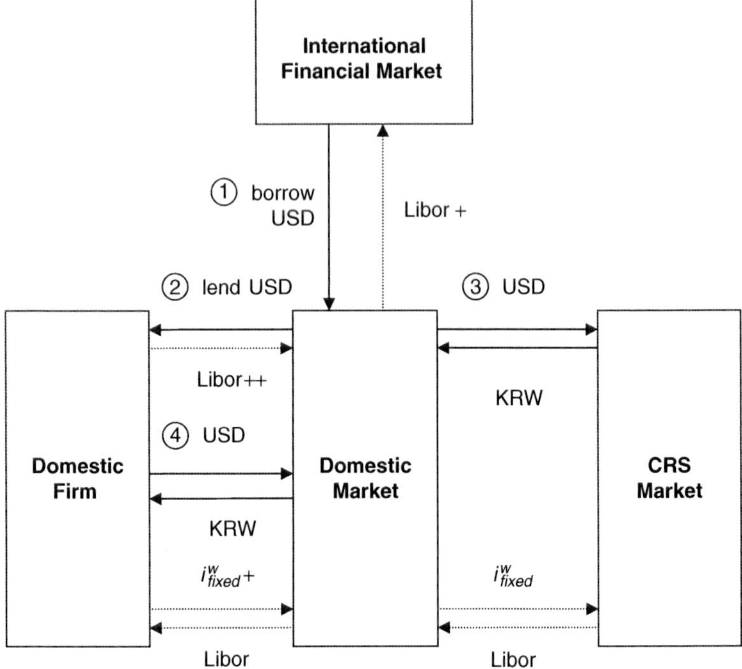

Figure 4A.7　Foreign currency lending by domestic bank

Profit from lending = {(Libor++)-Libor+} + $\{(i^{w}_{f}+) - i^{w}_{f}\}$

Example 8

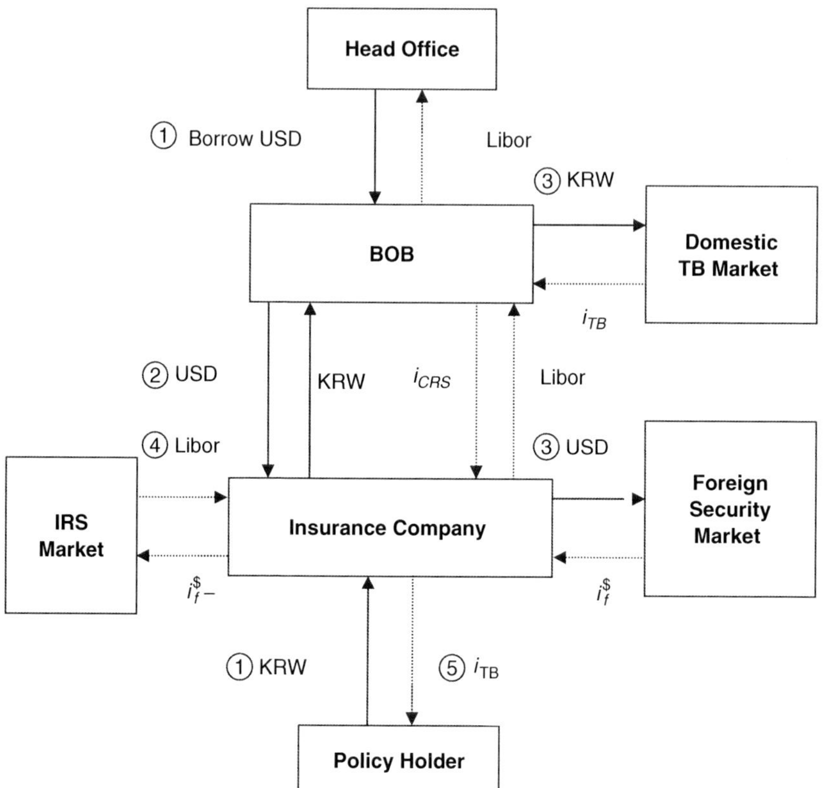

Figure 4A.8   Arbitrage activity of insurance company

BOB's profit rate = $i_{TB} - i_{CRS}$
Insurance company's profit rate = $(i_{CRS} - i_{TB}) + \left\{ i_f^\$ - (i_f^\$ -) \right\}$
Joint profit rate = $i_f^\$ - (i_f^\$ -)$

Appendix 2: Brief review of the South Korean government's foreign exchange liberalization policy

The first phase of the foreign exchange liberalization

In April 1999 regulations on capital account transactions were converted into a negative system, lifting all restrictions except for those limited by law. These include purchase of overseas real estate properties by corporations and financial institutions for business purposes and direct investments, overseas borrowing and issuance of foreign-currency denominated bonds with maturity of less than one year by domestic corporations, making deposits and open trust accounts denominated in Korean won with maturity of more than one year by non-residents, and abolishing the *bona fide* (real demand) principle in forward and derivative transactions.

Also regulations on foreign exchange institutions were revised. Requirement to engage in foreign exchange activities was changed from licensing to registration system, thereby liberalizing the establishment of money changers. Instead, safeguard measures in the event of a sudden increase in either capital inflow or outflow or an extremely unfavorable market situation were established. Safeguard measures include freezing of transaction, the reintroduction of a permission-based capital transaction system, the funneling of foreign currency to the Bank of Korea (BOK) and the activation of a Variable Deposit Requirement (VDR) system that requires a certain percentage of capital flows to be deposited in non-interest bearing accounts.

There were three important safety measures. The obligatory repatriation of external claim regulation was put in place. A limit on non-resident won funding was put in place to curb large-scale speculative attacks of short-term capitals. Restrictions on short-term external borrowing by financially unsound corporations were imposed.

The second phase of the foreign exchange liberalization

In January 2001, the South Korean government implemented the second phase of the foreign exchange liberalization.

Alleviating obligatory repatriation of overseas claims

Restrictions on obligatory repatriation of external claims have been eased to enhance the league efficiency of overseas economic activities for both individuals and businesses and to provide adequate ex post facto control measures. Overseas claims exceeding US$50,000 were still subject to obligatory inbound repatriation. However, the criterion for exemption and the period extension of inbound repatriation have been extended to include service and capital transaction claims in addition to the previous export claims.

In addition overseas deposits, portfolio investment and trusts, would be reported to the BOK by the designated bank; portfolio investment and trusts, overseas direct investments, and the acquisition of real estate must be notified to the BOK.

Eliminating ceiling on overseas payments and monetary possessions when leaving the country for residents

Ceilings on overseas payments for residents were eliminated. Instead, the ex post facto control measures were introduced. They were bank designation, automatic reporting to the National Tax Service (NTS), customs declaration, and prior confirmation of large overseas payments with the BOK and its subsequent notification.

Easing the regulation on purchase and sale of foreign exchange

The previous US$20,000 ceiling on foreign-currency purchase by residents for holding purposes was lifted. Also foreign-currency purchase by non-residents from foreign exchange banks was liberalized. Regulations on the purchase and sale of foreign exchange transactions both among residents and between residents and non-residents have been eased.

Relaxing the limitation on deposits and trusts

The restrictions on Korean won denominated deposits by non-residents with less than a one year maturity were lifted. Furthermore, restrictions on deposits and withdrawals of overseas deposits and trusts by residents were liberalized by introducing control measures, such as bank designation, notification requirement at the BOK, and automatic reporting scheme to NTS.

Greater allowance for overseas borrowing and Korean won lending

Short-term and long-term overseas borrowings by individuals and non-profit organizations unless they involve a third party as payment guarantee were allowed as long as they were reported to the BOK. Restrictions were maintained on short-term overseas borrowing by domestic businesses with financially unsound structure. The ceiling on the Korean won denominated borrowing by non-residents was raised from KRW 100 million to KRW 1 billion.

Further liberalization of securities investment

OTC securities transactions between residents and non-residents were liberalized.

Allowing acquisition of overseas real estates

In addition to the liberalization of purchases of overseas real estate properties by corporations and financial institutions for business purposes, residents were allowed to acquire overseas real estate for the purpose of establishing schools, hospitals or places of worship on condition that this was reported to and accepted by the BOK.

Expanding foreign exchange businesses

Insurance traders and facility rental services were allowed to register as foreign exchange business institutions and they were subject to prudential regulation.

Expanding methods of corporate settlement

Multi-netting between a corporate headquarters and its branches was allowed to reduce settlement cost of overseas claims and liabilities.

In January 2006, facing strong pressure of appreciation of the won the South Korean government encouraged capital outflows such as purchase of overseas real estate property and raising ceiling on individual overseas investment.

In May 2006, furthermore, the South Korean government brought forward the implementation schedule of the on-going foreign exchange liberalization from the initial timeline. Specifically, the government focused on (1) the won's internationalization, (2) liberalizing foreign exchange transactions and (3) easing regulations on foreign exchange position and further revitalizing the autonomous market-making by market participants.

Internationalization of the won

In order to promote the Korean won's internationalization during the first phase, with effect from May 2006, the ceiling on won-denominated loans to non-residents has been raised and the threshold amount subject to prior reporting to the BOK was adjusted upward from the previous KRW 1 billion to KRW 10 billion. The KRW/USD futures and options have now been listed on the Chicago Mercantile Exchange. Subject to developments and the likely impact on the foreign exchange market, the government is going to review the possibility of physical delivery of the won. Furthermore, to facilitate freer transactions involving the won by non-residents, won-denominated accounts of a similar nature held by non-residents should be integrated into "free won account." The threshold amount of reporting compliance (US$1 million) is expected to be completely scrapped in the course of 2007. In the second phase (2008–9) of the liberalization plan, the government will expand the scope of the won transactions exempted from reporting compliance.

Liberalization of foreign exchange transactions

Capital outflows are deregulated to promote freer overseas investment and business activities such as acquisition of overseas real estate by residents.

With regard to collection obligation on external credits, the amount exempted from the mandatory collection obligation is to be adjusted upward and it is expected to be completely abolished by 2009. Instead, the government will institutionalize "a reporting" system for the purpose of sound "monitoring" on overseas lending and/or capital transactions of such nature exceeding a certain amount. Also due safeguards will be added to the Foreign Exchange Transactions Act in time of emergency. The government will fully liberalize acquisition of overseas real estate by residents in the second phase of liberalization.

With exceptions solely for the stability and soundness of the foreign exchange market the government has softened procedural requirements involving capital transactions, such as reporting, step by step. Exceptions will be applicable exclusively to such cases as the won-denominated funding by non-residents and some credit derivatives transactions whose movement has direct implications on foreign exchange market stability. By 2009 most capital transactions are executed with simple reporting to 'foreign exchange banks' with a few exceptions including won-denominated fund raising by non-residents and some credit derivatives.

Financial institutions are free to undertake foreign exchange businesses. The limit of foreign-currency lending permitted to insurers and equipment lease companies was repealed in May 2006.

In the second phase (2008–9) of the liberalization plan, financial institutions are allowed to undertake in foreign currencies all kinds of financial businesses that are already available on a won-denominated basis and provided for pertinent financial legislation.

Upgrading of the foreign exchange market

In order to upgrade the microstructure of the foreign exchange market deregulatory measures such as raising the foreign exchange position ceiling are expected to be implemented. The pertinent regulation governing the exchange position will be integrated into prudential regulations under the corresponding laws and/or decrees in connection with the implementation of the Basel II Accord.

The government also seeks to boost the foreign exchange market with the introduction of a depositing foreign-currency denominated margin call in futures transactions. The margin call for futures transactions now is payable with foreign currencies, departing from the current system where the won is the only permitted currency.

In order to upgrade Korea's foreign exchange market and to boost the market-making function of market participants, several measures are implemented including the introduction of a differentiated brokerage fee schedule, disclosure of the volume of orders at the best bid/offer, and announcement in the public domain of the league table of market participants.

Notes

This chapter was prepared as a paper for HKMA conference, *Currency Internationalization: International Experiences and Implications for the Renminbi*, Hong Kong, October 15–16, 2007. We have been benefited from H. R. Park at J. P. Morgan Chase, S. S. Kang, Y. H. Yang, at the BOK for their useful comments. K. S. Jang, S. J. Hong, J. D. Lee and J. W. Chun at the BOK provided very useful data. We also would like to thank participants at the conference for their helpful comments. This chapter should not be reported as representing the views of the BOK.

1. Institute of Monetary and Economic Research, Bank of Korea, Seoul 100-794 Korea.
2. School of Economics, Kookmin University, Seoul 136-702, Korea.
3. In Korea, a non-resident (or foreign investor) is defined as a person whose economic interest lies abroad. A domestic firm setting up a paper company offshore can earn the status of non-resident. Also, a hedge fund opening an office in Korea becomes a resident.
4. The ceiling on won-denominated borrowing has been raised to KRW 10 billion, though.
5. Since the East Asia financial crisis, Korea's government bond market has exploded. In 2006, the listed amount was KRW677.8 trillion and the trading volume was KRW588.2 trillion.
6. Unfavorable tax treatment is another reason.
7. The results from pair-wise co-integration tests can be given upon request.
8. For example, between January 2005 and April 2007 the shipbuilding industry sold US$79.5 billion forward.
9. BOB are not considered juridically as entities eligible to issue bonds.
10. The foreign branches have also served as a market maker when export firms hedge their export revenues via domestic banks. This is because they have lower hedging costs than domestic banks.
11. These include, among others, HSBC, JP Morgan Chase, Deutsche Bank, ING, UBS, ABN Amro, BNP, CSFB.
12. At the end of 2006, non-residents comprised 1737 institutions and 399 individuals.
13. Non-residents own 7% of TB outstanding.
14. Numbers in parentheses denote percentage shares held by non-residents.
15. As a matter of fact, the non-residents' share of the stock market capitalization has been reduced from the peak of 43.9% in July 2004.
16. At the end of March 2007, the credit default swap premium for treasuries was 16bp.
17. During April through October in 2004 the swap rate far exceeded the interest rate differential.

References

Bank for International Settlement, "Triennial central bank survey of foreign exchange and derivatives market activity," Monetary and Economic Department, March 2004, December 2007.

Cho, Y. and J. Suh, "Interest rate differential and capital flows," *Foreign Exchange International Financial Review*, The Bank of Korea, December 2005. (In Korean.)

Debelle, G., J. Gyntelberg and M. Plumb, "Forward currency markets in Asia: lessons from the Australian experience," *BIS Quarterly Review*, September 2006.

Garber, P., "Derivatives in International Capital Flows," *NBER Working Paper*, No. 6623, 1998.

Johansen, S., "Statistical analysis of cointegration vectors," *Journal of Economic Dynamics and Control*, Vol. 12, pp. 323–38, 1998.

Kaminsky, G. and C. Reinhart, "When it Rains, it Pours: Pro-Cyclical Capital Flows and Macroeconomic Policies," NBER Macroeconomics Annual 2004, MIT press, 2005.

Korean Financial Supervisory Service, *Monthly Financial Statistics Bulletin*, various issues.

Lee, S., "The impact of NDF transaction on the domestic foreign exchange market," *Foreign Exchange International Financial Review*, The Bank of Korea, May 2003. (In Korean.)

Ma, G., C. Ho and R. McCauley, "The market for non-deliverable forwards in Asian currencies," *BIS Quarterly Review*, June 2004, pp. 81–94.

McCauley, R., "Internationalizing a Currency: The Case of Australian Dollar," *BIS Quarterly Review*, December 2006, pp. 41–54.

OECD, OECD Code of Liberalization of Capital Movements, 2007.

Ryu, S. and Y. Kim, "Foreign Exchange Risk Premium and its Implications," *Foreign Exchange International Financial Review*, The Bank of Korea, December 2006. (In Korean.)

Shin, S. and S. Jang, "Implications of the recent arbitrage transaction," *Foreign Exchange International Financial Review*, The Bank of Korea, December 2006. (In Korean.)

Suh, H., "Covered parity theory and capital mobility in Korea," *Foreign Exchange International Financial Review*, The Bank of Korea, May 2005. (In Korean.)

PART II Issues on International Use of the Renminbi

5
The Potential of the Renminbi as an International Currency

Hongyi Chen and Wensheng Peng

5.1 Introduction

China is now the fourth largest economy in the world and the third largest trading partner. In particular, China is the largest trading partner of many Asian economies, and has become an increasingly important source of investment in the region. As the rapid economic growth continues and the restrictions on international financial transactions are gradually liberalized, China's importance in the global economy and financial system will increase further. This begs the question of what role the Chinese currency, the renminbi, will play in international trade and finance, particularly in the Asian region.

There are already early forms of international use of the renminbi. It has been used in the settlement of border trade between China and some neighboring countries, and renminbi banknotes are accepted by shops in many tourist places in the region. More significantly, in 2004 banks in Hong Kong started to offer renminbi banking services such as deposits, remittance, currency exchange and debit/credit cards. The scope of the renminbi business in Hong Kong has been expanded twice, in 2005 and in 2007, with Hong Kong now possessing a renminbi bond market outside Mainland China.

The use of the renminbi in international trade and financial transactions is of course limited when compared with the major currencies such as the US dollar, the euro, the pound sterling and the Japanese yen. But the current situation reflects the limited capital account convertibility of the renminbi, and the examples cited above are best seen as pointing to the *potential* of the renminbi as an international currency. Government policies play a role to the extent that the pace of the renminbi attaining full convertibility would affect the ability of residents and non-residents to use the currency in settling international transactions and acquire renminbi-denominated assets. On the other hand, currency internationalization would have implications for domestic monetary policy and financial market development, entailing both benefits and risks. Thus, the potential international role of the renminbi would be a significant factor to consider in the formulation and implementation of measures on increasing currency convertibility and financial market liberalizations.

There is an increasing literature on the potential of the renminbi as an international currency, the associated benefits and risks and the appropriate government policies in promoting, facilitating or inhibiting the growth of such a role (李稻葵, 2006; 刘力臻等, 2006; Li, 2006; Eichengreen, 2005; He and Li, 2005; 姜波克, 2005; 李瑶, 2003; 巴曙松, 2003). This chapter considers some of these issues by drawing on the experiences of other major currencies. Specifically, we estimate determinants of the shares of five major currencies (the US dollar, the euro, the British pound, the Japanese yen and the Swiss franc) in reserve holdings of the world's central banks, and the model is then used to gauge the potential demand for the renminbi as official reserves, applying the relevant indicators of the determinants for China. Some of the policy issues related to currency internationalization are then discussed.

The remainder of the chapter is organized as follows. The next section (5.2) provides a definition of an international currency and a brief review of the main determinants of the international currency status that are suggested in the literature. Section 5.3 estimates a quantitative relationship between the shares of the five international currencies in reserve holdings and the main determinants, such as the size of the economy and financial market, and presents a counterfactual exercise to gauge the potential share of the renminbi in the reserve holdings if the currency were freely convertible. Section 5.4 considers some policy issues in the international use of the renminbi, and the final section offers some conclusions.

5.2   The main determinants of the international use of a currency

An international currency is one that is used outside its home country. The classical three functions of money domestically – medium of exchange, store of value and unit of account – can be transferred to the level of international money, as summarized in Table 5.1 (Chinn and Frankel 2005), which was originally introduced in Kenen (1983). Under each function, there are examples of how official authorities and private sectors sometimes choose to use a major international currency that is not their own. These functions are distinct from each other, and their respective importance may vary somewhat depending on specific factors. For example, short-term changes in reserve holdings may be influenced by exchange rate and interest rate movements. However, in the longer term the functions of an international currency are related and determined by more fundamental factors (see below).

Table 5.1   The international use of a currency

	Official Use	**Private Use**
Medium of Exchange	Vehicle currency for foreign exchange intervention	Invoicing trade and financial transactions
Store of Value	International reserves	Currency substitution (dollarisation)
Unit of Account	Anchor for pegging local currency	Denominating trade and financial transaction

Source: Chinn and Frankel (2005).

Full convertibility is required for a currency to play any significant role in international trade and financial transactions, but it is not a sufficient condition. The international use of a currency is ultimately determined by market forces. What follows briefly discusses four main economic determinants that are often listed in academic research and policy discussions (Lim, 2006; Yam, 2005, 2007; Eichengreen, 2005; Mundell, 1998; Talvas and Ozeki, 1992; Tavlas, 1991).

5.2.1   The size of the economy

International currencies are usually associated with large, competitive economies with extended trade and financial ties. A large domestic economy allows exploitation and reinforcement of economies of scale and scope involved in using a currency over a wider domain. A common measure of the size of an economy is gross domestic product (GDP). Based on time-series estimates, Eichengreen and Frankel (1996) found that every 1 per cent of GDP in the world total leads to 1.33 per cent of central bank reserve holdings in the corresponding currency. This is a point estimate rather than an average ratio, and it explains variations in the relative role of a currency such as the US dollar, but not its actual proportion. However, cross-country evidence also confirms a positive relationship between the share of GDP in the world total and the share of central bank reserve holdings in the corresponding currency, although the relationship is likely to be non-linear (Chinn and Frankel, 2005).

Economic size matters first through the share of the country in international trade. Large-scale trade activities usually generate a large market in foreign exchange transactions with at least one leg in the domestic currency. Also, well-diversified economies can often rely on their own currency for settling transactions with non-residents as they offer the latter a high-density network of trading relationships potentially involving the same currency, thereby lowering foreign exchange transaction costs. Thus, economic size brings a *de facto* limitation of international use of small economies' currencies.

The economic size of the euro area is close to that of the US, in terms of GDP as well as its population and share in international trade. Japan is the third largest, but is significantly smaller than the US and the euro area. Mainland China is the fourth largest economy in terms of the market exchange rate measured GDP, but is already the third largest by the measure of purchase power parity (PPP) based the exchange rate and in terms of the volume of international trade (Table 5.2). As China is expected to grow faster than the more developed economies, her economic weight in the world should continue to increase. Thus, as policy restrictions on the convertibility of the renminbi are increasingly lifted, it would be reasonable to expect the currency to play some role in international trade and finance, even though it is unlikely to challenge the position of the US dollar and the euro in the foreseeable future.

5.2.2   Size and development of financial markets

Size also matters in terms of financial development, and international currencies are usually associated with large, liquid and open financial markets. Large and developed financial markets give access to more investment and borrowing opportunities and allow effective arbitrage owing to low transaction costs. In particular, a deep and liquid secondary market of a wide range of securities would attract international investors, including central banks to do asset allocation in their reserve management according to their risk, liquidity and return requirements. Such markets would offer a wide range of financial services, which can help international investors to effectively hedge currency risk and manage their portfolio more efficiently (Greenspan, 2001). Because of the limited size and underdevelopment of the market, it is sometimes more cost effective for some market participants to borrow or invest abroad in an international currency and then exchange the proceeds for domestic currency, rather than conduct the transaction directly at home.

The US financial system is the most advanced globally, with deep and diversified financial markets, and with New York being a dominant financial centre. This is an important factor underlying the US dollar's position as a reserve currency. The pound sterling used to be the world's dominant reserve currency in the late nineteenth and early twentieth centuries, a time when Britain had the world's most developed financial system and London was the most important financial centre. The introduction of the euro has helped to integrate the financial markets within the euro area, and in particular the euro area has seen a strong growth of the bond market. The development of China's financial markets lags behind other major economies mainly in two ways. First, the domestic financial markets are still subject to some restrictions, including the remaining floors and ceilings on bank lending and deposit interest rates. Second, the market is by and large closed to international investors. However, important reform efforts are under way and the rapid growth of the stock market and short-term corporate bond market in recent years had shown the potential for China to develop into one of the largest financial markets in the world in the not too distant future (see below).

Table 5.2 Currency share of reserve holdings and determinants: Some indicators

	US	Euro Area	UK	Japan	Switzerland	Mainland China	Hong Kong SAR	Date
Currency Share in Foreign Reserves (%)	64.2	26.1	4.5	3.1	0.2	NA	NA	Apr 2007
Size of economy and financial market								
GDP (US$, bn)	13,202	10,527	2,345	4,340	380	2,668	190	2006
GDP (PPP, bn)	11,651	8,700	1,845	3,737	244	7,642	212	2004
Foreign trade (US$, bn)	2,958	3,478	976	1,230	274	1,761	651	2006
Stock market capitalization (US$, bn)	19,919	10,231	3,854	4,721	1,246	3,089	2,276	Aug 2007
Government bond outstanding (US$, bn)	6,415	6,805	835	6,854	114	915	20	Mar 2007
Foreign exchange turnover (total = 200%)	86.3	37	15	16.5	6.8	0.5	2.8	Apr 2007
M2 (US$, bn)	7,257	9,660	3,051	5,901	366	5,067	701	Jul 2007
Monetary Stability								
10-year average inflation (%)	2.54	1.91	2.64	−0.06	0.82	0.88	−0.37	1997–2006
Exchange rate volatility	4.49	5.44	5.02	8.15	5.98	4.40	4.58	1997–2007
Average annual appreciation of exchange rate against SDR (%)	−1.2	2.7	0.7	−0.4	1 .4	−1.3	−0.8	1997–2007

Source: World Bank; IMF; BIS; CEIC; Bloomberg; WFE; authors' calculations.
Notes:
1. Government bond outstanding is the outstanding amount of international and domestic debt issued by the governments; that for the euro area does not include Luxembourg and Slovenia due to data limitation.
2. Exchange rate volatility is the annualized standard deviation of daily percentage changes of the exchange rate against the SDR over the 10-year period.
3. For the euro/SDR exchange rate, the sample period is 1999–2007.

5.2.3   Stable value of the currency

Confidence in an international currency is important for it to be held as a store of value. Two possible indicators of currency stability are inflation and exchange rate volatility. The higher the inflation, the bigger the loss in the purchasing power of the currency. Often, a measure of the inflation differential from the average of developed economies is taken to indicate the relative stability of a currency. Exchange rate volatility is often measured with reference to the Special Drawing Rights (SDR); the more volatile the exchange rate, the higher the risk in holding reserves in that currency.

Since the turn of the century, the average annual inflation rate in China has been about 0.9%, which is much lower than that of 2.5% in the US, 1.9% in the euro area and 2.6% in the UK. Japan, on average, recorded a price decline during this period. The renminbi's volatility against the SDR was close to that of the US dollar, and lower than that of the euro, the British pound and the Japanese yen. This of course reflects the relatively close link of the renminbi with the US dollar.

Overall, it is probably fair to say that the stability of the renminbi in both the domestic and external value has been comparable to other major currencies over the past decade, following relatively high inflation and exchange rate depreciation in the earlier reform period.

5.2.4   Network externalities

It is often argued that once a currency becomes an international currency, this status is unlikely to be lost in a short period of time (Greenspan, 2001). This can be explained by persistence and network externalities. An international currency is usually associated with a deep and flexible financial market, and a good market infrastructure brings loyalty. Market participants in general would like to stick to the platform that they know well, as they have invested substantially over time to accumulate the knowledge of the platform. Another factor that supports a currency's status is network externalities. As more and more market participants use a currency to conduct transactions, others will find it convenient to follow suit. This becomes a reinforcing process, which generates a positive network effect (Eichengreen, 2005).

5.3   Data and empirical estimates

5.3.1   Data and stylized facts

Ideally, the international use of a currency should be assessed on each of the functions listed in Table 5.1. The empirical analysis of this chapter focuses on reserve currency holdings, as data are much more limited on indicators of the other international roles. The assumption is that reserve currency holdings are a good proxy for the overall international role of a currency. While interest rate and exchange rate movements may have an impact on the currency allocation of central banks' reserve holdings in the short run, in the longer term, the international roles of a currency tend to be related and jointly determined by more fundamental factors. There are economies of scope in this case. If a currency is widely used to invoice trade, it is more likely to be used to invoice financial transactions. If it is used as a vehicle currency, it is more likely to be used as a currency to which smaller economies peg, and it is more likely to account for a larger share of reserves holdings by the central banks.

The data on reserve holdings are from the IMF Currency Composition of Foreign Exchange Reserves (COFER) database. The currencies identified in the COFER data are the US dollar, euro, pound sterling, Japanese yen, Swiss franc, and a category of all 'other currencies'. In September 2005, the IMF changed the way it reports the reserve data and released revised statistics extending back to 1995. The main change was to separate the total reserves into allocated reserves and unallocated reserves. Because some member countries choose not to report the currency compositions of their foreign reserves, the IMF used to estimate the currency composition for these countries. Since the change, the IMF now includes the reserves of these countries in a category called 'unallocated reserves', which is the difference between the total world reserves and 'allocated reserves'. The share of allocated reserves in total world reserves is about 70%.[1] For our purpose, the currency composition of the allocated reserves is taken as the variable of reserve currency share.

This study uses quarterly data covering the period 1999–2006. The relatively short sample period is dictated by the data break due to the introduction of the euro in 1999. In some way, this study is complementary to Chinn and Frankel (2005) who used annual data before 1999. It is noted that the reliability and accuracy of data on reserve currency shares should be much improved in recent years, as an increasing number of central banks have disclosed information on reserve holdings.

The determinant variables discussed above, such as the GDP and trade share, inflation differentials and exchange rate volatility, are computed using data obtained mainly from the IMF International Financial Statistics (IFS), supplemented by CEIC and Bloomberg. It is difficult to find a good measure of financial market development that covers all the aspects, such as depth, breadth and efficiency of a market. Several measures, among them foreign exchange turnover and stock market capitalization, have been used in the literature (Chinn and Frankel, 2005). This study makes use of the stock market capitalization as a share of five major financial centres combined: New York, London, Tokyo, Euronext and Zurich.[2] It is expected that the stock market capitalization would be positively related to the share of that market's home currency in total world reserves. The data on stock market capitalization are from the World Federation of Exchanges (WFE).

As the sample period is short, there is a concern that variations in the data were too limited to derive a significant relationship using a regression analysis. Figures 5.1 and 5.2 show that reserve shares of the major currencies did have material changes over the eight years. The US dollar's share fell from 71.1% to 65.6%, while that of the euro increased from 18.1% to 25.2%. The share of the British pound rose from 2.7% to 4.3%, while that of the yen dropped from 6.0% to 3.2%.[3] Overall, the increase in the share of the euro is mainly at the expense of the US dollar and the Japanese yen.

Figure 5.3 plots the panel data points and shows that a higher reserve currency share is generally associated with a higher GDP share. It is often argued that reserve currency shares are not sensitive to changes in the determinant

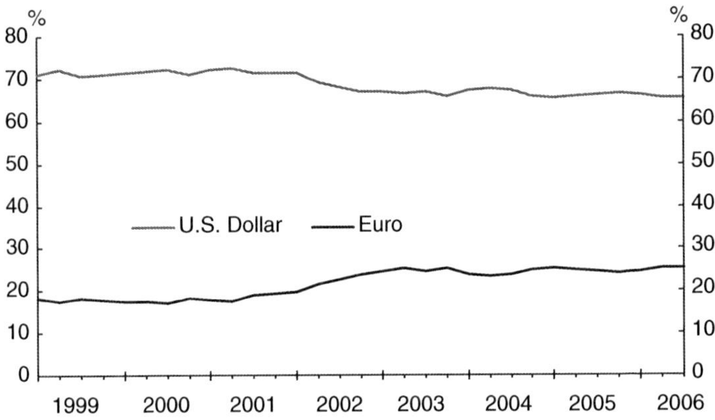

Figure 5.1   Shares of reserve currencies: US dollar and euro
Source: IMF; authors' calculations.

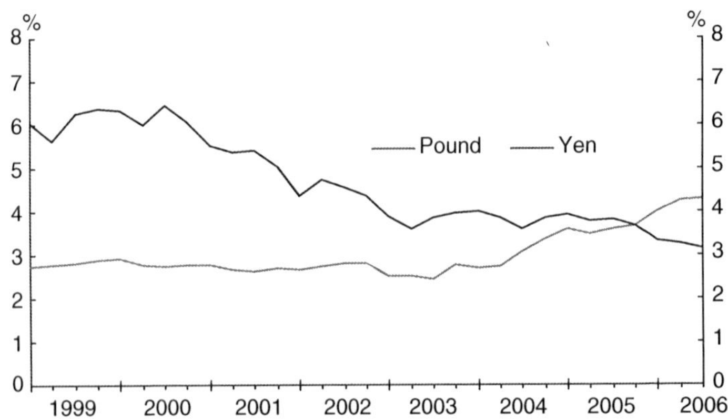

Figure 5.2   Shares of reserve currencies: British pound and Japanese yen
Source: IMF; authors' calculations.

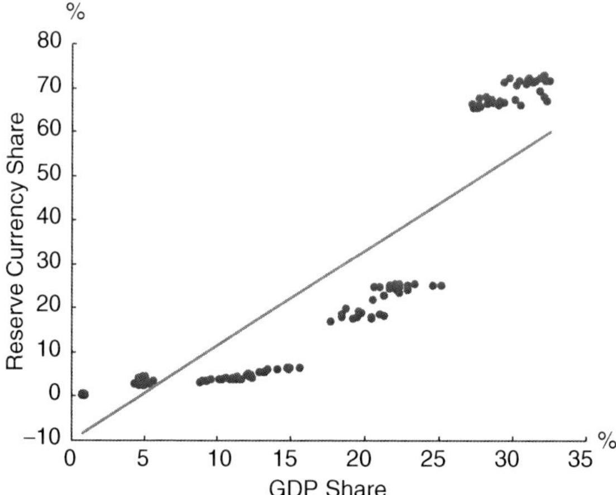

Figure 5.3   Reserve currency share vs. GDP share
Source: Authors' calculations.

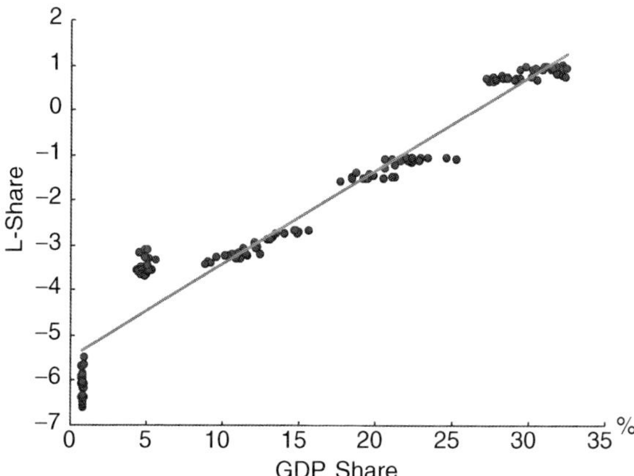

Figure 5.4   Logistic transformation of reserve currency share vs. GDP share
Source: Authors' calculations.

variables when the share is at a very low or a high level, reflecting the inertia or persistence feature noted above. Only when the reserve currency share reaches a certain threshold level will changes in the determinant variables have a significant impact. To capture this 'tipping phenomenon', the logistic transformation of the reserve currency share is used in the literature (Chinn and Frankel, 2005).[4] Figure 5.4 plots the logistic transformation of the reserve currency share against the GDP share, which also shows a positive relationship.

Similarly, the reserve currency share and share of stock market capitalization are also positively correlated (Figures 5.5 and 5.6).

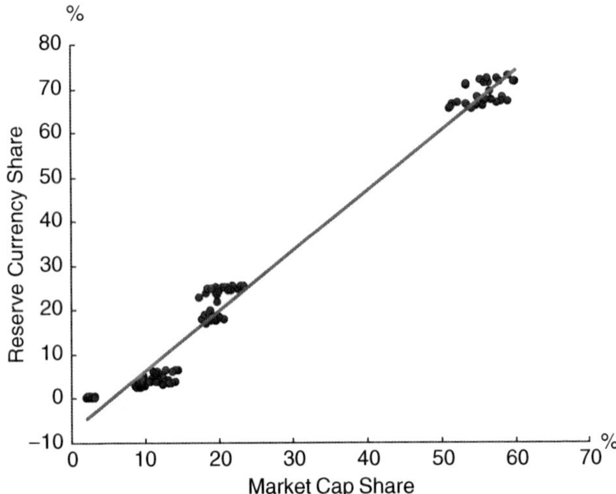

Figure 5.5   Reserve currency share vs. market cap share
Source: Authors' calculations.

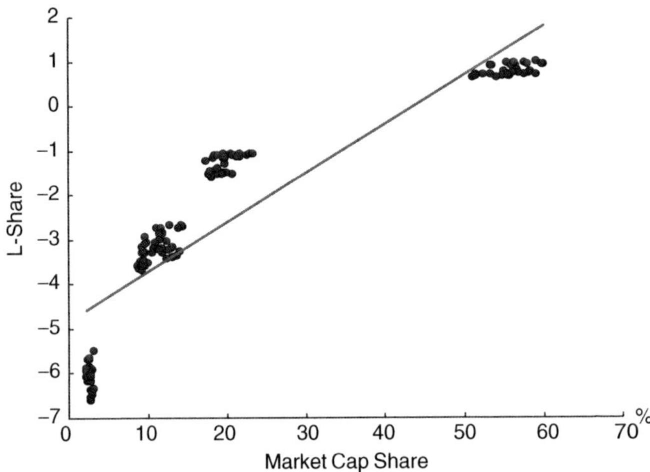

Figure 5.6   Logistic transformation of reserve currency share vs. market cap share
Source: Authors' calculations.

The relationship between the reserve currency share and exchange rate volatility and inflation differential (with the average inflation in G7 economies) is not obvious (Figures 5A.1–5A.4 in the Appendix). This suggests that exchange rate volatility and inflation differential are unlikely to be significant variables in explaining variations in reserve currency shares over time and across currencies in our sample. It probably reflects the limited variation in inflation and exchange rate volatility across currencies and over time during the short period. The logistic transformation of currency shares of reserve holdings seems to be positively correlated with the trade shares, but the relationship seems not as strong as that for the GDP share (Figures 5A.5–5A.6 in the Appendix).

5.3.2 The empirical model and estimation

The empirical estimation follows closely the model used in Chinn and Frankel (2005). That paper uses annual data from 1973–1998 to regress currency shares of reserve holdings on different combinations of explanatory variables, and finds that the share of GDP and inflation differential are statistically significant in explaining variations in the dependent variable.

The model to be estimated can be represented by the following equation:

$$SHARE_{it} = \alpha_i + \beta_1 GDP_{it} + \beta_2 INDIFF_{it} + \beta_3 MARKET\_CAP_{it}$$
$$+ \beta_4 VOL_{it} + \beta_5 TRADE_{it} + \beta_6 SHARE(-1) + \varepsilon_{it} \qquad (1)$$

In the equation, *i* refers to the different reserve currencies, including the US dollar, euro, Japanese yen, British pound and Swiss franc. *SHARE* denotes a currency's share in the total allocated world reserves. *GDP* and *MARKET_CAP* are *GDP* share in the world total and the share of stock market capitalization in the total of five financial centres respectively. *INDIFF* denotes the difference between inflation in a currency and the average inflation of the G7 economies. *VOL* is the annualized standard deviation of daily percentage change of the exchange rate of a currency against the SDR over the past five years. *TRADE* denotes the share of international trade in the total world trade.[5] The lagged dependent variable is included to capture the persistence effect, whereby the impact of shocks to the other explanatory variables accumulates in the equilibrium value of the dependent variable. To capture possible specific characteristics or conditions of each reserve currency, a cross section fixed-effect model is used in the panel regression. It is expected that β_1, β_3, β_5, β_6 have positive signs and β_2, β_4 have negative signs. The data are of quarterly frequency covering the period 1999 Q1 to 2006 Q3.

As noted above, there might be a 'tipping phenomenon' in changes in the currency shares of reserve holdings. To capture this non-linear relationship, the model is also estimated using the logistic transformation of the reserve share (*LSHARE*) as the dependent variable. Equations (2) and (3) are the final estimates obtained after dropping the insignificant variables from the preliminary estimates.

$$\widehat{SHARE} = \underset{(0.82)}{-0.001} + \underset{(0.01)}{0.080}\,GDP + \underset{(0.00)}{0.044}\,MARKET\_CAP$$
$$+ \underset{(0.00)}{0.910}\,SHARE(-1) \qquad (2)$$

$$LS\hat{H}ARE = -0.365 + 0.935\,GDP + 0.912\,LSHARE(-1) \tag{3}$$
$$\underset{(0.01)}{} \quad \underset{(0.03)}{} \quad \underset{(0.00)}{}$$

The numbers in the parentheses are p-values of the estimated coefficients, and the equations are estimated over the mean of the fixed effects.

In the linear model, only the coefficients of the GDP share, share of market capitalization, and the lagged reserve share are statistically significant. In the non-linear model, only the GDP share and the lagged dependent variable turn out to be significant.[6]

The two models suggest that the size of the economy as measured by the share of GDP in the world total is more important than other fundamental variables in determining the currency shares of reserve holdings. In particular, the trade share variable is not significant, consistent with the results in Chinn and Frankel (2005). A possible explanation is that the GDP and trade shares are correlated and the former better captures the size effect.

The lagged dependent variable is significant and its estimated coefficient has a value of 0.9. This supports the hypothesis that the currency shares of reserve holdings tend to be persistent and a shock, arising from say a change in GDP share, leads to a change in the reserve share only gradually. Specifically, our linear model estimates suggest that a rise in the GDP share by 1 percentage point would lead to an increase in the reserve currency share by 0.9 percentage point in the long run. But, it takes about seven years for half of the impact to complete.

The share of stock market capitalization is significant in the linear model but insignificant in the non-linear model. This probably reflects the difficulties in finding a good and comprehensive measure of the size of the financial market.[7] To take our linear model estimates literally, an increase by 1 percentage point in the share of stock market capitalization would raise the reserve currency share by 0.5 percentage point in the long run, and it takes about seven years for half of the effect to complete.

Neither inflation differential nor exchange rate volatility is statistically significant, probably reflecting the short sample period. In the long run, the stability in the value of a currency should be a significant factor affecting the international demand for the currency. In Chinn and Frankel (2005), inflation differential and exchange rate volatility are statistically significant in some of the regression models.[8]

5.3.3   Counterfactual exercise for the renminbi

Currently there are restrictions for renminbi capital account transactions, especially portfolio investment, although liberalization measures have been taken through schemes of Qualified Domestic Institution Investors (QDII) and Qualified Foreign Institution Investors (QFII). If the renminbi were to become fully convertible, some economies might choose to hold part of their foreign reserves in renminbi assets, especially those having close trade and investment ties with Mainland China. To gauge the potential significance of the renminbi as a reserve currency, below we conduct a counterfactual simulation using the estimated models presented above.

Applying the current levels of China's share of GDP (at the market exchange rate) in the world total and that of the stock market capitalization in the total of the six markets, which is 5.6% for GDP and 3.5% for stock market capitalization, the renminbi's share in the world reserves would be about 5% according to the linear model, and 3% based on the non-linear model. The relatively low estimate from the non-linear model partly reflects the 'tipping phenomenon', whereby the reserve currency share increases slowly when it is at a low level.

For comparison purposes, we calculated the potential reserve share of the renminbi using the estimated models in Chinn and Frankel (2005). Specifically, we employed the two models presented in Table 1 and 2 in the appendix of that paper:

$$\hat{SHARE} = \underset{(0.02)}{0.098}\,GDP - \underset{(0.17)}{0.071}\,INFDIFF - \underset{(0.16)}{0.028}\,EXVOL + \underset{(0.00)}{0.956}\,SHARE(-1) \quad (4)$$

$$\hat{LSHARE} = \underset{(0.00)}{-0.506} + \underset{(0.00)}{2.285}\,GDP - \underset{(0.09)}{1.565}\,INFDIFF - \underset{(0.34)}{0.445}\,EXVOL$$
$$+ \underset{(0.00)}{0.879}\,LSHARE(-1) \quad (5)$$

In the equations, *INFDIFF* denotes inflation differential and *EXVOL* denotes exchange rate volatility. In the calculation for the share of renminbi, the differential of China's average inflation over the past ten years from that of G7 countries is used for *INFDIFF*, and the annualized standard deviation of the log first difference of the renminbi-SDR exchange rate over the past ten years is used for *EXVOL*. Equation (5) is the non-linear version of equation (4), using the logistic transformation of the reserve currency share as the dependable variable. Chinn and Frankel (2005) use foreign exchange turnover to measure the size and development of the financial market, and it turns out to be significant in only one of the models. Considering that the foreign exchange turnover in the case of the renminbi is limited by the restrictions on the capital account transactions, we chose the two models in which the foreign exchange turnover is not included.

Applying China's data, the renminbi's share in the world reserve holdings would be 12.7% according to the linear model and 4.4% based on the non-linear model. Again, the non-linear model gives a lower estimate. Overall, our estimates are broadly in line with the estimates derived from the models of Chinn and Frankel (2005). They suggest that the renminbi's potential as a reserve currency would be comparable to the case of the Japanese yen and British pound should the renminbi become fully convertible today.[9]

5.4 Some policy considerations

It is perhaps not unreasonable to say that the renminbi has the potential to play a role in international trade and investment transactions, owing to the large size of the Chinese economy. The limited convertibility of the renminbi and the partial opening of China's financial market are restrictive factors for the international role of the renminbi. The liberalization of the restrictions on currency convertibility should of course obey the overall development and reform strategy, not necessarily for the purpose of promoting the international use of the renminbi, but a higher degree of currency convertibility may lead to an increased use of the renminbi in international transactions. This brings both benefits and risks.

Thus, the international role of the renminbi, along with the associated concerns, would be part of the consideration given by the authorities in determining the pace and form of attaining the capital account convertibility of the renminbi. As summarized in Table 5.3 (Chinn and Frankel, 2005), the main benefits of an international role include increased business for domestic financial institutions, reduced transaction costs and avoidance of exchange rate risks for residents in conducting international trade and investment activities, plus the ability of domestic institutions to issue foreign debt in the domestic currency at the prevailing interest rates. The risks are mainly associated with the external demand for renminbi assets, which may vary significantly over time, complicating the domestic monetary policy formulation and implementation (Hai & Yao, 2009).

It is beyond the scope of this chapter to provide a comprehensive analysis of the policy considerations in relation to the process of potential internationalization of the renminbi. Drawing on the international experiences, three issues are considered here, namely (i) the implications of an international role of the renminbi for domestic monetary policy, (ii) the relationship between currency internationalization and domestic financial market development, and (iii) the importance of promoting regional integration and cooperation in trade and finance.

5.4.1 Domestic monetary policy

The implication for domestic monetary policy is often cited as the main reason for caution in promoting or facilitating an international role for the renminbi. There are two concerns. The first is related to the volatility of the international demand for the renminbi which complicates the central bank's task in assessing monetary conditions and pursuing domestic monetary stability objectives. Second, considering the general market expectation of renminbi appreciation, an increase in the access of international investors to renminbi assets could lead to a trend of increasing demand for the currency, exacerbating the appreciation pressure on it. However, there is potentially an offsetting force: as the renminbi becomes increasingly

Table 5.3 Benefits and risks of the international use of renminbi

Benefits	Risks
1. Seignorage: foreign holdings of renminbi are essentially low interest loans to China, and allow China to borrow in the international market in its own currency.	1. Fluctuations in the international demand for the currency would complicate domestic monetary policymaking by increasing exchange rate volatility under a flexible exchange rate regime and variations in the demand for money under a pegged exchange rate arrangement.
2. Increase of business for domestic financial institutions: the international demand for renminbi assets would bring business for domestic financial institutions, which are the main sources of renminbi liquidity.	2. Increase in the average demand of the currency; this in general will put appreciation pressure on the exchange rate, which is especially the case in an environment of strong expectations of renminbi appreciation.
3. Avoiding exchange rate risk: the use of its own currency in international trade and finance allows domestic residents to avoid exchange rate risk.	3. Burden of responsibility: internationalization of renminbi would increase China's responsibility and obligations to maintain financial stability in the region, which would limit the freedom of using monetary policies for domestic objectives.
4. Convenience and prestige: an international currency will bring convenience and prestige for domestic residents.	

Source: Authors' compilation.

convertible, domestic investors may move part of their assets out of China for diversification purposes.

In this respect, it is interesting to look at the experiences of Japan and Germany. For many years leading up to the mid-1970s, the Japanese monetary authorities attempted to discourage the international use of the yen owing to concern that extensive foreign holdings of their currency would reduce their degree of control over money supply and increase the variability of the exchange rate (Tavlas and Ozeki, 1992). Similarly, between the late 1960s and the early 1980s, the Bundesbank attempted to limit the international use of the Deutsche mark for fear that substantial swings in capital flows could interfere with domestic stabilization (Thimann, 2009; Tavlas, 1991). The measures that the Bundesbank took were to control the capital inflows, such as restrictions over the issue of Deutsche mark obligations in the external bond market and international money market. Indeed, it is argued that the non-internationalization policies pursued by the German and Japanese authorities partly explain the persistence of the dominant US dollar position despite the increased importance of Japan and Germany in the world economy (Eichengreen 2005).

In China's case, the limited variation in the renminbi's exchange rate against the US dollar and the early stage of the development of the financial market are probably the main factors that explain the concerns about the potential destabilizing effect of the external demand for the renminbi on domestic monetary conditions. However, the increasing exchange rate flexibility and the progress of interest rate deregulation and financial sector development and reform should increase the domestic economy's resilience to external shocks over time.

5.4.2   Financial market development

This leads to the issue of the relationship between financial market development and an international role for the renminbi. In general, a large and developed financial market increases the capacity of the domestic economy in buffering against shocks arising from the varying external demand for the domestic currency. Thus, limitations in the domestic market are often taken as a risk factor in capital account opening and international use of the domestic currency. On the other hand, an increasing use of the domestic currency for conducting international trade and investment activities would increase the depth and breadth of the financial market by drawing more market participants and increasing linkages with the international market. In considering the balance of pros and cons of an international currency, one should not focus solely on the risk to the domestic financial market and by doing so understate the potential benefits.

Moreover, as the size of the financial market increases, the influence of the financial sector on policymaking would rise, with pressures for liberalization measures to improve efficiency, including opening up to the international market. After all, it is the financial sector that would benefit most from an international role for the domestic currency.

The experiences of Germany and Japan are again enlightening in this respect. In Japan, the large government budget deficits contributed to a rapid growth of the primary and secondary bond markets in the 1970s, which led to pressures from the financial community for improvement in the efficiency in the financial market. Beginning in the late 1970s, financial liberalization measures were implemented, leading to development of new instruments and deregulated interest rates. In May 1984, a new phase began with the release of a report by the Yen-Dollar Committee and an accompanying report by the Ministry of Finance entitled 'Current Status and Future Prospects for the liberalisation of Financial and Capital Markets and the Internalisation of the Yen'. These two documents noted the importance of financial liberalization and internationalization of the yen to the Japanese economy, and proposed reform measures to liberalize international transaction of the currency. The process of Deutsche mark internationalization was similar. By the mid-1980s, the Bundesbank's position had changed substantially, partly because German financial markets had developed markedly and were better insulated from external disturbances. It acknowledged the difficulty of inhibiting the operation of market forces underlying the demand for assets denominated in the Deutsche mark. Consequently, most restrictions on the issuance of foreign Deutsche mark bonds were lifted.

China's financial market has been growing rapidly in recent years, accompanied by significant progress of reform of the financial sector, including the listing of the major commercial banks. The A-share market has recorded a strong rally and, as of September 2007, the stock market capitalization had increased by 4.6 times from January 2004. In 2007, the A-share market is likely to become one of the largest IPO fundraising centres in the world. The share redesignation reform has been largely completed, removing previous concerns over the overhang of state holdings of non-tradable shares and improving corporate governance by better aligning the interests of majority and minority shareholders. Helped by strong economic growth and abundant liquidity, the bond market has also seen strong growth, particularly in short-term commercial papers. By the end of 2006, the total outstanding amount of bonds had reached 44% of GDP. In 2007, the authorities released new and much liberalized regulations on the issuing of corporate bonds, paving the way for rapid growth of the corporate bond market.

In the process of financial market development and liberalization, China has a unique advantage when compared with other economies. Under the 'one country, two systems' arrangement, China has Hong Kong, a developed and highly open international financial centre. Hong Kong is in an ideal position to develop a renminbi market outside Mainland China, providing a testing ground for the international use of the renminbi. This can be achieved by expanding the scope of the renminbi business in Hong Kong in terms of participants, products and services. There is also an increasing recognition of the need to strengthen market linkages between Hong Kong and the mainland. Recent initiatives include expanded scope for the qualified domestic institutional investors (QDII) scheme and the announced pilot scheme of allowing mainland China investors to invest directly in Hong Kong-listed securities. There are also discussions ongoing about arrangements under which Hong Kong-listed instruments can be traded on the mainland China market, and even talks of listing and trading renminbi-denominated shares on the Hong Kong Stock Exchange. All this activity will foster the integration of the two markets over time, and a larger and more liquid Chinese financial market would provide a solid base for the renminbi to play an international role. Already, combining the Hong Kong and Mainland China stock markets, the total capitalization exceeds that of Japan and is the largest in Asia.

5.4.3 Regional integration and cooperation

Finally, it is important that financial integration and cooperation are promoted in the region, since an international role for the renminbi starts with its use in conducting trade and investment activities in the Asian region (Wu, 2007; Gao, 2009). If the emergence of the euro can be considered as an extension of the internationalization of the Deutsche mark, the mark's internationalization has clearly been more successful than the Japanese yen. This was in no small part due to the cooperative arrangement within Europe. The stable value of the mark and the relatively large size of the German economy led to the use of the mark as the currency peg in the European Monetary System (EMS) before the euro was launched. In contrast, the yen experienced large swings in its exchange rate against the US dollar in recent decades, while most of the Asian currencies maintained some form of a link to the US dollar, leading to stabilizing effects on the Asian economies and hurting the regional use of the yen.

China has extensive trade and investment with the regional economies (Table 5.4). Financial integration and cooperation over arrangements that may prevent large swings in exchange rates among the Asian currencies are beneficial to all economies in the region. The exchange rates of most Asian currencies have become more flexible against the US dollar. Indeed, following the renminbi exchange rate reform in July 2005, there are signs that the renminbi has had an increasing influence on the exchange rates of the other Asian currencies (Shu, 2009). As the renminbi's exchange rate becomes more flexible and China's economic links with the region grow further over time, there would be increasing need to strengthen regional cooperation on trade and financial issues.

Table 5.4   Trade linkages in the Asian region (in per cent, as of 2006)

	China	Japan	South Korea	ASEAN	Hong Kong	Group Total
Mainland China		11.8	7.6	9.1	9.4	38.0
Japan	17.2		6.3	12.8	3.1	39.5
South Korea	20.1	12.4		10.3	3.3	46.1
ASEAN	10.0	11.2	4.3		4.4	29.8
Hong Kong SAR	46.4	7.7	3.4	9.5		67.0

Source: IMF Direction of Trade Statistics; authors' calculations.

Note: The numbers in the first row are the shares of trade with other Asian economies in China's total trade as recorded by China, the second row Japan's, and so on.

5.5   Concluding remarks

This chapter assesses the potential significance of the renminbi as an international currency by drawing on the experiences of the other major currencies. Built on the study of Chinn and Frankel (2005) and using data on five major reserve currencies, we first estimate an empirical relationship between currency shares of reserve holdings and main determinants such as the economic size of the issuing country. The empirical result shows that the size of the economy including market development and persistence and network-externality effects are the key determinants for a currency's share in the world reserves in our sample. Using the empirical relationship, a simulation is conducted to gauge the potential share of the renminbi in the total world reserves if it were to become fully convertible today. According to the linear model, the renminbi's share in the total world reserves would be 5%. According to the non-linear model, the renminbi's share would be 3%. These results suggest that at present the renminbi's potential as a reserve currency would be comparable to that of the Japanese yen and the British pound.

Whether the renminbi realizes its potential as an international currency that is in line with the size of the Chinese economy will be a market decision. Government policies in financial liberalization and currency convertibility could facilitate or inhibit the process. In this respect, the authorities, in formulating and implementing policy, need to weigh the benefits and risks associated with an international role for the renminbi. As the size of the economy and financial market increases and the monetary policy frame-work including exchange rate flexibility becomes more firmly established, the benefits should increasingly dominate costs. Overall, the international role of the renminbi and the associated benefits and costs should be part of policy considerations on the pace and form of attaining capital account convertibility for the currency.

Hong Kong, being an international financial centre, can play a significant role in the development and opening up of the Mainland China financial market. Indeed, the renminbi business in Hong Kong provides a useful testing ground for the expanded use of the renminbi in the region. In the long run, an integrated and much larger financial market that includes both Mainland China and Hong Kong markets would help to promote the international role of the renminbi.

Notes

Corresponding author, Wensheng Peng, Head of China Research, Barclays Capital. Tel: (852) 2903 2651. Email: Wensheng.Peng@barclayscapital.com. This chapter was written when Hongyi Chen and Wensheng Peng were staff members of the Hong Kong Monetary Authority. We are grateful to Rina Suo and Brian Ng for research assistance. The usual disclaimer applies.

1. All industrial countries report to the COFER database, but some developing countries choose not to do so. Thus, all the unallocated reserves are attributed to developing countries. Currently, the allocated reserves account for about 52% of developing countries' total reserves, and the ratio has been declining in recent years. This is probably a reflection that the foreign reserves of those developing countries choosing not to report to the COFER database have been increasing. Nevertheless, the allocated reserves still take up a majority share of the total reserves, and the currency shares of the allocated reserves for developing countries is similar to that of industrial countries.
2. These are the major international financial centres, which correspond to the five major reserve currencies studied in this paper. The total market capitalization of these five centres accounts for about 80% of the world total.
3. The Swiss franc's share fell marginally and there was little change in the share of all other currencies.
4. The logistic transformation of reserve currency share S is $\log(S/(1 - S))$.
5. In calculating the share of the euro area's trade in the world total, the intra-euro area trade is taken out in both the numerator and denominator, so that the definition of trade share is consistent with that for the other four currencies.
6. The use of the market exchange rate in calculating both the dependable variable and some explanatory variables such as GDP and market capitalization shares may raise concern about endogeneity. However, such concerns are unwarranted since exchange rates do not enter the equation directly on the right-hand side, see Chinn and Frankel (2005).
7. In Chinn and Frankel (2005), foreign exchange turnover was used as the indicator of financial market development. It turns out that only in one of the seven regressions is it statistically significant. In our case, quarterly data on foreign exchange turnover were not available.
8. Chinn and Frankel (2005) tried the long-run depreciation trend of the exchange rate against the SDR and found it to be insignificant.
9. Li and Liu (2009) used a similar approach and estimated an empirical model of reserve currency share using annual data from 1967–2004. Their simulation suggests that the renminbi would be the third major reserve currency behind the US dollar and the euro in 20 years' time, assuming China's rapid economic growth continues.

References

Chinn, M. and J. Frankel (2005). 'Will the Euro Eventually Surpass the Dollar as Leading International Reserve Currency?', NBER Working Paper, No. 11510.

Eichengreen, B. (2005). 'Sterling's Past, Dollar's Future: Historical Perspectives on Reserve Currency Competition', NBER Working Paper No. 11336.

Eichengreen, B. and J. Frankel (1996). 'The SDR, Reserve Currencies, and the Future of the International Monetary System', in M. Mussa, J. Boughton and P. Isard (eds), *The Future of the SDR in Light of Changes in the International Financial System*. International Monetary Fund.

Greenspan, A. (2001). 'The Euro as an International Currency', paper presented at the Euro 50 Group Roundtable, Washington, DC, November 30.

Hai, W. (2007). 'Pros and Cons of International Use of RMB for China', presentation at Hong Kong Institute of Monetary Research Conference, *Currency Internationalization: International Experiences and Implications for the Renminbi*, 15–16 October 2007, Hong Kong.

He, F. and J. Li (2005). 'The Experience and Lessons from the Internationalization of US dollar', *Chinese Social Sciences Studies*, January 2005, Beijing.

Kenen, P. (1983). *The Role of the Dollar as an International Currency*, Occasional Papers No. 13, Group of Thirty, New York.

Li, D.D. and L. Liu (2007). 'RMB Internationalization: An Empirical Analysis', Presentation at Hong Kong Institute of Monetary Research Conference: *Currency Internationalization: International Experiences and Implications for the Renminbi*, 15–16 October 2007, Hong Kong.

Li, J. (2006). 'RMB as a Regional International Currency: Cost-benefit Analysis and Roadmap', *Centre for European Studies*, Fudan University, Shanghai.

Lim, E-G. (2006). 'The Euro's Challenge to the Dollar: Different Views from Economists and Evidence from COFER (Currency Composition of Foreign Exchange Reserves) and other Data', IMF Working Paper, WP/06/153.

Mundell, R.A. (1998). 'What Makes a Great Currency', *Central Banking*, Vol. 9 (August), pp. 32–42.

Shu, C. (2009). 'Impact of Renminbi on Asian Currencies', *China Economic Issues*, June 2007, Hong Kong Monetary Authority.

Tavlas, G.S. (1991). 'On the International Use of Currencies: The Case of the Deutsche Mark', *Essays in International Finance*, No. 181, Princeton University.

Tavlas, G.S. and Y. Ozeki (1992). 'The Internationalization of Currencies: An Appraisal of the Japanese Yen', IMF Occasional Paper, No. 90.

Thimann, C. (2007). 'The Global Role of Currencies: Concept, Development and Policies', paper presented at Hong Kong Institute of Monetary Research Conference, *Currency Internationalization: International Experiences and Implications for the Renminbi*, 15–16 October 2007, Hong Kong.

Truman, E.M. (1999). 'The Evolution of the International Financial System', Remarks at the Institute for International Monetary Affairs Eighth Symposium, Tokyo, 6 December.

Wu, B. (2007). 'Financial Market Development and International Use of Renminbi', presentation at Hong Kong Institute of Monetary Research Conference, *Currency Internationalization: International Experiences and Implications for the Renminbi*, 15–16 October 2007, Hong Kong.

Yam, J. (2005). The World's Reserve Currency. View Point article, January 2005. Hong Kong Monetary Authority website: http://www.hkma.gov.hk.

Yam, J. (2007). 'China as a Player in International Financial Markets', View Point article, April 2007. Hong Kong Monetary Authority website: http://www.hkma.gov.hk.

Yu, Y. and H. Gao (2007). 'Internationalization of the Renminbi and Its Implications for Monetary Policy', presentation at Hong Kong Institute of Monetary Research Conference, *Currency Internationalization: International Experiences and Implications for the Renminbi*, 15–16 October 2007, Hong Kong.

巴曙松, 人民币国际化从哪里切入,《金融经济》, 2003 年第 8 期.

姜波克、张青龙: 国际货币的两难及人民币国际化的思考,《学习与探索》, 2005 年第 4 期.

李稻葵, 人民币国际化: 势在必行, 宜于速行,《新财富》, 2006 年 6 月.

李瑶: 非国际货币, 货币国际化与资本项目可兑换,《金融研究》, 2003 第 8 期.

刘力臻: 徐奇渊等著,《人民币国际化探索》, 北京: 人民出版社, 2006 年 10 月.

Appendix

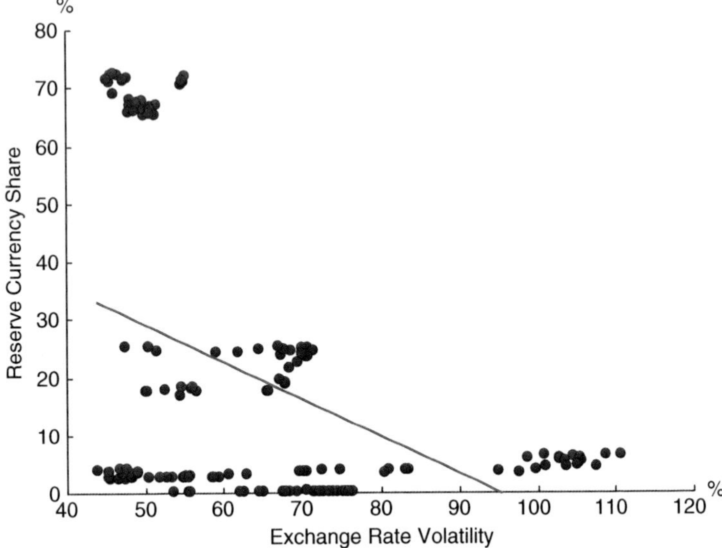

Figure 5A.1   Reserve currency share vs. exchange rate volatility
Source: Authors' calculations.

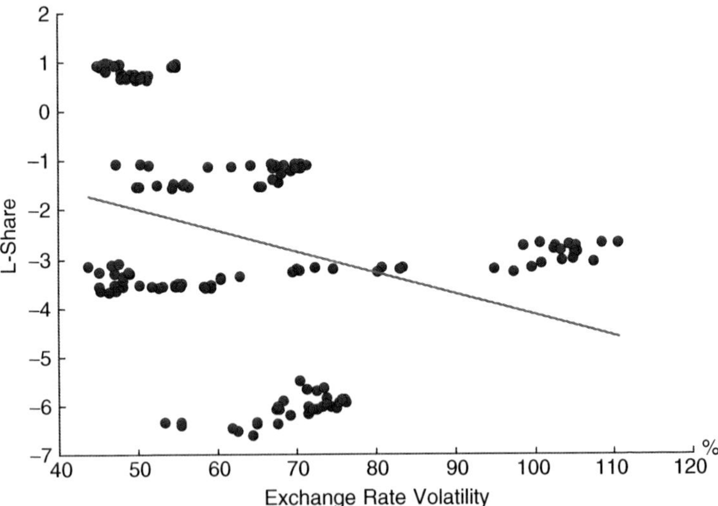

Figure 5A.2   Logistic transformation of reserve currency share vs. exchange rate volatility
Source: Authors' calculations.

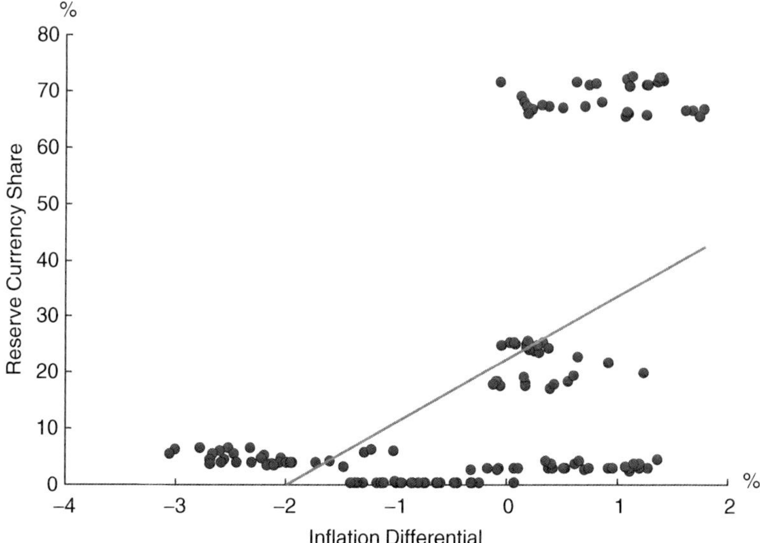

Figure 5A.3   Reserve currency share vs. inflation differential
Source: Authors' calculations.

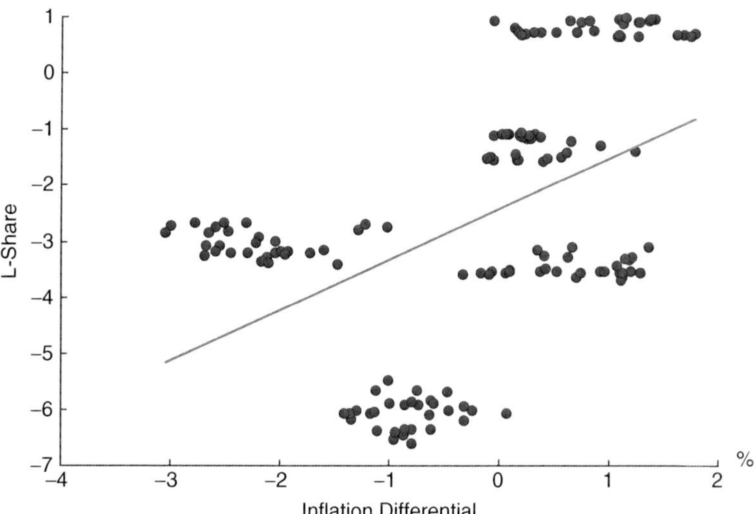

Figure 5A.4   Logistic transformation of reserve currency share vs. inflation differential
Source: Authors' calculations.

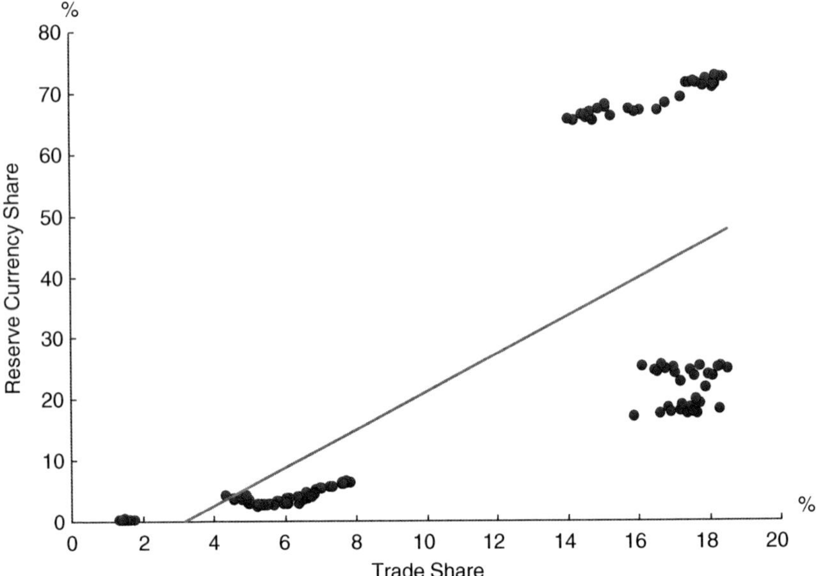

Figure 5A.5   Reserve currency share vs. trade share
Source: Authors' calculations.

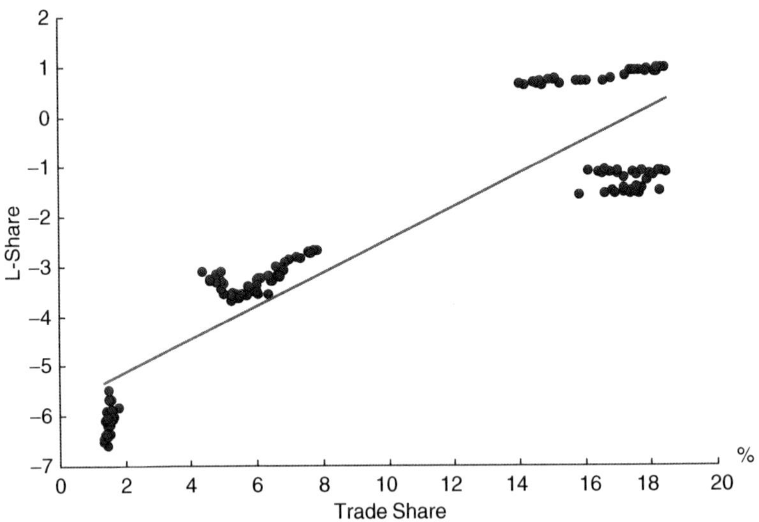

Figure 5A.6   Logistic transformation of reserve currency share vs. trade share
Source: Authors' calculations.

6
Pros and Cons of International Use of the RMB for China

Wen Hai and Hongxin Yao

6.1　Introduction

Along with economic globalization and international financial integration, currency internationalization has been an important issue in the study of international finance. Even though there is still no consistent definition for the internationalization of a currency, the various definitions actually share some common points. Tavlas (1998) and Hartman (2002) argued that if a currency is received by the institutions or individuals of other countries, and it functions as the medium of exchange, unit of account and store of value, then it can be considered as an international currency. Since the 1990s, the reputation of the Chinese renminbi (RMB) in the international market has given greatly. Its influence has extended to neighboring countries such that the RMB is widely accepted as the settlement currency in border trades with Vietnam, Thailand, Burma, Cambodia, North Korea, Mongolia, Russia, Pakistan and Nepal. The Philippines, South Korea, Cambodia, Malaysia and Nepal have already accepted the RMB as their foreign exchange reserve. Bergsten (1975) analyzed both the internal and external economic conditions of an international currency, as they affected the US dollar. The internal conditions include robust economic growth, price stability, comparative advantages of international scale, and highly developed financial markets. The external conditions include foreign confidence in the stability of the convertibility regime, as well as the maintenance of a reasonable mobility ratio and the healthy balance of payments. Based on these factors, the achievement of the international status of the RMB relies on the aspects outlined in the following sections.

**The high-speed growth of China's economy
over the past 30 years**

The development of China's economy is of great importance for the circulation and stability, in terms of value, of its currency. The country's enormous output and stable growth rate can create more opportunities for trade and provide more capital for monetary markets. Without the enormous output as

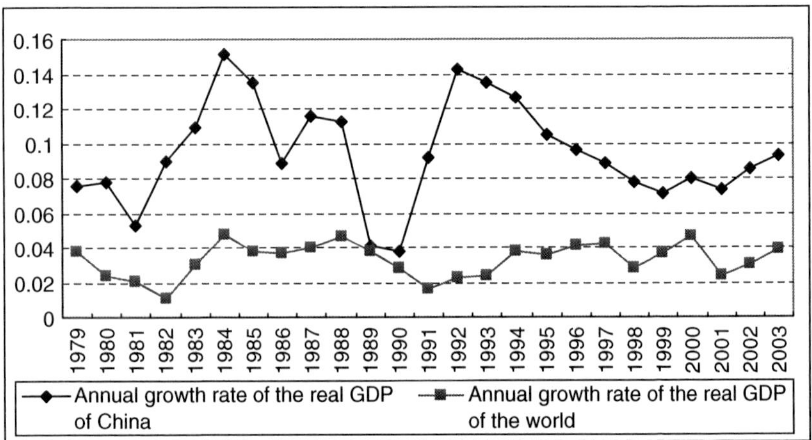

Figure 6.1   The comparison of the GDP growth rate between China and world
Source: China Economic Statistics Database, ERS International Macroeconomic data set, authors'
compilations.

a support, the flow of international capital could wreak havoc on domestic
macro-economic stability. For example, the strong economies of the United
States, Japan and the European Union are the important guarantee of the
international use of the US dollar, the yen and the euro respectively. With the
economic reform, China's economy maintained a high-speed and sustainable
growth from 1979 to 2004, with an average GDP growth rate of 9.5%—much
higher than the world level during the corresponding period (Figure 6.1). In
2004, China's total GDP even ranked in the top six in the world.[1] It is owing
to this exceptional economic growth that the international use of the RMB
can expand greatly over the next few years.

6.1.1   The rapid development of China's international trade

Page (1981) showed that along with the increase of a country's trade volume, its currency would be more frequently used in international transactions, thus further motivating the currency's circulation. The importance of
a currency in the international market is directly related to its proportion
of the world trade volume. If a country's businesses participate in international trade more frequently, then the country's currency is more likely to
be used for payment, settlement and storage. In recent years, China's international trade has developed rapidly. Both export and import volume have
maintained a high growth rate, while the trade surplus too has continued to
increase. Since 1996, the trade growth rate of China has been much higher
than that of the world level (Figure 6.2), and by the end of 2007, the export
earnings has contributed US$1 trillion for China's foreign exchange reserve.[2]

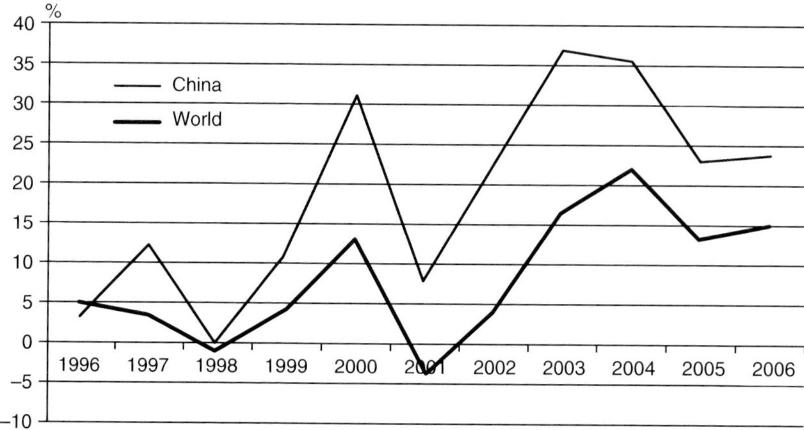

Figure 6.2 The comparison of the growth rate of trade volume between China and world
Source: UNCTAD, authors' calculations.

By observing the trend of export and import growth rates, there is no doubt that the international use of the RMB has already gained strong support within international trade, providing a sound base for further expansion of the renminbi as an international currency in the future.

6.1.2   The long-term stability of China's macro-economy

The core of long-term stability of a country's macro-economy is control of the inflation rate. Maintaining high-speed growth and a low level of inflation is essential requirements for the international use of a currency. A high-level inflation rate would result in the depreciation of the nominal and real exchange rate, which can impair the functioning of an international currency, such as a unit of account. Furthermore, a high inflation rate can reduce the purchasing power of residents, thereby affecting other functions of a currency for international use, such as medium of exchange and store of value. Thus, the long-term stability of a country's macro-economy is the innate basis for the stability of a currency, giving both overseas and domestic citizens the confidence to invest in the currency. In recent years, the Chinese government has not only emphasized the resource allocating function of the market, but also the effect of economic policy. So, while maintaining a high-speed growth rate, the inflation rate, for instance, was far below the growth rate after the "soft-landing" policy was announced in 1996 (Table 6.1). The long-term stability of China's macro-economy is another factor for the international use of RMB.

6.1.3   Reform of the foreign exchange system

Along with the development of trade with neighboring countries or regions, the Chinese government has gradually recognized the importance of promoting the

Table 6.1 Comparison of growth rate and inflation rate in China

Year	1996	1997	1998	1999	2000	2001	2002	2003	2004
Inflation rate	8.3	2.8	−0.8	−1.4	0.4	0.7	−0.8	1.2	3.9
GDP growth rate	9.6	8.8	7.8	7.1	8.0	7.5	8.3	9.5	9.5

Source: China Economic Statistics Database; Authors' calculations.

international use of the RMB, and in 1994, the government began to implement a number of institutional reforms in the field of economy and finance to achieve this. On 1 January 1994, the government announced that the official exchange rate and the market exchange rate of the RMB would merge, and the managed floating rate system based on the market mechanism was established. In the same year, the conditional convertibility of the current account was realized. On 21 July 2005, the managed floating rate system based on market supply and demand, with reference to a basket of currencies, was implemented. Since the exchange rate mechanism forms a basis for the international use of a currency, all three of these foreign exchange reforms aimed at realizing the free convertibility of the RMB, vital for establishing the international use of the currency.

By using CEIC data, Li et al. (2004) estimated that the overseas stock amount of the RMB was around RMB5–8 billion. In 2002, the outflow amount of the RMB resulting from cross-border trade and cross-border travel was estimated to be RMB120 billion. Taking into account the underground exchange and statistical errors, the real cross-border flow amount of the RMB was more likely to be between RMB120 and RMB140 billion. Two years later, in 2004, a survey report put the cross-border flow at RMB771.3 billion, RMB390.6 billion of which was outflow and RMB380.7 billion of which was inflow (The Investigation Team of the Cross-border Movement of RMB Cash, 2005). The net effect of 2004 was an outflow of RMB9.9 billion, which is 2.1 times that of 2001, and 5.8% of the increment of money supply that year. Therefore, even though the cross-border flow of the RMB was still small compared to the expansion of money supply, the absolute amount maintained an upward trend. While international use of the RMB is still in its early stages, more and more neighboring countries are gradually becoming aware of the value of the RMB as an international currency.

6.2   The benefits of the international use of RMB on China's economy

6.2.1   Earning the international seigniorage

One of the features of a modern currency is its departure from its true value. A government that issues a specific currency has the right to exchange with its citizenry paper money for real resources, and to benefit from the resulting gains. The profit that is the difference between the face value of a currency and the cost of its production is called seigniorage. Based on this definition, the international seigniorage is that gained when the currency is held by other countries. Olivier (1997) defined seigniorage as,

$$s_n = \Delta M_r / p$$

where s_n is the real seigniorage, ΔM_r is the increment of money supply and p is the inflation rate; when considering the international seigniorage, ΔM_r is the increment of money supply held by other countries. Since the overseas outflow of the RMB is mainly sourced from border trade, cash payments made in cross-border travel, and underground foreign exchange, we define the difference between the cash payments in border trade and in overseas travel as ΔM. Also, the change in the CPI (consumer price index) is defined as p. Thus, the seigniorage from border trade is,

$$s_n = \left(\Delta M_r / p \right) \times 100$$

Due to the difficulty in data collection, accurate information about the total outflow of the RMB overseas is still unavailable. Even though some researchers have estimated the cumulative amount in neighboring countries, the results by different methods are inconsistent because of the problems in gathering the data.

6.2.1.1 Estimation of the international seigniorage of RMB

In estimating as accurately as possible the international seigniorage of the RMB in our research, we have taken into consideration the border trade balance, the cash amount carried by Chinese citizens traveling in Asian countries and the cash amount carried by Hong Kong and Macau citizens traveling in mainland China. Some means of estimation are as follows:

1. In the estimation of the cumulative amount of the RMB, the ratio of RMB settlement in border trader before 2000 was set at 10 per cent, and after 2000 at 50% (figures based on research by the People's Bank of China in 2000 and State administration of Foreign Exchange in 2001).[3]
2. Since the cash amount carried by Chinese citizens when traveling in other Asian countries, and especially neighboring countries, accounts for an essential part of the cash amount carried by Chinese citizens for traveling overseas, we use the former as a substitution for the latter. Furthermore, owing to insufficient data, we had to estimate the number of Chinese citizens traveling in Asian countries after 2002 by multiplying the total number of overseas travelers by 85%.[4] We also assumed that the average per capita consumption in traveling between 1996 and 1998 was approximately RMB3000–5000, and specifically that for 1996 it was RMB3000, for

1997 it was RMB4000, for 1998 it was RMB5000, and for subsequent years it was RMB6000.[5] This assumption was based on the fact that per capita consumption keeps increasing.
3. Since most of the overseas citizens entering Mainland China with the RMB are Hong Kong or Macau citizens, we used the entry number of Hong Kong or Macau citizens to estimate indirectly the RMB cash inflow. Additionally, with regard to the impact of Hong Kong's return to Chinese ownership on cash amounts held by people entering China, prior to Hong Kong's reentry the per capita RMB cash-carrying limit was 200, after which the amount was set at RMB300 for 1998, RMB400 for 1999, RMB500 for 2000, and RMB600 for the period 2001–2005.[6]

The estimation of RMB inflows and outflows from cross-border trade and travel is presented in Table 6.2. It shows that from 1996 the cross-border flow of the RMB keeps increasing, reaching RMB66.551 billion in 2006 because of the dramatic increase in the number of people entering and departing China between 2001 and 2006. It is worth noting that our estimation is

Table 6.2 Estimation of total international seigniorage revenue of RMB (in billion yuan) (1996–2006)

Year	Net value of RMB outflow to other countries	Expense of resident out to other Asian countries	Expense of compatriots from Hong Kong and Macao	Consumer price index (1996 = 100)	Seigniorage revenue
1996	0.19569	6.156	8.5	100.00	−2.148
1997	0.29586	6.222	9.59	102.79	−2.989
1998	0.3342	8.136	16.22	101.98	−7.600
1999	0.5721	21.756	24.67	100.54	−2.329
2000	7.8704	28.716	35.05	100.95	1.522
2001	10.1104	35.430	45.21	101.65	0.325
2002	8.4472	51.378	48.65	100.84	11.082
2003	3.4231	75.536	46.49	102.05	31.818
2004	2.5744	117.198	53.05	106.02	62.929
2005	−6.9262	128.214	57.56	107.93	59.047
2006	−14.9162	146.820	58.99	109.56	66.551
Total	11981	625.562	344.98	–	218.208

Note: Expenses of residents traveling in other Asian countries = number of residents × personal expenses of the resident; expenses of compatriots from Hong Kong and Macao in Mainland China = number of compatriots × personal expenses of residents.
Source: China Economic Statistics Database; Authors' calculations.

rather conservative, and that the amount would be around RMB70 billion if we had taken such factors as underground transactions and statistical errors into consideration. The overseas RMB stock amount is estimated to be RMB292.554 billion, which generates a seigniorage of RMB218.208 billion.

6.2.1.2   *Estimation of the international seigniorage of RMB in future years*

In the above estimation, we consider only the seigniorage from trade with neighboring countries. Along with the rapid development of China's economy, the stable state of the RMB's appreciation and the increasing potency of the Chinese government's financial policies, more and more international trades are being priced and settled in the RMB. Consequently, the international use of the RMB will in future have a much larger dimension than at present, and the international seigniorage of the RMB will experience a further increase.

Currently, owing to close economic ties and the sharp increase in regional trade and investment, the ten members of the ASEAN are the main potential countries that will accept the RMB as the denominated and settlement currency. At the ASEAN-China "10 + 1" heads-of-state meeting in Brunei in November 2001, agreement was reached on establishing the ASEAN-China free trade area, which further promotes trade between China and the ASEAN member countries. During the past few years, the level of trade has increased year on year, and the stability of the RMB has earned the currency a good reputation among Asian countries, two factors which have helped provide a solid foundation for the further international use of the RMB. Also, RMB services, such as the cross-border Yuan trade settlement and RMB deposit business, have been corporated in Vietnam, Thailand, Burma, Malaysia, Philippines, and Singapore successively.

To estimate the international seigniorage of the RMB, let us assume that trade between China and the ASEAN member countries is priced in the RMB from year 2008. Based on the growth rate of trade balances from 1996 to 2006, we can first estimate the trade balances for the years 2008 to 2015. Inflation rates for this period is estimated according to the historical inflation rates from 1995 to 2007. The estimation of the international seigniorage for future years is shown in Table 6.3 (note that cross-border trade is not included to avoid overestimation). If 10% of the trade between China and the ASEAN countries is settled in the RMB, the international seigniorage for 2015 would reach RMB17.572 billion, and the total international seigniorage for 2008 to 2015 would be RMB123.026 billion.

In addition, with the development of regional trade and investment, currency cooperation is promoted further. In May 2000, at the 33rd annual meeting of the Asian Development Bank, ASEAN countries, Japan, Korea and China signed the "Chiang Mai Initiative," agreeing on the establishment of a bilateral currency swap system to avoid or mitigate future crises. To date, the bilateral swap credit funds under this agreement have reached US$80 billion. In May 2007, the 10th ASEAN "10 + 3" Finance Ministers

Table 6.3 Estimation of seigniorage revenue if RMB is used as the invoicing currency in trade with ASEAN countries, 2008–15

Year	2008	2009	2010	2011	2012	2013	2014	2015
Balance of trade with ASEAN counties (billion yuan)	16.245	17.539	18.832	20.126	21.42	22.713	24.007	25.301
Consumer price index 1996 = 100	125.35	127.86	130.41	133.02	135.68	138.39	141.16	143.99
Seigniorage revenue from trade with ASEAN counties (billion yuan)	12.960	13.718	14.440	15.130	15.787	16.412	17.007	17.572

Note: The CPI in this table is calculated through iteration based on the China average CPI inflation rate from 1996 to 2007; the CPI for 2007 is calculated from the average of January–June; 1 US dollar = 7.5 RMB yuan.
Source: China Economic Statistics Database; Authors' calculations.

Meeting agreed to establish the East Asian foreign exchange reserve, for use when any member country is faced with a crisis.

Thus, the ASEAN–Japan–Korea–China currency cooperation area has taken shape, and from 2008, 3% of the transactions within the region will be denominated and settled in the RMB. Using the same estimation method stated above, the international seigniorage would reach RMB24.43 billion in 2015, and the total amount from 2008 to 2015 would be RMB172.717 billion (Table 6.4). Nevertheless, it should be noted that this seigniorage level is still far below that of the US and some other developed countries. Also, since our estimation is based on the assumption of a stable growth rate, which would be discounted once the current trade deficit of those Asian countries with China has improved, the estimation may not be realized.

6.2.2 Promoting China's international trade

6.2.2.1 *Reducing the currency risk*

Usually, the exporter is faced with two kinds of foreign exchange risks. First, when the denominated currency that is not the domestic currency depreciates, the exporter will receive less after the exchange rate has changed. Second, if the value of the denominated currency is of great volatility, the importer holding the currency will face more uncertainty. The US dollar is a common invoicing and settlement currency in China's exports, and hence the appreciation of the RMB since July 2005 has resulted in some loss for those exporters. Moreover, since the exporters

Table 6.4 Estimation of seigniorage revenue if RMB is used as the invoicing currency in trade with the East Asian currency cooperation countries, 2008–15

Year	2008	2009	2010	2011	2012	2013	2014	2015
Balance of trade with East Asian counties (billion yuan)	23.13	24.85	26.57	28.29	30.01	31.74	33.46	35.18
Consumer price index 1996 = 100	125.35	127.86	130.41	133.02	135.68	138.39	141.16	143.99
Seigniorage revenue from trade with East Asian countries (billion yuan)	18.453	19.437	20.375	21.27	22.121	22.931	23.7	24.43

Note: The CPI in this table is calculated through iteration based on the China average CPI inflation rate from 1996 to 2007; the CPI for 2007 is calculated from the average of January–June; 1 US dollar = 7.5 RMB Yuan.
Source: China Economic Statistics Database; Authors' calculations.

Table 6.5 Comparison of the fluctuation of the RMB and US dollar between July 2005 and October 2007

	EUR	JPY	AU$	GBP	CA$
RMB	13.2%	21.6%	16.5%	15.2%	15.8%
US$	22.7%	14.2%	28.4%	21.2%	26.9%

Note: The fluctuations shown were the largest in foreign exchange rates during the period July 2005 to October 2007.
Source: China Economic Statistics Database; Authors' calculations.

need to hold a large amount of foreign currency for transactions, they will be under a high currency risk owing to foreign exchange fluctuations. The value of the RMB, however, is less volatile. As shown in Table 6.5, after the announcement of the managed floating exchange rate system in China, almost all the fluctuations in the RMB against the major foreign currencies were less than the US dollar against those same currencies, indicating the stability of the RMB.

6.2.2.2 *Reducing the transaction costs*

When the invoicing currency is not the domestic currency, the transaction cost of the business deal is not a trivial amount. Currently, China's trade with both developed countries and neighboring developing countries is always denominated and settled in a third-party currency (usually the US dollar). A large amount of transaction costs are generated in the transaction process. Especially in cross-border trade, small companies have to exchange in the underground market, and hence have to pay more and face the risk of being swindled.

To estimate a transaction cost, we used a trade between a Chinese mainland company and a Hong Kong company as an example. The total payment is assumed to be US$0.5 billion. First of all, the mainland company buys this amount of US dollars with the RMB, paying about RMB15.02 million as a transaction fee at 0.4%. Also, the Hong Kong company needs to sell the US$0.5 billion for HK dollars, leading to a transaction cost of about RMB0.58 billion. Hence, the total transaction fee is about RMB15.6 billion, which could be saved were both companies to use the RMB as the invoicing and settlement currency. It is thanks to this cost reduction effect that the internationalization of the RMB could further promote international trade.

6.2.2.3   *Providing an alternative settlement currency for trading partners*

It is worth noting that most of China's neighboring states, with which China keeps a trade surplus, are developing countries that are short of foreign exchange reserve. This reality actually restricts the bilateral trade between China and these countries. If these countries were to accept the RMB as the settlement currency, they could export more products and services to China, and thereby change their current state of trade deficit. At the same time, since most of these nations are abundant in natural resources but short of market supply, promoting trade between China and these countries will help considerably towards solving the problems of market oversupply of trading partners and resource scarcity in China. Therefore, the promotion of the RMB as a settlement currency and the enhancing of bilateral trade will benefit all parties.

6.2.3   Increasing the ability of Chinese firms to invest abroad

Generally, investors prefer their domestic currency, where allowed, because it is more convenient and less expensive for them to hold. In the future, along with an increase of direct and indirect investments by countries, China's RMB will function more as an international currency in contracts and claims documents. Thus, China's capital and financial account may show a big deficit, something experienced in the past by both the US and Japan. From 1953 to 1971 (except for 1968 and 1969), the deficit of the US capital and financial account increased dramatically, with that for 1971 being 51.39 times more than in 1953. Since 1981, when Japan began to promote the international use of the yen, Japan's capital and financial account has been in deficit, with the deficit from foreign investment increasing from 4.71 trillion yen in 1981 to 21.35 trillion yen in 1998.[7]

Even though China's foreign direct investment does not have a long history, its foreign investment flows already rank first among developing countries. Nevertheless, most of the current foreign direct investment is in the form of US dollars, which could be replaced by the RMB when investing in neighboring countries in the future. The RMB enjoys a high reputation in neighboring states and the wider region, and this lays a solid foundation for direct investment in the RMB. Were the RMB to be used directly in foreign investment, the current problem of supply of foreign currency in foreign investment would be readily solved. In addition, the fact that China's current account maintains a surplus and the RMB keeps appreciating against the US dollar motivates investors to use RMB in their foreign investments.

6.2.4   Optimizing China's economic structure

6.2.4.1   Earning foreign currency will no longer be the main objective of export

"Earning foreign currency" has been an important strategic goal in past years. Under this strategy, exporting companies have rapidly developed as profits have increased dramatically. The trade surplus in 2005 exceeded US$100 billion, while the cumulative amount at the beginning of 2007 reached US$1 trillion. Some negative effects, however, have appeared in recent years. From a theoretical viewpoint, the bigger the country, the less dependent on trade it is; the more developed the country, the less dependent on trade it is. However, China, as a big country, is increasingly dependent on international trade. In 2004, for instance, the dependence of China's GDP on foreign trade amounted to 70%[8] which indicates that China's economy largely depends on international markets and does not follow the normal development path. Internationalization of the RMB will help in adjusting and enhancing China's trade strategy and economic structure.

6.2.4.2   Patterns of production and international trade will be based more on China's comparative advantage and stage of development

The essence of the international use of RMB is to exchange the currency for real resources. Therefore, the currency's promotion internationally will be of great benefit to Chinese enterprises in obtaining scarce raw materials and primary products. Most of the ASEAN countries, for example, are abundant in mineral and plant resources. Moreover, since the cost of foreign investment to technology-intensive enterprises would be less impacted by RMB appreciation than it would for labor-intensive enterprises, foreign capital will be more motivated to participate in China's newly emerging industrial structure. Hence, the international use of the RMB might not only strengthen the cost advantage, but also boost the transformation of technology- and capital-intensive patterns within the economic structure.

6.2.5   Increasing the efficiency of financial markets and financial institutions

6.2.5.1   Promoting the development of financial markets

With the deepening internationalization of RMB, the financial market reform in China becomes increasingly vital. While on the one hand, the internationalized financial environment provides a foundation for the international use of RMB, on the other hand, the international use of the RMB is also facilitating the internationalization of China's financial system. Since the international use of a currency actually results in increasing cross-border transactions, deepening internationalization of that currency requires that the country's financial system be in line with international standards. Based on the experiences of other countries, some of the adjustments and changes required in China are as follows.

1. **Internationalization of the banking industry:** The first step is commercialization. This means that China's banks seek to maximize their profits in accordance with international commercial banking norms, namely: the marketization of interest rates, the diversification of financial services and the modernization of internal management systems. However, since the country's current banking system is still far from robust and competitive, and the RMB as an operating currency is not yet fully developed, foreign banks have not entered the Chinese market in more broadly. It has to be said that, apart from the Bank of China, domestic commercial banks have not yet reached international standards.
2. **Internationalization of the security market:** This requires that there be no nationality limitation on both investors and debtors, and that products include both domestic and overseas securities. The level of internationalization of a country's security market is a reflection of the development of a country's financial system, and is of significance for the country's economic development. Hence, to realize the internationalization of China's security market, it is crucial that the reform of the financial system is accelerated .
3. **Internationalization of China's financial institutions:** This requires that China's financial institutions and companies are not limited by national boundaries and are free to operate internationally. This includes the opportunity to establish overseas branches and the opening up of the country to foreign institutions, in particular admitting foreign banks to the domestic marketplace.

6.2.5.2   Establishing the RMB offshore market in Hong Kong, and the Shanghai International Financial Center

To become an international currency, the RMB needs not only to be widely accepted, but also to function sustainably as an international currency. In other words, the RMB needs not only to be the settlement currency in cross-border trade, but also to function as the invoicing currency and the transaction instrument of the international investment and credit markets. A robust financial environment requires both a developed domestic financial market and a mature offshore financial market. Achieving this will ensure that China and its currency lie at the core of international finance, opening up the channel for international currency exchange and the mechanisms that will enable the RMB to become an international settlement currency.

1. **Establishment of the Hong Kong RMB offshore financial market:** Access to offshore financial markets, or overseas markets, separate from the domestic financial market, free non-residents from the restrictions imposed by domestic taxation and foreign exchange regulations when trading or investing. Launch of the RMB financial market in Hong Kong will offer an institutional arrangement for the inflow and outflow of the currency, facilitate economic cooperation and personal consumption, and generally enhance financial services. This will both strengthen Hong Kong's status as an international finance center and facilitate the process of opening the RMB capital account.
2. **Establishment of the Shanghai International Finance Center:** With financial markets for securities, foreign exchange, gold and futures, Shanghai is developing into an influential financial center. This will help capture up-to-the-minute information on international markets as well as allow best use of international resources, thereby boosting the national economy and affording greater protection for the RMB as an international currency.

6.3   International use of RMB and its challenge to the Chinese economy

6.3.1   The challenge to monetary policy of China

Today, Chinese monetary policy relies appropriately on the issuance of base money, affecting the real economy through interest rates, fiscal expenditure and credit facilities among others. Although China has implemented its managed floating exchange rate system, the international use of the RMB is still at an early stage. However, with the opening of the Chinese current account, use of the RMB is increasingly used in the invoicing and settlement process of border trade, and this has led to the expanding amount of RMB in circulation. Theoretically, the increasing demand for international use of the RMB may interfere with policy effectiveness in China, such that control of the money supply may become harder for the Central Bank, the People's Bank of China. Though there are different explanations for the transmission mechanism of monetary policy according to the Keynesian and Monetarist theories, for China, it can be divided into three parts: impulse factor, intermediate target and final target. Here, the impulse factor is the increment of money supply issued by the Central Bank; the intermediate target includes interest rate, investment, credit facility, fiscal expenditure, asset prices and so on; and the final target is constituted by targets such as industrial added value, GDP, fiscal income, etc. If the increment of money supply has an influence on the country's economic growth through the intermediate targets, then the amount of RMB in cross-border circulation could be regarded as an exogenous currency increment that may result in a similar policy disturbance. But, since the RMB in cross-border circulation is only a small proportion of the monthly increment of money supply, its influence could be very limited.

Assumption 1 *The cross-border circulation of the RMB will affect China's economy, but because of its relatively small volume, the disturbance to monetary policy effectiveness will be very limited.*

To testify this assumption we have established a concise vector autoregression (VAR) model to analyze whether RMB cross-border circulation will disturb the policy effectiveness of money supply decided by the Central Bank. Owing to the absence of direct data about the amount of the RMB being used in cross-border business, in this model we have instead used the monthly data on the balance of border trade since 1996. A border trade deficit may imply the RMB outflow and a trade surplus may imply the RMB inflow. At the same time, we use the monthly increment of M2 from January 1996 onwards as the expanding amount of money being supplied by the Central Bank. We also assume that through the increase or decrease of money supply, the Central Bank wants to achieve a balance between inflation and economic growth. Let $rmbr = deficit/\Delta m2$; here *deficit* is defined as the net import of the RMB in border trade. If we assume that all transactions in border trade use the RMB, then the *deficit* could also be used as the net outflowing amount of the RMB. Accordingly, the *rmbr* could measure the ratio of increment in cross-border circulation to the expanding amount of money supply. If a change in this *rmbr* ratio could cause a corresponding deviation in the final economic target, then we may conclude that the circulation of the RMB in the frontier regions could affect the effectiveness of monetary policy through the monetary transmission mechanism. This chapter uses two variables—*investment* and *interest*—to represent intermediate targets, where *investment* stands for the monthly growth rate of total fixed asset investment, and *interest* for the monthly real interest rate. To represent the final target, we use *price* and *output* to indicate the growth rate of industrial added value and consumer price index respectively. According to the results of an ADF (augmented Dickey-Fuller) and PP (Phillips-Perron) test (Table 6.6), variables like *rmbr invest price and output* are all stationary series,

Table 6.6 The results of ADF and PP tests

Variable	ADF test			PP test		
	With trend	Without trend	Without trend and constant	With trend	Without trend	Without trend and constant
rmbr	−10.722***	−10.764***	−10.644***	−10.722***	−10.764***	−10.648***
interest	−2.169	−4.214***	−3.228***	−2.310*	−5.011***	−3.395***
invest	−14.997***	−14.958***	−10.743***	−15.643***	−15.667***	−10.824***
price	−10.277***	−10.037***	−10.017***	−10.273***	−10.032***	−10.015***
output	−7.643***	−7.603***	−7.613***	−7.643***	−7.038***	−7.140***

Source: China Economic Statistics Database: Authors' calculations.

except for *interest*, which might only be a non-stationary sequence. Thus we have the following VAR system:

$$Y_t = c + \sum_{i=1}^{n} A_i(L)Y_{t-i} + u_t \quad \text{and} \quad E[u_t\, u_t'] = \Theta$$

Here $Y_t = (rmbr, interest, invest, price, output)$; $A(L)$ is the five-order polynomial matrix in lag operator; u_t is a (5×1) vector of simplified residuals; Θ is the variance of residuals – the covariance matrix. According to the result of a Granger-causality test (Table 6.7), we could get the Cholesky decomposition in the following order:

$$rmbr \rightarrow interest \rightarrow invest \rightarrow price \rightarrow output$$

Based on the stationary conditions (see Figure 6.3) and the Akaike information criterion (AIC), Schwarz information criterion (SIC), Final prediction error (FBE) rules, the first order VAR model should be chosen (Table 6.8). However, the coefficients estimated by using that model are not so significant; hence we turn to the second order VAR model to find the dynamic structure of the impacts of *rmbr* from its impulse response functions. Listed below are the figures of orthogonal and cumulated orthogonal impulse response functions, which examine the effect of innovation of *rmbr* on the final target *price* and *output*.

From the above figures, we can see that the increase of the RMB net outflow (inflow) ratio does have an influence on the output level and the consumer price index. Note that all the variables in this model have already been translated into growth rates. Then, if we standardize the structural innovation as 1, the change of other variables after the shock could accordingly be regarded as the elasticity. Figures 6.4 and 6.5 show that one standardized unit innovation of *rmbr* may have a significant impact on the consumer price and output level in the second and third period. This influence on output would probably fade after four months, accumulating to a roughly 4% change. Meanwhile, the influence on prices would last for a longer time, say ten months, and

Table 6.7   The result of Granger causality test

Variables	Lag length									
	Lag1	lag2	Lag3	Lag4	Lag5	Lag6	Lag7	Lag8	Lag9	Lag10
output										
rmbr $\nRightarrow$ *output*	3.87**	1.70	1.20	0.97	0.77	0.63	0.52	0.86	0.46	0.41
interest $\nRightarrow$ *output*	0.12	0.08	0.05	0.48	0.57	0.49	0.43	0.36	0.33	0.24
invest $\nRightarrow$ *output*	0.48	0.31	0.19	0.17	0.25	0.71	0.93	1.23	1.78	1.90*
price $\nRightarrow$ *output*	6.71***	3.57**	2.67**	2.40*	1.87*	2.11**	2.17**	2.52***	2.99***	2.80**
price										
rmbr $\nRightarrow$ *price*	0.74	0.63	0.43	0.24	0.30	0.36	0.30	0.27	0.27	0.25
interest $\nRightarrow$ *price*	11.60***	7.64***	5.53**	3.59***	2.86**	2.38**	1.79*	1.45	1.18	1.27
invest $\nRightarrow$ *price*	0.48	0.23	0.96	0.76	0.98	0.95	1.05	0.95	1.35	0.71
output $\nRightarrow$ *price*	0.35	1.50	5.07***	3.62***	2.71**	2.20**	1.95*	1.82*	1.66*	1.65*
invest										
rmbr $\nRightarrow$ *invest*	0.31	0.13	1.00	0.78	0.60	0.40	1.07	0.99	0.99	0.32
interest $\nRightarrow$ *invest*	0.66	0.29	0.16	1.03	1.09	1.16	1.15	1.90*	2.70***	16.03***
interest										
rmbr $\nRightarrow$ *interest*	0.38	9.56***	6.17***	4.70***	4.15***	3.86**	3.66**	3.19**	2.61**	1.94**

Source: China Economic Statistics Database; Authors' calculations.

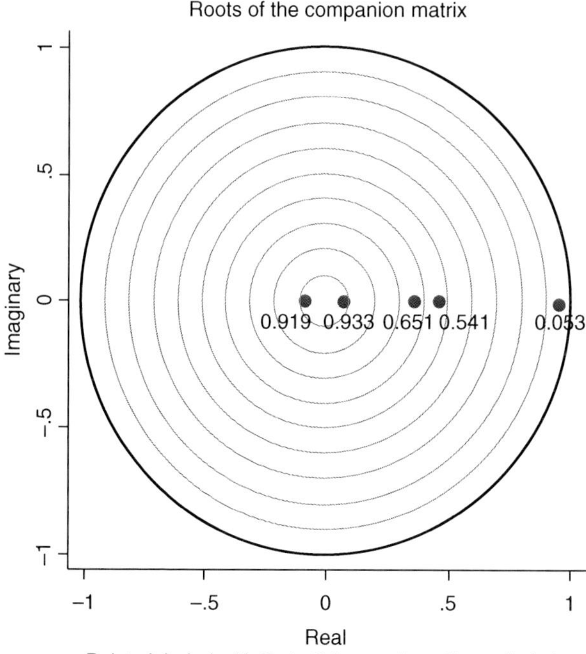

Figure 6.3   The test of stationary conditions of VAR System
Source: China Economic Statistic Database, authors' calculations.

Table 6.8   The lag order test of a VAR system

lag	LL	LR	df	p	FPE	AIC	HQIC	SBIC
Var(0)	207.436				1.1e-09	−6.427	−6.359	−6.256
Var(1)	359.984	305.09	25	0.000	1.9e-11*	−10.476*	−10.0743*	−9.45513**
Var(2)	374.073	28.179	25	0.300	2.8e-11	−10.129	−9.393	−8.258
Var(3)	383.731	19.315	25	0.008	7.9e-20	−27.003	−25.6772	−23.7044
Var(4)	402.736	38.011	25	0.046	6.2e-11	−9.452	−8.047	−5.880
Var(5)	417.298	29.123	25	0.259	9.8e-11	−9.120	−7.381	−4.698
Var(6)	450.744	66.892*	25	0.000	9.2e-11	−9.389	−7.315	−4.116

HQIC: Hannan-Quinn information criterion; LR: sequential modified LR test statistic (each test at 5% level); SBIC: Schwarz' Bayesian information criterion.
Source: China economic statistic database, authors' calculations.

may accumulate to a roughly −0.4% shock. Moreover, according to Figure 6.6, after the variance decomposition, the contribution of *rmbr* to *output* and *price* could accumulate to 3.8% and 6.6% in the fifth and tenth periods. Since we have only defined two intermediate variables in this model, *investment* and

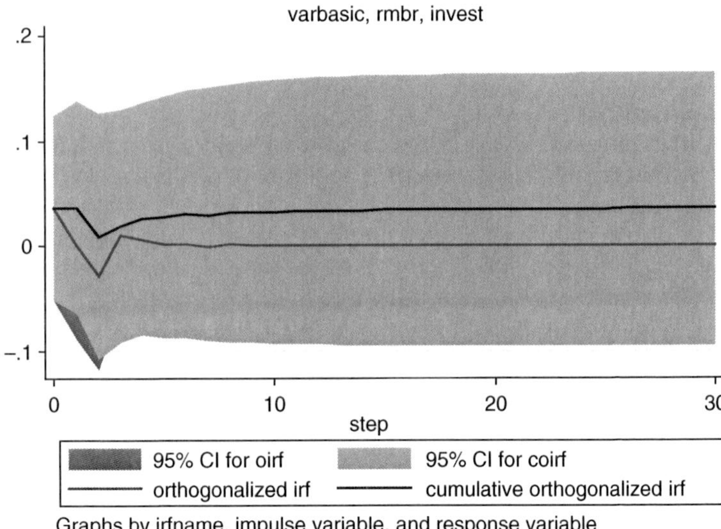

Figure 6.4   The orthogonal and cumulated orthogonal impulse response functions of *output* to *rmbr*
Source: China Economic Statistic Database, authors' calculations.

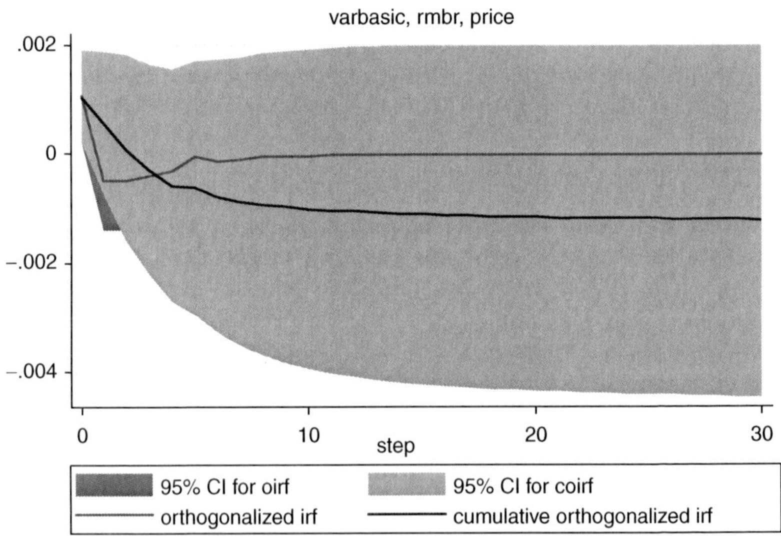

Figure 6.5   The orthogonal and cumulated orthogonal impulse response functions of *price* to *rmbr*
Source: China Economic Statistic Database, authors' calculations.

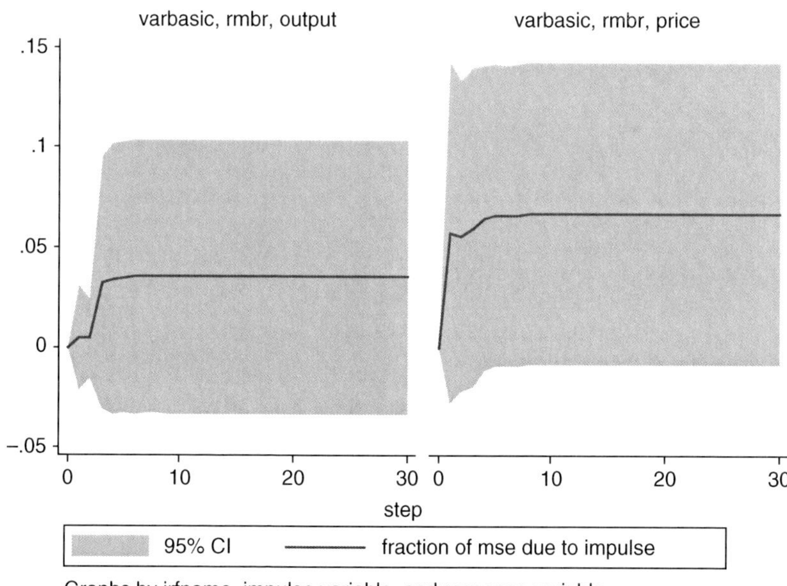

Figure 6.6   Variance decomposition of *output* and *price* to *rmbr*
Source: China Economic Statistic Database, authors' calculations.

interest, to determine the effect of *rmbr* on final targets, we should note that by adding in new intermediate variables, the contribution ratio of *rmbr* might fall correspondingly.

Although, according to the results of the VAR model, the influence of *rmbr* does exist, it is very small. One unit innovation of *rmbr*, say 1%, might cause very little fluctuations in *output* and *price*, approximately 0.02% and 0.003% respectively. Moreover, the increment of monthly border trade is small, especially compared to China's expansion of money supply, which today makes the influence even smaller in China. Figure 6.7 demonstrates that most of the *rmbr* increment is between −2.5% and 2.5%. Ignoring other intermediate targets that may contribute to *output* and *price*, we can safely conclude that in the short to medium term, the innovation of *rmbr* will not have a significant influence on the effectiveness of Chinese monetary policy, and this verifies Assumption 1, above. However, given the ever growing scale of RMB cross-border circulation, this kind of exogenous shock may increasingly affect the stability of the Chinese economy through endogenous monetary transmission mechanisms.

6.3.2   The economy may be more difficult to maintain external balance

The "Triffin dilemma" was introduced in the late 1950s by Professor Robert Triffin of Yale University. He believed that any currency, if afforded

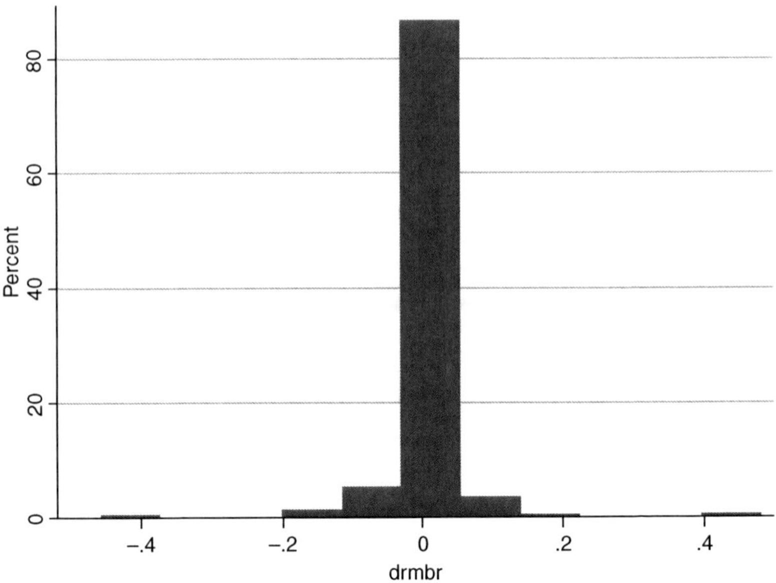

Figure 6.7 The frequency distribution of increment of monthly *rmbr*
Source: China Economic Statistic Database, authors' calculations.

international status, would face a dilemma in stabilizing its value. On the one hand, a continuous trade deficit and domestic currency outflow would favor other countries by strengthening their international liquidity, leading to depreciation of the international currency in question and possibly undermining its international standing. On the other hand, if the country balances its trade deficit to stabilize its currency value, other countries may then incur the problem of a lack of international liquidity. The fundamental idea behind the dilemma is this: international liquidity cannot always be built on the deficit of an international currency. A broader implication of the Triffin dilemma is that when the issuing country provides other countries with international liquidity and reserves by maintaining a trade deficit, the depreciation pressure on the currency domestically conflicts with the target to stabilize its value, and this conflict might shock the exogenous balance of the economy. The high growth rate of the Chinese economy, the stabilization of its currency and the increasing volume of China's trading in the global economy have assured the international use of the RMB. This explains why many Chinese researchers–for example, Li, Guan and He (2004) and Xu (2004)–who hold optimistic expectations about the international use of the RMB, have made the following theoretical assumption.

Assumption 2 *As the international use of the Chinese currency increases, the RMB may face the Triffin dilemma.*

Although this assumption is based on rational understanding of China's potential economic growth, it might not be valid if conditions change. First, after the collapse of the Bretton Woods system of monetary management, the Jamaica system, an international reserve system with the US dollar as the core along with a basket of other currencies, became established. As a consequence of the diversification of international reserves, the US dollar is no longer the sole currency of international liquidity and payment. This, to some extent, has solved the Triffin dilemma facing the US dollar. At the same time, the rapid economic recovery of the United Kingdom and the euro zone, with less risk in their growth potential, has forced central banks and global investors to keep adjusting their investment structures, from single, dollar reserves to multi-currency portfolios. Because global investors are more concerned with economic growth and stabilization of currencies, those currencies with depreciation potential lose their attractiveness, while those with stable value are more favorable for global investors to maintain their liquidity. Therefore, the foundations on which the Triffin dilemma is based have changed. Under the multi-currency reserve system, if the US dollar depreciates as a result of a trade deficit, central banks in other countries and global investors do not have to keep dollars for maintaining liquidity as was the case under the Bretton Woods system. Instead, they can substitute dollars with other currencies. Under this theory, should the RMB becomes an international currency as a result of the rapid growth of the Chinese economy, it offers a new alternative for central banks and global investors. However, if the RMB's value becomes unstable, investors would switch to other currencies in their portfolio.

Data show that the US dollar, as a foreign currency reserve in central banks, is shrinking year on year. Meanwhile the euro, with optimistic anticipation, is gaining ground (see Figure 6.8), though the US dollar still retains its dominant position in international finance and investment. IMF statistics show that Europe's capital market has a total value of US$27 trillion, compared to US$23 trillion in the United States and US$16 trillion in Japan, including bonds, stocks and bank deposits.[9] This indicates that the diversification of international reserves offers more currency alternatives to central banks and that the basis of the Triffin dilemma has changed.

Second, it is unlikely that the RMB will attain the same position as did the US dollar under the Bretton Woods system. Two factors have determined the dollar's dominant place in international reserves. First, the Second World War remodeled the economic world. The UK suffered huge losses during the war, and the US became the largest creditor and the biggest

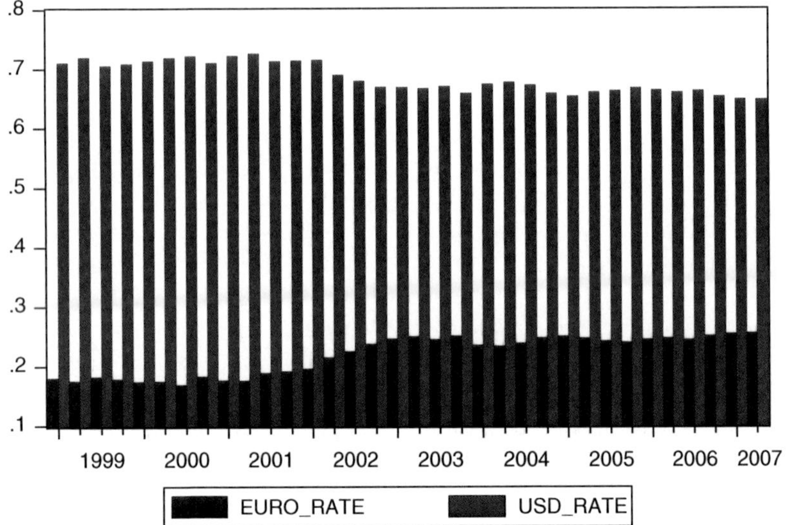

Figure 6.8   The weight change of the USD and euro in international reserve from 1999–2007
Source: BIS, authors' calculations.

economy. This provided an essential qualification for the dollar to become the international core currency. Second, the internationalization of the dollar was closely bound with the developed economy and advanced market system in the US. While China is experiencing rapid growth, this kind of developing economy still cannot be compared with the economic giant that has the largest manufacturing base, the most developed financial system and the largest GDP in the world. As is well known, the total value of the US treasury and stock market almost equals the sum of all the other six major financial markets. These strong economic foundations provide the critical conditions that support the dollar as an international currency (Tavlas, 1997). At the same time, the dollar is the most popular currency in international trade as the invoicing unit and settlement instrument. The total international trade priced in dollars is three to four times as much as in the US itself. Moreover, 90% of exports to the US and 80% of imports from it are denominated and settled in dollars. And in international trade between other countries, the dollar is the currency of choice where one or the other's currency is not selected.[10] In addition, in international trade, oil and other resources are all priced in US dollars. So, even if the dollar is loosing its weight in international reserves, in June 2007 it still accounts for 65% of the total (see Figure 6.8), a situation unlikely to be achieved by other currencies in the near future.

Because it is hard for the RMB to achieve the conditions enjoyed by the dollar in its internationalization, and it will take a long time for the Chinese economy to match that of the US, there is little support for Assumption 2. Furthermore, since China holds a strong position in its trade balance and a surplus in both its current account and capital account, with abundant foreign exchange reserves, it can avoid the Triffin dilemma when providing RMB assets to neighboring countries. With regard to international trade, China's surplus with the US and other developed countries has balanced the deficit with Asian countries and stabilized its currency value. If this favorable trading structure continues, the conflict between depreciation pressure caused by a trade deficit and the objective of a stable currency value can be avoided, and the RMB can become more widely used in international trade.

6.3.3   Possible shocks arising from international capital flows

As international use of the RMB widens, the amount of international capital flow will increase accordingly. A moderate amount of international capital inflow can facilitate economic growth. For example, long-term capital inflow not only satisfies the need of capital for economic development, but also brings advanced technology and management experience. However, a high volume of short-term capital inflow, especially speculative capital, will have a negative effect on the Chinese financial market. For this, many Chinese monetary researchers (e.g. Gan, 2002; Liang, 2003) have raised the following assumptions.

Assumption 3 Capital flows may cause large fluctuations in the RMB exchange rate.

High capital inflows raise the supply of foreign currency and are likely to force appreciation pressure of the RMB, whereas high capital outflows make foreign currency scarcer, causing depreciation pressure.

Assumption 4 Capital flows may have an effect on the interest rate of the Chinese capital market.

High capital inflows would raise demand for the RMB, which would place upward pressure of the market interest rate for the purpose on controlling the excess liquidity.

Assumption 5 Capital flows may cause large fluctuations in domestic asset prices.

Short-term capital inflows are invariably invested in the monetary and security market. A high volume of short-term capital inflows may cause inflation in asset prices, even causing bubbles at times. Once the short-term capital retreats, asset prices may fall sharply, causing a "negative wealth effect," reducing individual consumption and leading to a shortage of effective demand, thereby resulting in economic depression.

Assumption 6 *Capital flows may cause a sharp reduction in Chinese foreign exchange reserves.*

High capital outflows would have a negative effect on China's foreign exchange reserves. Once the effect is anticipated by the market, speculative money may escape, causing further reduction of foreign exchange reserves and forcing depreciation pressure on the RMB. To avoid such crises, the Central Bank may raise interest rates to attract foreign investment. However, this measure could damage the domestic economy.

The above assumptions are all reasonably inferred from macroeconomic theories, and are the reasons why the Chinese government takes a cautious attitude toward the opening of capital account. However, since convertibility is a prior condition of internationalization of the RMB, the Chinese capital account must be gradually opened. In general, there are four steps to the freeing-up of currency exchange: (i) a convertible current account; (ii) a convertible capital account; (iii) domestic convertibility; and (iv) convertibility across the board. To date, China has completed step one and is in process of releasing constraints on the capital account. The remaining steps will be taken at the appropriate time to achieve internationalization of the RMB. That said, the formulation of an appropriate schedule would help to widen and increase international use of the RMB. Conversely, opening the capital account too early, when conditions are not satisfactory, would not only show the weakness of the financial system, but also increase the possibility of financial crisis. That is why process of opening the Chinese capital account should happen gradually and be implemented sequentially. To achieve this, the Chinese government has the option of adopting the following two measures to avoid the possibility that assumptions 3 to 6, above, occur in the future.

1. **No specific timetable for the opening of a convertible capital account:** For a large developing country like China, the implementation of convertible capital account may have requirements, such as economic strength and advanced financial regulatory framework. At present, the latter is still at an initial level. The financial market has limited volume, and some firms are not well self-disciplined. As such, completely opening a capital account now might lead to financial upheaval. Hence, the Chinese government at present offers no specific timetable during which financial organizations and businesses can prepare and improve their systems, objectives, techniques and human resource structure to deal with the potential disorder brought about by international capital flows.
2. **Setting an appropriate sequence for the opening of convertible capital account:** The general principle is to take removing constraints of capital inflows as a priority, with long term capital inflows prior to short term inflows. With regard to long-term capital inflows, direct investment is

needed prior to bank loans and security investments, since it has less liquidity; during financial turbulence, direct investment cannot be withdrawn in the short run, while the liquidation of security investments can worsen a situation. Concern over short-term capital inflows makes it favorable to delay the onset of speculative capital flows for as long as possible.

In conclusion, considering that China has maintained constraints on a capital account, international capital flow has had a limited effect on the Chinese financial markets. The Chinese government can schedule the opening of a capital account and strengthening of the financial regulatory framework in advance in order to minimize the negative effects arising from the opening of the domestic financial market to international capital. As the country's financial market matures, it could establish risk resistance ability, as in developed countries, such that the constraints on a capital account are no longer needed.

6.4   Conclusion and recommendations

As an international currency, the RMB has influenced every aspect of the Chinese economy. Thanks to the high rate of economic development and the accelerating pace of globalization, China has gained more and more flexibility to overcome the unavoidable difficulties inherent in the internationalization of its currency. First, as with many other developed countries, China can obtain scarce resources for which there is high demand by providing an international currency, at the same time optimizing its industrial structure and improving export competence. Second, the expansion of the RMB as an international currency can enable the government to improve the efficiency of the country's financial institutions and markets, opening the way for China's banking, security and financial industries to fully enter the global market, and creating opportunities for Chinese firms to invest directly in foreign countries. The long-term benefits would cover any short- to middle-term losses. Moreover, the Chinese government has many strategic alternatives to avoid the risks associated with RMB internationalization. From this standpoint, the worldwide use of the RMB is in reality an opportunity rather than challenge.

Of course, there is a need to reform China's political and economic system to meet the many challenges posed by internationalization of its currency. To achieve higher efficiency within the economic system in particular, speeding up of the pace of reforms in the financial market is most needed, for which the following recommendations should be considered:

1. **Building up the service system for cross-border use of the RMB:** Cross-border cooperation is critical in deciding the scale and level of RMB circulation overseas. To help RMB regionalization progress in a more

direct and active way, the banks in China should selectively offer standard and regulated RMB services in the border areas. Meanwhile, China should enhance the multi-level cooperation of central banks and commercial banks with neighboring countries, establishing bilateral negotiation mechanisms similar to Sino-Russian banking cooperation. More agencies should offer RMB exchange services abroad, and more commercial bank branches overseas should offer RMB retail and loan business.

2. **Developing small- and medium-sized banks and optimizing the banking system:** Small- and medium-sized firms are the basis of cross-border trade. At the same time, they have created a huge amount of industrial value-added, altogether equal to 55.6% of Chinese GDP. In order to expand the scale of international use of the RMB, it is critical to solve the financial problems faced by small- and medium-sized firms. Big banks are not able to provide adequate financial services to them because of the operating costs and risk control problems involved. Judged by the experience of other developed countries, however, small- and medium-sized banks could offer a more efficient way of solving their financial problems.

3. **Accelerating the construction of Shanghai as an international finance center:** To begin with, the interbank borrowing rate in Shanghai should become the basis of all short-term rates in China, at the same time making Shanghai the real capital financing center. When the opportunity comes, China's Central Bank should build its open market operation center in Shanghai, from where it can issue treasury notes. This would cultivate the adjustment mechanism needed in the short-term financial market and lay the foundations for using economic instruments to adjust money supply. Second, Shanghai should perform free exchange of the RMB. When this becomes possible, firms and foreign banks will rush to participate in Shanghai's short-term capital market, bond market, stock market and exchange market, as well as the gold market, sequentially.

4. **Gradually allow non-Chinese residents to hold and trade RMB assets:** Step by step, China should allow non-residents to hold a certain amount of treasury bonds or other RMB-denominated bonds, and allow the trading of RMB assets under supervision. Using the offshore RMB center in Hong Kong as an experimental area, China could try to implement more RMB-denominated asset trading. The national monetary authority should work closely with the Hong Kong Monetary Authority to supervise this new RMB business and minimize any risk that may occur.

5. **Gradually enlarge the use of the RMB in capital account trading:** The Chinese government should loosen the restrictions on capital accounts and encourage domestic firms to invest directly in surrounding countries by using the RMB. China should also encourage domestic commercial banks using the RMB to offer buyer's credit for overseas importers and permit the RMB as the bid currency for investment and financial aid to

neighboring countries. The government could also permit developing countries to use the RMB to repay their debt, and allow foreigners to invest in the Chinese stock market by using the RMB, while the holders of the RMB in surrounding areas should be allowed to open the RMB accounts in Chinese domestic banks.

Notes

This chapter was originally presented as a paper at the Conference on "External Use of Currency: International Experience and Implications for Renminbi," 15–16 October 2007, Hong Kong, organized by the Hong Kong Institute for Monetary Research. The research was financially supported by the Hong Kong Monetary Authority. Xiaolu Liu and Xiaoying Xie provided excellent research assistance.

1. China Economic Statistics Database, education version.
2. China Economic Statistics Database, education version.
3. The references are He, Yu, and Huang (2000); The Team of State Administration of Foreign Exchange Yunnan Branch (2001); and The Investigation Team of the Cross-border Movement of RMB Cash (2005).
4. The ratio of the number of Chinese citizens traveling in Asian countries to that of Chinese citizens traveling elsewhere overseas is quite stable.
5. This estimation is slightly higher than the offshore currency limit set by China's customs regulation.
6. The data are based on the People's Bank of China 2000 survey report and estimated according to the daily consumption trend in mainland China.
7. IMF, International Financial Statistics Yearbook, 1997, 2000.
8. China Economic Statistics Database, monthly trade.
9. BIS.
10. BIS.

References

Bergsten, C. Fred, 1975, *The Dilemmas of the Dollar*, New York University Press, New York.

Blanchard, O., 1997, *Macroeconomics* (3rd edn), Beijing: Prentice-Hall International, Inc.

Fuchs-Schundeln, N., and Funke, N., 2001, "Stock Market Liberalization: Financial and Macroeconomic Implications," IMF Working Paper 2001/193.

Gan, Xindi, 2002, "The Impact of the Short-Term International Capital Movement on the Policy and Coordination of RMB & Foreign Currency," *Word Economy Study* (Chinese journal) (6) pp. 37–40.

Hartmann, P., 2002, The International Role of Euro, *Journal of Policy Modeling*, 24 (1), pp. 347–54.

He, Jianxiong, Yu, Manling, and Huang, Hao, on the economic and trade relations between Guangxi, Yunnan and Vietnam, Burma, Laos and the use of offshore RMB, the PBOC 2000 survey report, pp. 11–13.

Li, Jing, Guan, Tao, He, Fan, 2004, "The Status Quo of Transnational Circulation of RMB and its Impact on China's Economy," *Management World* (Chinese Journal), (9) pp. 46–52.

Liang, Qinxin, 2003, "The thinking about RMB internalization," *Southwest Finance* (Chinese Journal), (7), pp. 11–12.

Page, S. A. B., 1981, "The Choice of Invoicing Currency in Merchandise Trade," *National Institute Economic Review*, Vol. 98 (1), pp. 60–72.

Tavlas, G., 1998, "The International Use of the US Dollar: An Optimum Currency Area Perspective," *The World Economy*, 20 (9), pp. 709–47.

Tavlas, G. and Ozeki, Y., 1992, "The Internationalization of Currencies: The Case of the Japanese Yen," IMF Occasional Paper no. 90, Washington DC, International Monetary Fund.

Tomoyuki, Nakagawa, 2004, "Internationalization of the Renminbi Yuan and its Impact on East Asia," IIP Policy Paper, (1).

Xu Hongsui, "On the Internationalization of the Renminbi – Based on the Analysis of the Renminbi Peripheral Circulation," *Shanghai finance* (Chinese Journal), 2004 (5), pp. 43–5. The Team of State Administration of Foreign Exchange Yunnan Branch (2001). "Analysis on RMB internationalization of the peripheral circulation," *China Foreign Currency Management* (Chinese journal), Vol. 12, p. 25.

The Investigation Team of the Cross-border Movement of RMB Cash (2005). "The Cross-border Movement of RMB Cash in 2004," *China Finance* (Chinese journal) Vol. 6, pp. 38–9.

7
RMB Internationalization: Empirical and Policy Analysis

David Daokui Li and Linlin Liu

7.1 Introduction

China is now one of the largest economies and largest trading partners in the world. With the restrictions on international financial transactions gradually being liberalized, the emergence of the Chinese economy has aroused speculation on the future landscape of the world economy. One of the most interesting aspects is the possible rise of the Chinese renminbi (henceforth RMB) as an international currency, as the RMB is already widely used in cross-border trade between China and neighboring countries.

At present, compared to the important international currencies such as the US dollar, the euro, the pound sterling and the Japanese yen, the RMB is far from being internationalized, though its position in the international currency system has gradually been enhanced over the last ten years. The RMB has held a significant position as a settlement currency in trade between China and some neighboring countries, and RMB banknotes are accepted by local shops in some tourist destinations. Furthermore, from 2007, Hong Kong have possessed a renminbi bond market outside Mainland China—the first international bond in the Chinese currency targeted at non-residents.

With deep financial reforms continuing in China and the country growing more and more open to the rest of the world, full convertibility of the RMB is required for the currency to play a significant role in international trade and financial transactions. At present, though, the RMB is not fully convertible and the Chinese government maintains control of the capital account.

In this chapter we consider three measures of the internationalization of a currency: (i) the share of the currency in the reserve of the world's central banks; (ii) the currency composition in international trade settlements; and (iii) the currency composition in international bonds and notes. Specifically, we estimate the determinants of the share of the major currencies in these three perspectives, and the results are then used to calculate the differing international demands for the RMB. Some policy issues as to the feasibility and most advantageous approach to RMB internationalization are then discussed.

The chapter is organized as follows. Section 7.2 is a summary of the recent literature on international currencies. Section 7.3 gives an econometrical estimate of the shares of the major currencies in the three perspectives, and attempts to uncover the main determining factors behind the internationalization of a currency. Section 7.4 presents a counterfactual exercise to calculate the potential international demands for the RMB under different assumptions aside from the currency being freely convertible. Section 7.5 considers some policies on the possible approach to the internationalization of the RMB.

7.2   Overview

There is an increasing literature on currency internationalization. Chinn and Frankel (2005) econometrically estimated the determinants of the share of major currencies in the reserve holdings of the world's central banks over the period 1973–98. Significant factors include the size of the home country, inflation rate, exchange rate variability and size of the relevant home financial center. Under two possible scenarios—the remaining EU members, including the United Kingdom, joining the euro zone by 2020 and the recent depreciation trend of the dollar persisting into the future—the euro may surpass the dollar as the leading international reserve currency by 2022. Chen and Peng (2009) applied a similar framework and explored the potential role of RMB as an international currency. Our work is related closely to their study and also includes some predictions on the RMB's role in non-reserve functions.

The PBOC Study Group (2006) established an index of the internationalization of the different currencies, with the US dollar set at 100. Against this, they listed the euro at 40, the Japanese yen at 28.2 and the RMB at just 2. Lim (2006) examined opposing views on the euro's challenge to the dollar as an international currency. Lim's paper used foreign exchange market data from 1999–2005, and the result supported the view that "network externalities," were responsible for the dollar's continued dominance.

Eichengreen (1998) presented historical and econometric evidence that the euro will only slowly come to rival the dollar as a reserve currency. In addition, creating a market with sufficient stability to be attractive to international investors requires continuous liquidity management and periodic lender-of-last-resort operations by the issuing central bank.

Others pointed out that because the attractiveness of any vehicle currency grows as its liquidity increases, and that an international currency has the tendency to become a natural monopoly, a necessary condition of an international currency was that a currency's future value in terms of goods and services be viewed as predictable. Other factors would govern the selection from among the body of sound currencies. One is a strong, competitive economy open to, and active in, international trade and finance.

In the above literature, we found a number of different factors that affect currency internationalization. For the most part, economic analysis of the international currency is based on the euro challenge to the US dollar, especially on the share of the currency in central banks. However, there is little research on the internationalization of the RMB. The contribution of this chapter is to advance the understanding of the factors behind currency internationalization under different measures and to predict the share of the RMB by assuming full convertibility.

The definition of an international currency is one that is used outside the country. The classical three functions of money are medium of exchange, store of value and unit of account, which we can use to transfer to the level of international currency. Cohen (1971) and Kenen (1983) summarized the international use of a currency, as shown in Table 7.1.

These functions can offer various ways to measure the lever of the internationalization of a currency. For the "store of value" function, we can use the currency composition of international reserves to measure which currency is more internationalized. The more a currency is worth storing, the larger the proportion of that currency in a government's reserve. The "medium of exchange" function can be assessed on the settlement of currency composition in international trade between two countries. An owing to limited data, we only compared the US dollar to the euro in international trading settlements between countries. Finally, the data on currency composition in international bonds and notes offer some perspective on the "unit of account" function (though international bonds and notes can also be ascribed to "store of value"). Using these international currency functions, we carried out a number of econometric regressions of the three measurements of currency internationalization, as described in the following section, to further to predict the share of an assumed fully convertible RMB.

Table 7.1   The international use of a currency

	Office use	**Private use**
Medium of exchange	Vehicle currency for foreign exchange intervention	Invoicing trade and financial transactions
Store of value	International reserves	Currency substitution
Unit of account	Anchor for pegging local currency	Denominating trade and financial transactions

Source: Cohen (1971); Kenen (1983); Authors' compilation.

7.3　Data and empirical estimate

7.3.1　Determinants of an international currency

The international status of a currency tends to be determined by different complex factors. Since an international currency has the three functions described above—store of value, medium of exchange and unit of account—and the use of an international currency is determined by market forces, a competitive economy and the stable value of that currency are important for it to be held as both a reserve and vehicle currency.

An international currency is established in a competitive domestic economy, one measured especially by the ratio of national GDP of the issuing currency against the global GDP total. As mentioned in the literature summary, some econometric estimates from cross-country data were used to find the relationship between GDP and currency composition.

The stable value of an international currency is crucial in terms of user confidence. The value of a currency can be measured from two perspectives. One is macroeconomic conditions such as inflation or the real interest rate, which have a huge influence on the future domestic economy and financial system. Potential investors in a currency would worry about an economy with high inflation or a large, long-term adverse balance of trade. These are especially important factors underlying any currency serving as a reserve currency. With regard to the second perspective, a currency with less volatility and an appreciating exchange rate in the long term will be more acceptable as an international currency. For example, a stable value currency will be acceptable to both partners in international trade, while foreign reserves and international bonds also need to lower the risk of volatility of the currency. Particularly in the long term, appreciation will be helpful to the store of value function of an international currency.

The factors discussed above are the main determinants of our empirical analysis. The data on the issuing economies are from the World Development Indicators database for the period 1967–2004. They include the GDP ratio, inflation rate, real interest rate and current account balance. We use a country's GDP share of total global GDP as the measure of the issuing country's economic scale, with GDP data in constant 2000 US dollars. The data on the stable value of the currency are from International Monetary Fund statistics on currency per special drawing rights (SDR). Appreciation of a currency is estimated as the 20-year average rate of change of the value of the currency against SDR. The volatility of a currency is estimated as the ten-year average rate of the standard deviation of the log first difference of the SDR monthly exchange rate.

7.3.2　Currency composition of foreign exchange reserves

The reserve currency holding is a good proxy for the international role of a currency, especially in the long term. Our study uses annual data

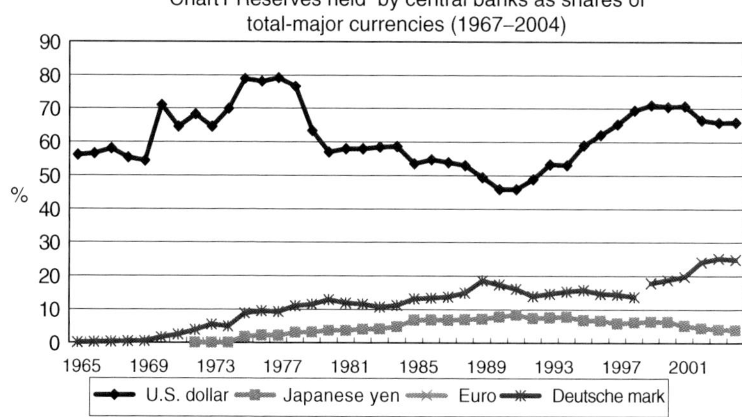

Figure 7.1   Reserves held by central banks as shares of total major currencies (1967–2004)
Source: IMF data; Authors' calculations.

from the IMF currency composition of foreign exchange reserves (COFER) database, for the period 1967–2004. The major currencies are the US dollar, euro, Japanese yen, pound sterling, Deutsche mark, Swiss franc and the Netherlands guilder. Figure 7.1 shows the changes in the reserve shares of the four major currencies for the period in question. The US dollar's share changed from a high of 80% to a low of less than 50%, while that of the yen has dropped gradually in recent years.

The empirical estimation basically follows the model used in Chinn and Frankel (2005). That paper used annual data from 1973 to 1998 to study the currency share of reserve holdings; we have extended the data period and made some improvements. As the dependent variable "currency share" is in the range 0 to 1, which is not robust for the econometric estimate, to begin with we had to make a logistical transformation (Figure 7.2) to the dependent variable in order to widen its range to $[-\infty, +\infty]$.

The model to be estimated can be represented by the following equation:

$$Logisticshare_{it} = \alpha_i + \beta_1 GDP\,raito_{it} + \beta_2 Appreciation_{it} + \ldots + \varepsilon_{it} \qquad (1)$$

where *i* refers to the different reserve currency, including the US dollar, euro, Japanese yen, pound sterling, Swiss franc, Deutsche mark and Netherlands guilder. *Logisticshare* denotes the currency share in the total allocated world reserve. As the run of data broke with the introduction of the euro in 1999, we added a dummy variable *year >1998* to the equation (1), in order to check if there are different coefficients following the euro entry after 1998—equation (2) below. If the dummy variable is significant, then we can conclude that determinant factors change after 1998.

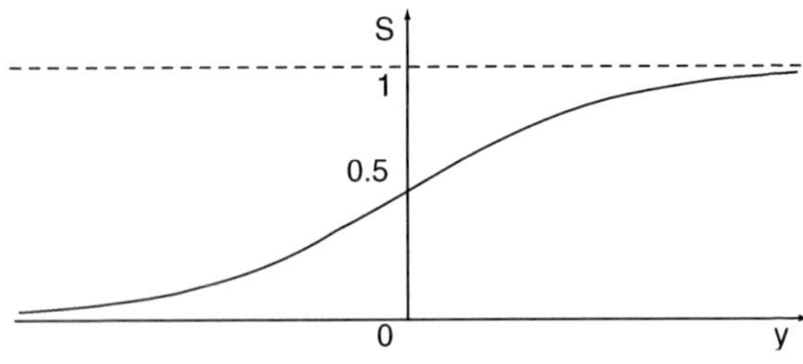

Figure 7.2   Logistic transformation
Source: Authors' calculations.

$$Logisticshare_{it} = \alpha_i + \beta_1 GDP\,raito_{it} + \gamma_1 GDP\,ratio_{it} * Dummy\_year > 1998$$
$$+ \beta_2 Appreciation_{it} + \gamma_2 Appreciation_{it} * Dummy\_year > 1998 + ... + \varepsilon_{it} \tag{2}$$

To allow for the impact of the collapse of the former Soviet Union on the rise of the US dollar in official reserves, we gave the dollar different coefficients. Thus, in equation (3) below, we have added a dummy US dollar to equation (1):

$$Logisticshare_{it} = \alpha_i + \beta_1 GDP\,raito_{it} + \gamma_1 GDP\,raito_{it} * Dummy\_US$$
$$+ \beta_2 Appreciation_{it} + \gamma_2 Appreciation_{it} * US > + ... + \varepsilon_{it} \tag{3}$$

The regression result is shown in Table 7.2.

The three models suggest that the size of the economy as measured by the share of GDP in the world total is significant. This result supports the hypothesis that the currency-issuing country needs to have a competitive economy in order to support its international currency. Moreover, the coefficient of the GDP ratio is larger than other fundamental variables in determining the currency share of reserve holding, which implies that a powerful economy is more important than any other determining factors.

The appreciation variable is positive and significant while the variation is negative and significant, suggesting that a stable value of the currency is also important for a currency to be stored. The same is true of the variable real interest rate. A puzzling variable is current account balance, which is negative, suggesting that the currency-issuing country with a worse trade balance has a higher share of reserve holding. Though we cannot yet explain it, this accorded with the fact that the US has a worse trade balance than Japan, while the former's currency is more internationalized than the latter's.

In model 2, the dummy *year > 1998* is not significant, and this supports the hypothesis that the determinant factors have no change before and after 1999, and that the birth of the euro has no significant impact on determining the currency composition in the reserve. In model 3, the dummy US dollar is significant in the coefficient of the GDP ratio and real interest rate, which suggests that the huge scale of the US economy is definitely supporting its

Table 7.2 Explanation of the composition of official reserves: regression result

Model 1		Model 2		Model 3	
GDP ratio	14.53***	GDP ratio	14.36***	GDP ratio	11.63***
	−0.58		−0.62		−1.17
Appreciation	9.18***	GDP ratio	2.88	GDP ratio	18.08
	−2.32	*Dummy year > 1998	−29.42	*Dummy US$	−42.8
Variation	−68.04***	Appreciation	11.13***	Appreciation	14.67***
	−14.88		−2.89		−2.64
Inflation	0.02	Appreciation	−7.51	Appreciation	5.68
	−0.02	*Dummy year >1998	−6.74	*Dummy US$	−28.8
Real interest rate	0.04**	Variation	−79.70***	Variation	−51.59***
	−0.02		−17.08		−19.66
Curr. acc. balance	−0.14***	Variation	57.87	Variation	57.32
	−0.02	*Dummy year >1998	−62.63	*Dummy US$	−56.1
		Inflation	0.02	Real interest rate	0.07***
			−0.02		−0.02
		Inflation	0.16	Real interest rate	−0.16**
		*Dummy year >1998	−0.19	*Dummy US$	−0.07
		Real interest rate	−0.06	Curr. acc. balance	−0.18***
			−0.21		−0.03
		Real interest rate	0.04*	Curr. acc. balance	0.22*
		*Dummy year >1998	−0.02	*Dummy US$	−0.13
		Curr. acc. balance	0.11	Dummy US$	−4.35
			−0.61		−13.16
		Curr. acc. balance	−0.15***		
		*Dummy year >1998	−0.03		
		Dummy year >1998	−1.67		
			−6.19		
No.	182		177		191
Adj. R2	0.89		0.89		0.87

Note: *Significant at 10%; **significant at 5%; ***significant at 1%.
Source: Authors' calculations.

currency's international standing, and that this support is greater than for any other country even where there is the same ratio of GDP.

7.3.3   Composition of currency settlement of international trade

With regard to international trade and financial transactions, the share of a currency in the settlement of invoices is an important measurement of the internationalization of that currency. The composition data of currency settlement come from Kamps (2006), which covers 42 countries in different continents over the period 1999–2005. Figure 7.3 shows the annual average share of the US dollar and the euro in the currency breakdown of exports and imports of the 42 countries. Figure 7.4 shows the share of the US dollar and the euro in EU countries.

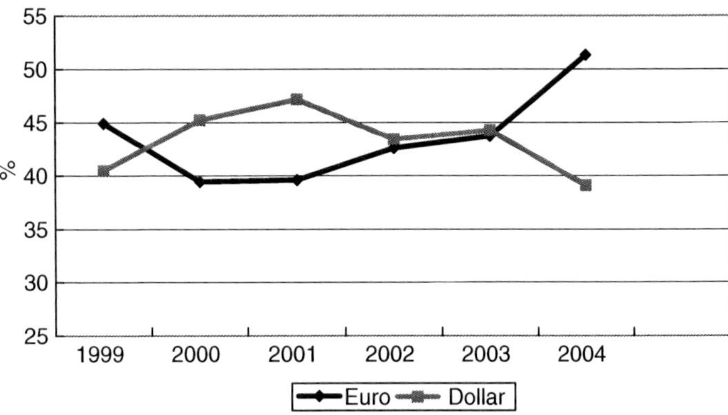

Figure 7.3   Currency breakdown of exports and imports
Source: Kamps (2006); Authors' calculations.

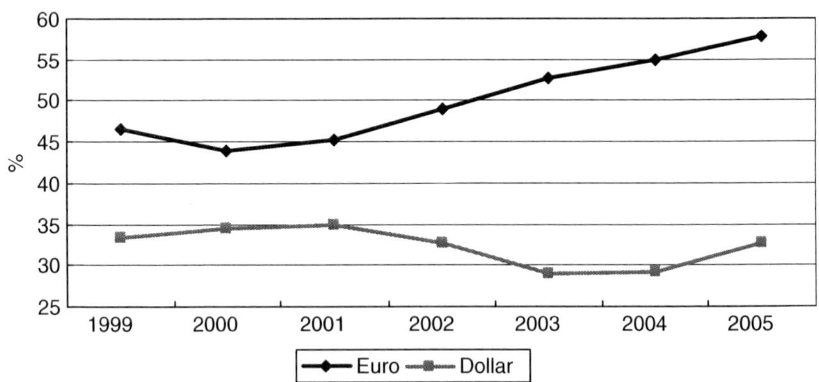

Figure 7.4   Currency breakdown of exports and imports of EU countries
Source: Kamps (2006); Authors' calculations.

The empirical analysis of the currency composition of international trade focuses on the euro and the US dollar. Figures 7.3 and 7.4 show that the share of the euro in trade settlements is gradually increasing, while that of the US dollar is decreasing slightly. We assume that currency composition is decided both by the total sum of trade with the currency-issuing country and the degree of internationalization of the currency. Hence, in trade between China and the US, the dollar is more likely to be used as the settlement currency, whereas the euro is more likely to be used where China trades with European countries, so we must control the variable "trading amount with the currency issuing country." The data on trading amounts are from the IMF's Balance of Payment Statistics. We used the ratio between the trade amount with the cur-rency-issuing country and total trade to denote the trade ratio. Similarly, we carried out a logistical transition to the share of currency in the settlements. The model is represented by the following equation. We established a time trend factor to reflect changes in the upheaval of the euro, which measures changes over time, as equation (1). To distinguish the US dollar from the euro, we also added a dummy US dollar to the equation, as in equation (2).

$$Logisticshare_{it} = \alpha_i + \beta_1 Time_{it} + \beta_2 traderaito_{it} + \beta_3 Appreciation_{it} + ... + \varepsilon_{it} \quad (1)$$

$$\begin{aligned} Logisticshare_{it} &= \alpha_i + \beta_1 Time_{it} + \gamma_1 Time_{it} * dummy\_US \\ &+ \beta_2 traderaito_{it} * dummy\_US + \beta_3 Appreciation_{it} * dummy\_US + ... + \varepsilon_{it} \end{aligned} \quad (2)$$

We used panel data under fixed effects, and the regression result is shown in Table 7.3.

Table 7.3   Regression results on international trade

	(1)	(2)	(3)	(4)	(5)	(6)
	import_share	export_share	trade_share	import_share	export_share	trade_share
Import ratio	2.461			2.073		
	(4.19)***			(3.46)***		
Export ratio		2.455			1.546	
		(2.93)***			(1.91)*	
Trade ratio			3.998			2.968
			(4.97)***			(3.65)***
Appreciation	2.161	2.918	2.5	1.043	1.203	1.12
	(7.58)***	(7.77)***	(8.24)***	(3.59)***	(3.27)***	(3.72)***
Variation	−7.552	−5.231	−5.313	−4.484	−0.874	−1.44
	(2.43)**	−1.29	(1.63)*	(1.87)*	−0.29	−0.59
Real interest rate	0.025	0.03	0.026	0.12	−0.237	−0.043
	(2.03)**	(1.83)*	(1.94)*	−0.78	−1.27	−0.27

(Continued)

Table 7.3　(Continued)

	(1)	(2)	(3)	(4)	(5)	(6)
Trade/GDP	0.023	0.028	0.027			
	(3.62)***	(3.34)***	(3.92)***			
Curr. acc.	0.049	0.114	0.071			
balance	−1.23	(2.15)**	(1.67)*			
Time				0.062	0.089	0.073
				(5.10)***	(5.85)***	(5.92)***
Time				−0.057	−0.13	−0.087
*dummy US$				−1.52	(2.73)***	(2.25)*
Appreciation				11.737	18.433	16.412
*dummy US$				(2.12)**	(2.53)**	(2.81)***
Variation				−48.009	−69.257	−62.19
*dummy US$				−0.8	−0.91	−1
Real interest rate				−0.066	0.253	0.08
*dummy US$				−0.42	−1.34	−0.49
Trade ratio						−8.45
*dummy US$						(3.11)***
Export ratio					−3.775	
*dummy US$					−1.5	
Import ratio				−6.591		
*dummy US$				(2.57)**		
Observations	264	283	283	286	307	307
Number of id	61	69	69	61	69	69
R-squared	0.47	0.43	0.5	0.53	0.54	0.58

Source: Authors' calculations.

The coefficient of the trade ratio is statistically significant, which suggests that the trade amount with the currency-issuing country has a strong influence on the determination of the settlement currency. The coefficients of the stable value factors—appreciation, variation, real interest rate, trade/GDP, currency account balance—are significant and make sense. Otherwise, the trend factor on the euro is positive and significant, while the trend factor on the US dollar is negative, which suggests the euro does have an upturn trend after 1999.

7.3.4　Currency composition in international bonds and notes

The international bond data are from the Bank for International Settlements (BIS). The BIS definition of international securities (as opposed to domestic securities) is based on three major characteristics: (i) the location of the transaction; (ii) the currency of issuance; and (iii) the residence of the issuer.

International issues comprise all foreign currency issues by residents and non-residents in a given country and all domestic currency issues launched in the domestic market by non-residents. In addition, domestic currency issues launched in the domestic market by residents are also considered as international issues if they are specifically targeted at non-resident investors.

These characteristics suggest international bonds carry the function of both store of value and financial transaction. From some perspectives, the currency composition of international bonds can show the status of internationalization of a currency.

Table 7.4 shows the classification of BIS securities.

Figure 7.5 shows the major currency share in international bonds and notes over the period 1993–2006. Figure 7.4 suggests the share of the euro in the currency share of international bonds is higher than that of the US dollar, which covered more than 40% of total international bonds and notes in 2006.

We use panel data under fixed effects, and the regression result is as shown in Table 7.5.

The regression result suggests the determinant factors of the composition currency of international bonds and notes are almost the same as

Table 7.4   Classification of BIS securities

In domestic currency	Targeted at resident investors	Targeted at non-residents	In foreign currency
Issues by residents	Domestic	International	International
Issues by non-residents	International	International	International

Source: BIS (2003); Authors' compilation.

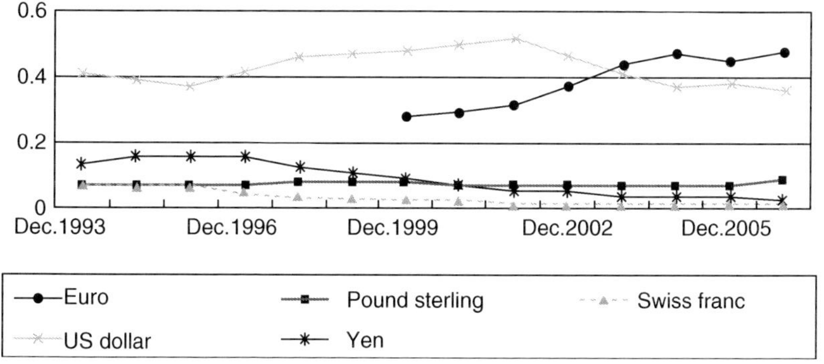

Figure 7.5   International bonds and notes by currency (1993–2006)
Source: BIS data; Authors' calculations.

Table 7.5 Regression results on international bonds and notes

Logistic bond share	GDP ratio	Appreciation	Variation	Real interest rate	Curr. acc. balance
Fixed effect	35.5	6.795	10.257	0.056	–0.078
	(8.408)***	(2.167)***	(0.536)	(0.033)*	(0.024)***

Source: Authors' calculations.

for international reserves, while the share of GDP is the most important factor in determining currency share. Furthermore, the positive coefficient of current account balance provides a confusing result on international reserves, while the coefficient of current account balance in this regression is negative and significant, which means that a worse current account balance in the US does have an influence on the internationalization of the US dollar.

7.4 Predictions for the RMB: Scenarios

In section 7.3 we gave an empirical analysis, focusing on the currency composition of international reserves, the currency settlements in international trade, and international bonds and notes. In the section, we predict the share of the RMB under the three measures in 2020.

Though the limited convertibility of the RMB and partial of opening of China's financial market are restrictive factors for the international role of the RMB, the liberalization of the restrictions on currency convertibility should of course follow the overall development and reform strategy. A higher degree of currency convertibility may lead to an increase in the use of the RMB in international transactions. In our forecast for the RMB, we make the assumptions that the RMB is fully convertible and China's financial sector is healthy enough to fend off pressures for capital flight.

Below, we first predict the share of RMB in international reserves in 2020, based on the following assumptions.

1. The economic circulation of other major currencies is the same as in 2004, accounting for currency appreciation, volatility, inflation and so on. Global GDP growth rate is taken as 3.5% during 2004 to 2020.
2. We make three alternative assumptions about the economy in China from 2004 to 2020 and predict the share of RMB in international reserves under each assumption.
   (i) The most optimistic prediction of 2020 GDP
      GDP growth rate is 9% in the first four years and 8 per cent in the following 11 years

RMB appreciation is 3% in the first four years and 1% in the following 11 years.
Current account balance is 1% of GDP in 2020.
  (ii) The medium prediction of 2020 GDP
GDP growth rate is 9% in the first four years and 8% in the following
11 years
RMB appreciation 3% in the first four years and 0% in the following
11 years
Current account balance is 4% of GDP in 2020
 (iii) The most pessimistic prediction of 2020 GDP
GDP growth rate is 8% in the first four years and 5 % in the following
11 years.
RMB appreciation 3% in the first four years and 0% in the following
11 years.
Current account balance is 4% of GDP in 2020.

The prediction of the RMB under the three assumptions is given in Table 7.6.

Table 7.6 suggests that under the assumption that the currency becomes
fully convertible, the share of RMB will be the third largest in the world at
about 17.54% (in the medium prediction) in 2020.

Using the same method, Table 7.7 predicts the percentage, under the
medium prediction, of RMB in the currency composition of international
bonds and notes in 2020.

Focusing only on the US dollar and the euro in the settlements currency
composition, we now turn to the share of the RMB in China's international
trade. Because the exact data on the currency composition of Chinese international trading are not available to us, we have had to make some assumptions about the share of US dollars in China's international trade. This we
set at 75%, 80%, and 90%. With an annual devaluation rate of the dollar
changing from 1% to 5%, Table 7.8 shows the changing percentage of the
share of the US dollar in the settlements currency composition of China's
international trade.

Table 7.6   Predicted currency composition of international reserves in 2020 (%)

	Optimistic	Medium	Pessimistic
RMB	21.45	17.54	15.15
US$	27.37	28.74	29.57
Euro	22.45	23.57	24.25
Jap Yen	13.43	14.10	14.51
Sw Fr.	1.53	1.61	1.66
GBP	13.76	14.45	14.86

Source: Author's calculations.

Table 7.7   Predicted currency composition of international bonds and notes in 2020 (%)

RMB	18.93
USD	19.39
Euro	19.33
Jap Yen	18.95
Sw Fr.	6.90
GBP	16.50

Source: Authors' calculations.

Table 7.8   Change in the share of the US dollar in China's international trade

US dollar share in the trade of China Annual devaluation of US dollar	75%	80%	85%
1%	−3.08%	−2.63%	−2.09%
2%	−6.15%	−5.25%	−4.19%
3%	−9.23%	−7.88%	−6.28%
4%	−12.31%	−10.50%	−8.37%
5%	−15.39%	−13.13%	−10.46%

Source: Authors' calculations.

Based on the result of the empirical analysis model, and assuming full convertibility of the RMB, under the three measures we suggest that the share of RMB will increase significantly.

7.5   Policy analysis

Following on from our empirical analysis, we can proceed to discuss two policy issues: (i) is it in China's interest to pursue rapid internationalization of the RMB?; and (ii) what would be an appropriate strategy for China to follow regarding RMB internationalization? We argue that China may not find it worthwhile to push for fast RMB internationalization. Instead, a twin-track approach may be preferable, one that takes advantage of Hong Kong as a financial center while maintaining financial stability in mainland China.

Before reaching our policy conclusions, it is necessary to first understand a few fundamental features of the Chinese economy that are relevant to the issue of RMB internationalization. It is also important to understand the major concerns of the Chinese central government when it comes to critical decisions on RMB internationalization.

Fundamental fact 1: Huge size of the economy and high degree of openness

The Chinese economy is already one of the top three economies in the world measured in nominal GDP. It is also one of the most open large economies in trade and foreign direct investment (FDI), with the import plus export and FDI to nominal GDP ratio in the neighborhood of 70% and 3%, respectively, in 2007. By 2015, it is widely expected that China will enter the rank of mid-income developing countries, with per capita GDP above US$8,000. By 2020, China is projected to be the largest economy in the world. More visibly, China is already the world's largest producer, consumer and trader of commodities and goods such as iron ore, steel, coal, lumber, textiles, etc. There are numerous implications. The most important is that the Chinese economy is and will continue to be an important component of the world economy. Fluctuations in the global economy are transmitted into the Chinese economy and changes in the Chinese economy will also have an increasingly significant impact on the world economy. Monetary policies in China will have to be coordinated with those in other major economies in order for the Chinese economy to grow in a smooth fashion. Thus, the Chinese government wants to retain a comfortable degree of control over its monetary policy.

Fundamental fact 2: Persistently high savings rate

Currently, China's national savings rate is about 50%, while the household savings rate is in the high 30s in percentage terms. There are many reasons for this, including a large proportion of the population recently lifted out of poverty but, out of habit, persistently consuming little; a young demographic structure; lack of a social safety net causing a high rate of precautionary saving; and a Confucian culture that emphasizes thrift and investment in child education. Whatever the reasons, observing the history of Japan and Korea, which share similar cultural and demographic features with China but "took off" economically several decades earlier than China, it is safe to assume that China's high savings rate will continue over the next 20 years.

What are the consequences of China's persistently high savings rate? An immediate effect is that, in the near future, the Chinese economy will to face the issue of a trade surplus with the rest of the world, since trade surplus, in essence, means extra savings in the economy. After that, RMB appreciation, either nominal or real, is inevitable. Also, China will become one of the largest—if not the largest—source of capital outflow in the world, simply because the country's high savings rate will not be absorbed by domestic consumption and investment.

Fundamental fact 3: An inefficient financial system—by design

It is an indisputable fact that China's financial system is still very inefficient, despite 30 years of reforms. However, it is not widely realized that it is an inefficient system by design; that is, the slow pace of financial reform in China is an outcome of the overall reform strategy. The country's financial system can be characterized as "mild financial repression," in which savers are not allowed to invest overseas and a state-monopolized banking sector dominates the entire financial system. As a result, the M2 to GDP ratio in 2007 was as high as 165%, and compared to the huge amount of M2, the equity markets are very small, with at most 50% of shares being tradable, commanding a very high earnings rate in the region of 50%. Such forms of mild repression serve the overall economic reform very well, providing the government with easy access to funds for borrowing and supporting the decreasing share of government tax revenue in GDP during most of the reform era.

One clear and important consequence of China's mild financial repression and inefficient financial system is vulnerability to full capital account convertibility in the near future. Given the current circumstances, which are likely to continue in the near future, this may cause a sudden and massive outflow of domestic savings to foreign currencies and foreign assets. In turn, financial institutions in China will face a liquidity crisis and China's financial markets will see a sudden and drastic price drop. Both will be extremely destabilizing for the Chinese economy.

Fundamental fact 4: Hong Kong

No other developing countries in the world are like China in having a highly developed economy bordering one of the world's most sophisticated and advanced financial systems—that of Hong Kong. As a result, China has at least two financial centers: a domestic one in Shanghai and an international one in Hong Kong. This obviously has far-reaching implications for China's financial development. In fact, Hong Kong has been China's most important source of foreign equity financing. In addition, many advanced financial transactions originating in mainland China are conducted in Hong Kong.

Implication 1: Relatively low benefit of borrowing internationally

Because of China's high savings rate and relatively high ratio of trade surplus to GDP (which reached as high as 7% in 2007), China have relatively few benefits from being able to borrow internationally. Since the need to borrow abroad is low, China is unlikely to assume a large amount of foreign debt, and therefore the chance of a balance of payments crisis for China should be very low in the future.

Implication 2: The seigniorage from internationalizing RMB may not be big

In fact, it may even be negative. The reason is that in order to internationalize the RMB, China's capital account needs to be convertible, which, given the circumstances of mild financial repression, may cause a significant amount of savings to leave the country in search of non-RMB-denominated assets.

Having recognized the fundamental facts of the Chinese economy and their implications, let us now turn to the concerns of central government policymakers about RMB internationalization. There seem to be three principal areas:

Fundamental concern 1: How to maintain financial stability (and therefore overall economic stability) while improving the efficiency of the financial sector

The last thing Chinese central policymakers want is economic instability, such that potential financial instability is an overriding concern. Recent years have seen the Chinese central government convening high-level meetings devoted specifically to financial reforms and financial stability. A special department—the department of financial stability—under the central bank was established to take charge of policies maintaining financial stability.

Fundamental concern 2: How to avoid major international attention and speculation that China is changing either the rules of the game or the landscape of the playing field in the world economy

China, as a newcomer to the club of the world's largest economies, is very uncertain about how to play its role. More importantly, Chinese leaders, following Deng Xiaoping's legacy of keeping a low profile in international affairs, have been trying hard to avoid any road-blocks to China's continued economic emergence. Internationalization of the RMB is one of the most visible international economic issues of the moment. Naturally, Chinese leaders would choose to avoid giving any impressions to existing international currency issuers that they have any clear intentions or strategic goals towards this issue.

Fundamental concern 3: How to maintain Hong Kong's continued economic success

This is an issue bigger than the welfare of Hong Kong's population, since this is about the credibility of the Chinese government, which has repeatedly maintained that the 'one country, two systems' principle is fundamentally workable. Moreover, Hong Kong's continued economic success will have implications for resolving the Taiwan issue peacefully.

Having discussed the fundamental facts of the Chinese economy and concerns of the central government, let us next analyze the future development of RMB internationalization. We call this the twin-track approach to RMB internationalization.

Track 1 The mainland Chinese economy

In this track, the government gradually lifts capital control through various means, including increasingly quotas for the programs of the QDII (qualified domestic institutional investor) and QFII (qualified foreign institutional investor). In addition, the program allowing Chinese mainland investors to convert the RMB into HKD in order to buy Hong Kong equity will also be given higher quotas. More interestingly, the central government may eventually invite foreign firms (such as Apple, IBM, Intel) to be listed in Shanghai/Shenzhen equity markets by allowing them to remit in US dollars after converting the RMB revenue they have raised. Also, the government may promote more contracts and settlement of international trade in RMB. The way to promote this is by subsidizing currency swap contracts offered by commercial banks, thereby lowering the costs faced by RMB holders.

Track 2 Hong Kong

The central government may implement three things simultaneously: (i) enlarge the size and scope of the issuance of RMB financial assets (for example, RMB sovereign bonds, corporate bonds, RMB-denominated equity); (ii) accommodate the settlement of trade in RMB securities by providing cash or credit in the RMB; and (iii) avoid creating a large RMB exchange market which would compete with that in Shanghai by restricting the participants in such a market in Hong Kong to traders of RMB securities.

7.6   Conclusions

In this chapter we have discussed the factors behind the internationalization of a currency, econometrically estimating determinants of the shares of major currencies in the reserve holdings of the world's central banks, in the exports and imports of the various countries, and in international bonds and notes. Significant factors include: the size of the home country, inflation rate, real interest rate, exchange rate variability, exchange rate appreciation and the trade ratio with the home country. Assuming the RMB to be fully convertible, we predicted the share of the RMB under the three measures, the results suggesting that the RMB share will increase significantly, based on the conclusion of the empirical analysis. The RMB portion of the world's currency reserves and long-term bonds may be as high as 20% by 2020.

Although prospects are bright, the main challenge facing China seems to be the undesirable consequences of full convertibility, arising from the fact that the country's domestic financial institutions may not be ready for full convertibility in the near future. It is feasible and desirable to adopt a twin-track approach to RMB internationalization: gradually make RMB convertible in mainland China, synchronizing it with the pace of financial sector reforms, and speed up the creation and trade of RMB securities in Hong Kong without having a huge offshore RMB exchange market.

References

Chen, Hongyi and Wensheng Peng (2007), "The potential role of the renminbi as an international currency," *China Economic Issues*, Hong Kong Monetary Authority, December 2007.

Chinn Menzie and Frankel Jeffrey (2007), "Will the Euro Eventually Surpass the Dollar as Leading International Reserve Currency?" NBER Working Paper No. 11510.

Cohen, Benjamin J. (1971), *The Future of Sterling as an International Currency*, New York: St. Martin's Press.

Eichengreen, B. (1998), "The Euro as a Reserve Currency," *Journal of the Japanese and International Economics*, Vol. 12(4), pp. 483–506.

Kamps Annette (2006), "The Euro as Invoicing currency in International Trade," Working paper series No. 665.

Kenen, Peter (1983), "The Role of the Dollar as an International Currency," Occasional Paper No. 13, Group of Thirty, NY.

Lim, Ewe-Ghee (2006), "The Euro's Challenge to the Dollar: Different Views from Economists and Evidence from COFER (Currency Composition of Foreign Exchange Reserves) and other Data," *IMF Working Paper*, WP/06/153, 2006.

Monetary and Economic Department (2003), "Guide to the International Financial Statistics," BIS Paper No. 14.

PBOC Study Group (2006), "The Timing, Path, and Strategies of RMB Internationalization," *China Finance*, 5, pp. 12–13.

8
Effects of RMB Internationalization on China's Finance Industry

Shusong Ba, Bo Wu, Ping Yuan, Miao Wang and Zhuqing Yin

8.1 Introduction and literature review

Under the accelerating trend of global financial integration, especially since China's entry into the World Trade Organization (WTO), the finance sector of China is faced with the inevitability of opening its door to the outside world. The internationalization of the Chinese currency, the renminbi (RMB)—an important channel through which to export China's influence to the outside world—is a gradual process affected by different factors.

Bergsten (1975) identified two conditions for currency internationalization: political and economic. External economic conditions are confidence in the currency's convertibility and liquidity, and a sound international balance of payment structure. Internal economic conditions, meanwhile, are growth of the economy, price stability, relative advantage of the economy, independence of monetary policy and a developed financial market. Krugman (1980) found that the currency with the lowest transaction cost and largest trade scale has the potential to become the international vehicle currency, whether or not the issuing country's position in the global economy falls. Krugman's work was continued by Rey (2001), in whose model the export of a country's goods expands the international demand for its currency, at the same time increasing the liquidity of the foreign exchange market and reducing transaction costs. Thus, a more internationalized market will make it easier to convert currencies with the outside world, and the currency of the particular country has a greater opportunity to become an international currency. The internationalization of a currency rests with the people's confidence in its stability, which is determined by the extent of the currency's circulation, the stability of monetary policy, the strength of regulation, the development and sustainability of the economy, and the value of the currency itself.

The main power influencing the international position of a currency is the market rather the government (Hu, 2003). But the financial environment in which RMB circulated is one of the drawbacks to its internationalization. Hence, the key problem is whether there is a market environment in which the currency can satisfy different conditions to be an international currency, such as its stability, convertibility, the advantage of the transaction cost and information cost. But Li and He (2004) found that the institutional and economic environment in China constrained the development of RMB internationalization, such as the convertibility of RMB, the process of the reform of foreign exchange regime, and the development of domestic financial system. There are different preconditions for RMB internationalization according to Xu (2005), such as the liberalization of capital account, stability of RMB exchange rate, the strong backing of China's economy, the development of the financial system and even some political foundation.

From the literature, it is evident that China's financial environment is stressed as the preconditions of RMB internationalization. By nature, the internationalization of the currency is a financial issue, and it is therefore necessary for this process to be consistent with the development of the Chinese finance sector.

On the one hand, financial institutions create the important channels for RMB business and for its cross-border circulation. The expansion of these financial institutions and the effectiveness of their operations determine the range and convenience of RMB in the world market. On the other hand, the financial market is the stage on which the RMB can perform different currency functions internationally. The acceptance of RMB by the world market relies on an open, stable and developed financial market. A developed financial system can ensure that the external price (exchange rate) and internal price (interest rate) of RMB are rational and stable, which is the precondition for RMB to be accepted by the international market. But as is well known, the Chinese financial market is currently neither efficient nor sufficiently open.

In this chapter we discuss the effects of RMB internationalization on different aspects of China's finance sector, and then analyze how the sector can lend support at different stages through its reform and innovation. As the micro-foundation and basic units of the country's finance sector, China's financial institutions reflect the close relationship between the internationalization of RMB and the finance industry. In section 8.2, the effects of the internationalization of the RMB on banking, securities and the insurance industry are discussed in detail. The influence of the internationalization of the currency on the macro-economy and financial market is discussed in section 8.3. By drawing on experiences on how the euro and the Japanese yen influenced their domestic markets, we examine the mutual influence between RMB internationalization and the Chinese financial market. In section 8.4, the process of internationalization of the RMB is divided into three stages. From the standpoint of how financial institutions support RMB internationalization, different approaches are put forward to boost the regionalization and globalization of RMB. The chapter closes with some brief conclusions.

8.2   The micro-effects on Chinese financial institutions

8.2.1   The effects of the internationalization of RMB on banking business

8.2.1.1   *Theory of currency substitution and the internationalization of RMB*

Chetty (1969) introduced the concept of currency substitution for the first time. In an open economy, the function of the local convertible currency would be partly or totally substituted by foreign currencies, either because the local currency had depreciated or because confidence in the local currency had collapsed. Rojas (1985) defined currency substitution more laconically as the need of foreign currencies by the national resident. To some extent, the holding of multi-currency portfolios is currency substitution.

Currency internationalization is the result of the substitution of vehicle currencies for foreign currencies. The phenomenon on currency substitution has appeared more and more in the banking system. For instance, the process of dollarization started with the advent of the Eurodollar deposit—and the real essence of the Eurodollar is the substitution of the US dollar for other foreign currencies.

Using the relative index of currency substitution, the extent of RMB substitution is shown in Figure 8.1.

Figure 8.1 shows that the degree of currency substitution for RMB has been falling since 2002. This is partly because the excess liquidity raises

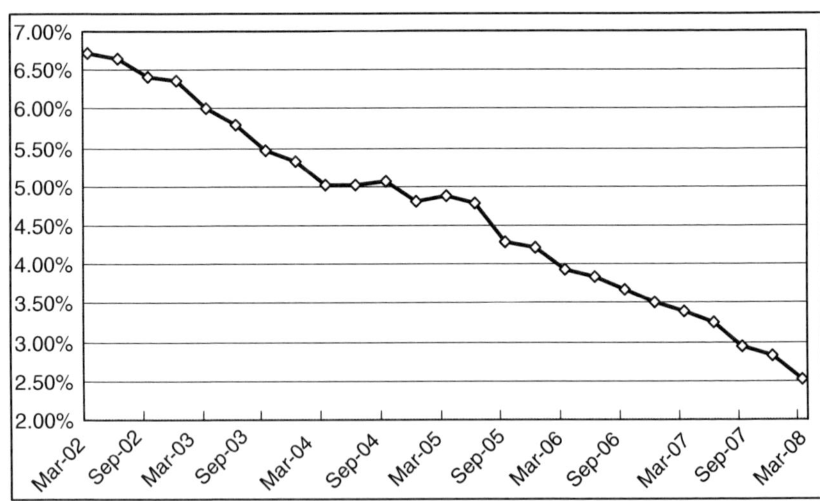

Figure 8.1   Currency substitution of RMB in 1996–2003
Source: PBoC; Authors' calculation.

M2 rapidly, and the appreciation of RMB leads to the reduction of the deposit in foreign currencies. This situation is characterized by the contrary substitution of RMB for foreign currencies—an important phenomenon of RMB internationalization which shows that the overseas desire for RMB is increasing.

8.2.1.2 *Effects on the banking system*

According to the theory of currency substitution, RMB internationalization is a process in which the demand for RMB assets abroad increases and RMB circulation expands. Of course, such a process will have significant effects on the operations of banks in China, at least in the following four aspects.

1. Effects on assets operation: In recent years, RMB assets operation abroad has developed but is still in its primary phase. This is because RMB is not convertible and the capital account has not yet been liberalized.

   Take the Bank of China for example, whose overseas branches and international operations are both considerably well developed. However, its domestic institutions have issued loans four times larger than its overseas branches in recent years, making it obvious that domestic loan expansion still dominates its assets operations. Moreover, in the last two years the structure of the Bank of China's loan expansion both at home and abroad has changed (Figure 8.2). Loan expansion overseas has decreased sharply, partly because the appreciation of the RMB has raised the exchange risk on RMB loans, thus reducing the demand for RMB loans abroad. In fact, the interest cost of RMB loans abroad will rise as RMB appreciates, so that foreign institutions and individuals will tend to substitute RMB loans with other currency loans.

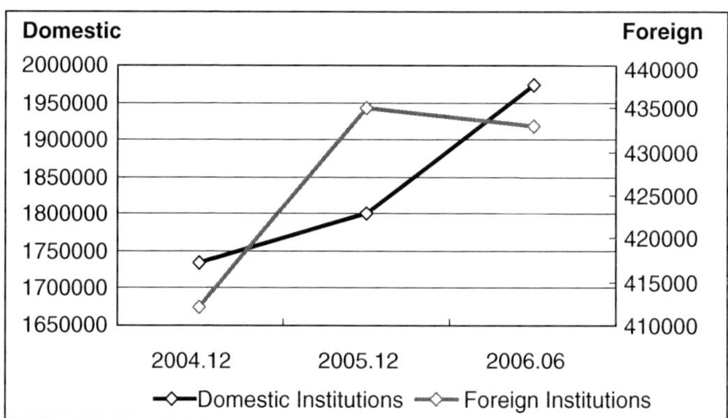

Figure 8.2 Change in the structure of loan expansion, Bank of China (billion yuan)
Source: Interim Report of Bank of China (2006); Authors' calculation.

2. Effects on liability operation: RMB liability operation mostly concerns RMB deposits. As China's capital account has not been entirely liberalized, the offshore finance market cannot be put into effect. The currencies Chinese banks are dealing with are mostly the US dollar, euro, yen, pound and Hong Kong dollar. As a result, the domestic liability operation can avoid external shocks, but may be affected more by the diversification of domestic financial assets, such as capital outflow from the banking system into stocks or real estate markets. As China's capital account liberalization and the internationalization of RMB move forward, so RMB offshore finance will finally step into the outside world.

    Looking at what happened with dollarization, the development of the Eurodollar market led to an outflow of domestic dollar deposits from the US, due to the interest rate spread between the domestic and offshore markets (Balbach and Resler, 1980). RMB internationalization may act in the same way, if the interest spread exists between domestic and offshore markets.

3. Effects on intermediary business: Since the 1950s, the intermediary business of western banks has developed rapidly, and the percentage of non-interest income in the total income of the banks has increased year on year. The development of intermediary business by banks in developed country was closely tied with their international trade and currency internationalization.

    The rapid development of China's economy and the rise of the RMB's global status led to the development of international trade settlement in RMB and capital inflow into the capital market. Accordingly, Chinese banks can develop their own intermediary business through international settlement, international cards, international fund custody, etc. What is more, with RMB internationalization, the exchange rate will increasingly depend on market forces, which will make RMB exchange more flexible. Chinese banks can then develop monetary derivatives, such as forward exchange contracts, foreign exchange futures, foreign exchange options, currency swaps and so on. As a result, the operational structure of Chinese banks will be improved and their ability in financial product innovation and profit-making will also be enhanced.

4. Effects on the expansion of overseas branches: Ma and Rao (2007) estimated the scale of cross-border circulation of RMB and found that the inventory of RMB abroad was about CYN31.05 billion, only 1.29% of the total RMB amount. While most of the RMB abroad will flow back to China, with the exception of a small amount used for liquidity management, there is almost no way to invest and gain interest overseas.

    The main route by which RMB flows back is non-banking, with a portion flowing back through banks. There are two main channels: foreigners, including those who reside in countries bordering on China, who deposit RMB directly with foreign financial institutions; and foreign banks that can redeposit RMB in Chinese local banks.

The infrastructure for cross-border circulation of RMB comprises the overseas branches of Chinese commercial banks. It is important to make RMB cross-border transactions flow through formal channels, thereby smoothing inflow and outflow routes of RMB and providing better tracking and inspection of the cross-border circulation of RMB. Such a system can enhance the efficiency of monetary policy affecting RMB internationalization. At the same time, using RMB more frequently in international trade settlement will reduce the pressure of RMB appreciation.

8.2.2   Effects on securities business

Internationalization of the RMB means that the currency will be used more extensively in capital markets both at home and abroad. In addition, liberalization of the capital account will enlarge the scale of overseas capital inflow, which will consequently deepen the extent of internationalization of the Chinese capital market.

8.2.2.1   Effects of RMB internationalization on the stock market

To some extent, the development of the stock market directly reflects capital efficiency. The currency internationalization must be accompanied by a gradual opening of the capital market. This will bring two opposing effects on the development of the capital market: both increasing its efficiency and causing its fluctuation.

Nowadays, the influential international currencies include the US dollar, euro, pound and yen. The euro is not concluded in the empirical study here, for there are only eight years of historical data since its coming into being on 1 January 1999.

Let us select the percentages of international currencies in the total foreign exchange reserve (R, the end-of-year data) as the variable which reflects the extent of the currencies' internationalization. In addition, the percentages of the total stock transaction in GDP (*eq*) are taken as the variable which reflects the extent of stock market development. As for the sampling, there are annual data on three currencies, the US dollar, pound and yen from 1987 to 2003.

First, in the regression analysis of the effects on the stock market of currency internationalization, R is taken as the explanatory variable which reflects the currency internationalization, and *eq* is taken as the dependent variable reflecting the extent of stock market development. The model of panel data is as follows:

$$eq_{it} = u_i + \beta_i R_{it} + \varepsilon_{it} \qquad i = \text{US, UK, JP}; \ t = 1, 2, \dots, 17$$

where the subscript of i reflects different currencies (or countries), and t reflects the time (year). Applying the unit root test to the residual under the fixed-effect model, we reach the following result:

ADF test statistic −3.947126	1% critical value	−4.0681
	5% critical value	−3.1222
	10% critical value	−2.7042

The residual under the fixed-effect model passes the ADF unit root test at the 95% confidence level, and thus is integrated of order zero. As a result, the fixed-effect model can be used in the analysis. The result of the regression is shown in Table 8.1.

As shown in the table, the goodness of fit in the model reaches 0.68438, so the model fits the data well. The t-statistic of R is 9.043, which passes the significance test. And this means that the explanatory variable can explain the dependent variable well.

In the output, the coefficient of R is positive, which reflects that currency internationalization plays a positive role in the development of the local stock market. So, we can draw the conclusion that the internationalization of RMB will play an important and useful role in the development of the Chinese stock market.

Second, in the regression analysis of the effects of the stock market on currency internationalization, *eq* is taken as the explanatory variable instead of R in the following model of panel data:

$$R_{it} = \alpha_i + \beta_i eq_{it} + \varepsilon_{it} \qquad i = \text{US, UK, JP};\ t = 1, 2, \dots, 17$$

Making the analysis in the same way as above, we reach the regression analysis shown in Table 8.2.

Similarly, the model fits the data perfectly. The t-statistic *eq* it shows that the explanatory variable can explain the dependent variable well. The

Table 8.1   Effects on stock market of currency internationalization

Variable	Coefficient	t-Statistic	Prob.
R	15.73704	9.043029	0.0000
Fixed effects			
US—C	−798.7289		
UK—C	19.42947		
JP—C	−49.46616		
R^2	0.68438		

Table 8.2 Effects on currency internationalization of stock market

Variable	Coefficient	t-Statistic	Prob.
eq	0.040352	9.043029	0.0000
Fixed effects			
US—C	53.40763		
UK—C	0.413948		
JP—C	4.404902		
R^2	0.994008		

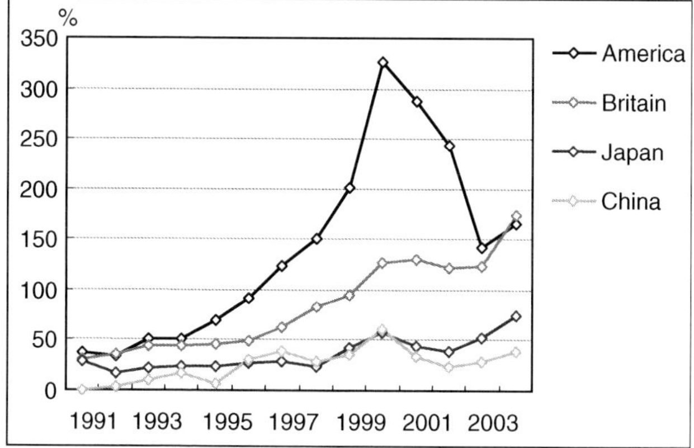

Figure 8.3 Percentage of the total stock transaction in GDP
Source: IMF; Authors's calculation.

coefficient of *eq* reflects that the development of the local stock market plays a helpful role in currency internationalization.

Thus, it can be concluded that a good external environment can be provided for the internationalization of RMB. Only if the scale of the capital market is enlarged can the efficiency of the stock market be enhanced. However, Figure 8.3 tells us there is a long way for the Chinese stock market to go compared with other developed countries.

8.2.2.2 *Effects of RMB internationalization on the bond market*

The extent of the internationalization of China's bond market is not high at the moment, and most of the bonds in RMB can only be issued domestically. This is not good for the development of financing overseas, and will block the internationalization of the Chinese capital market. RMB internationalization will enhance the stability of the RMB exchange rate and accelerate the cross-border circulation of RMB. Consequently, it will contribute to the issuance of RMB bonds. Cohen (2005) found that there was more bond issuance in a given currency when the long-term interest rate of that currency was high relative to other available currencies.

Figure 8.4 tells us that the US dollar is the main currency in the currency denomination of bond issues. The dollar was used in 44.3% of international bond issuance from the third quarter of 1993 to the forth quarter of 1998. Although the share of the dollar in the currency denomination of bond issues has fallen since the euro came into being, it still accounts for 42.8%. In addition, the substitution effect of the yen in the currency denomination of bond issues is most obvious.

According to Cohen (2005), the share of international debt issuance denominated in a given currency tends to be related to the strength of that currency. Areskoug (1980) considered that the stability of the exchange rate meant higher precision in forecasting the value of the currency; thus, it was easier to decide the real cost of the bond issuers and the real profit of the bond purchasers. The expectation of the exchange rate affects the circulation of bond issues and the liquidity of the bond market. As a result, the denominating currencies of international bonds bear close relation to their

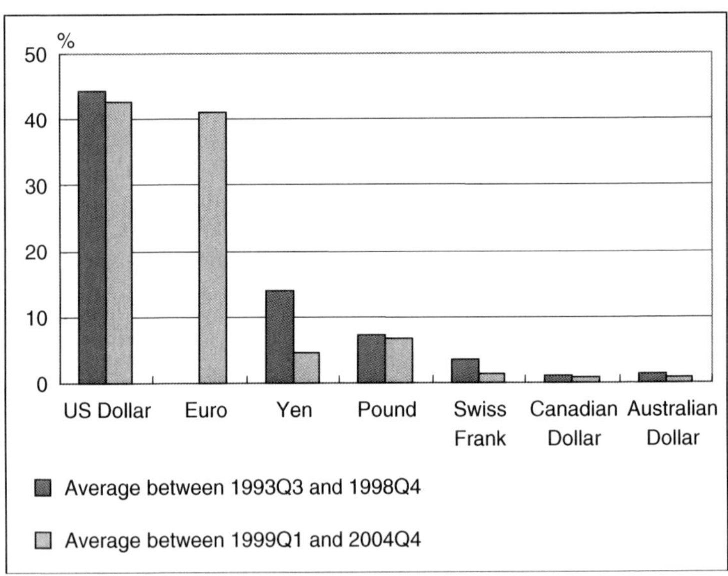

Figure 8.4   Share of the currency denomination of bond issues
Source: Dealogic; Euroclear; Thomson Financial Securities Data; BIS calculations: Authors' compilation.

international status and the strength and stability of the exchange rates. Hence it can be foreseen that RMB internationalization will enhance the international status of RMB and can thus enlarge the share of international bonds denominated in RMB. The development of international bonds denominated in RMB is decided by the extent of RMB internationalization and by the stability of the RMB exchange rate.

With the support of the international market and law, the international bonds denominated in RMB have had a good beginning. The People's Bank of China decided to expand RMB operations in Hong Kong in January 2007. Domestic financial institutions were allowed to issue RMB financial bonds in Hong Kong, with the Central Bank providing the settlement arrangement for it. The China Development Bank first issued RMB bonds in Hong Kong on 26 June 2007, in an amount of CYN5 billion. And the China Export-Import Bank issued a total of CYN2 billion RMB bonds in Hong Kong on 10 August 2007. The Bank of China and the China Construction Bank will follow suit.

As analyzed above, the development of RMB bonds will accelerate under several forces, especially RMB internationalization.

8.2.3 The effects on insurance business

China's domestic insurance companies expand to overseas market in recent years by overseas business operations and overseas financing. As a result, how to manage the increasing foreign exchange assets to prevent the risk of currency mis-match has received much attention.

Goldstein and Turner (2005) defined currency mismatch as an entity of rights and interests (including sovereignties, banks, non-banks and households) who uses different currencies in income and expense activities to make its net value or net income more sensitive to fluctuations in the exchange rate, where the structure of its assets and liability are in different currencies.

The primary problem with currency mismatch is the exchange rate risk. Analysis of currency mismatch provides guidance for the risk management of the foreign exchange assets of domestic insurance companies. Only if the pressure of the currency mismatch and maturity mismatch in the domestic insurance foreign exchange assets is released, will the exchange rate risk be prevented effectively, allowing the foreign exchange assets of insurance companies to be invested and operated more constantly (Xia et al., 2006).

Having looked at asset and liability figures, Ba (2007) pointed out that Chinese insurance capital had obvious problems with both maturity and currency mismatch. As overseas financing and operation of the domestic insurance sector have expanded, the problem has become more serious. In fact, by the end of 2005, the three Chinese insurance companies listed on overseas stock markets—China Life Insurance Company, Ping An Insurance Company of China, and Property and Casualty Company—had lost more than CYN1.3 billion due to RMB appreciation.

Here we offer some suggestions for insurance companies: In the short term, they can withdraw reserves to prevent exchange risk loss; China Life Insurance Company and Ping An Insurance Company of China withdrew reserves of CYN500 and CYN300 million respectively. In the mid-term, the ability of global assets collocation is the core-competitiveness of the insurance institutions. The efficiency of the foreign exchange assets operation is closely aligned with the continuous development of the insurance companies. Such a process can lead the capital structure of the insurance companies to be internationalized. For example, the share of the international securities of Japanese insurance firms increased from 2% in 1978 to 10% in 1997.

According to Ba (2006), there are three measures which can improve the problems of maturity mismatch and currency mismatch: (i) enlarge the scale and type of securitization products of insurance assets; (ii) develop a pilot project on insurance capital investment for estates and enterprises; and (iii) expand insurance investments overseas.

In fact, the Chinese authorities have paid great attention to the overseas application of the insurance foreign exchange asset. In September 2005, China opened the way for domestic insurance companies to invest foreign exchange capital in the stock exchanges in New York, London, Frankfurt, Tokyo, Singapore and Hong Kong.

In the long term, the appreciation of RMB will become more stable and the internationalization of RMB will help increase the use of RMB. Hence, for insurance companies the exchange rate risk to foreign exchange assets and the difficulty of investing overseas will decrease, while at the same time, the more convertible RMB will promote overseas investment. This will reduce the need for foreign exchange, which bodes well for the international business carried out by China's domestic insurance companies.

8.3   Interactive effects with Chinese financial market

8.3.1   Effects of currency internationalization on the financial market—in theory

Much literature is available on the conditions and effects of international currency (Bergsten, 1975; Lei, 2000), while there is far less research on partly internationalized currencies.

In the process of currency internationalization, the issuing country needs to take active measures to sustain and improve the status of the currency in the international marketplace. This includes promoting currency cooperation in the surrounding region, to the point of establishing a regional currency system. These measures can also help to expand the circulation of the currency, thus transforming it into a totally internationalized currency.

The analysis above indicates that RMB is at the beginning of its regionalization. So, based on the theories of optimum currency area (OCA) and currency integration, we can assess the effects of the internationalization of RMB on macro-economic finance. The OCA theory, which was put forward by Mundell (1961), is the primary theory on the regime choice of regional currency integration. From then on, Ingram (1962), Kenen (1980), McKinnon (1993), among others, joined the discussion on the OCA's criteria. With the establishment of European monetary union and the emergence of the euro in the 1990s, scholars began to focus again on the impact of currency integration on the currency area. In particular, they focused on how to create effective policies, especially monetary policy, to deal with the different impacts.

The optimal purpose of currency area cooperation is to achieve currency integration. Under the Pareto Optimum, there should be net positive benefits arising for each member country joining the currency area. Thus, a cost-benefit framework is helpful in analyzing the impact of currency internationalization on the issuing country.

1. Benefits of establishing a regional currency system: First, it is good to eliminate the uncertainty of the exchange rate. Such uncertainty results from the change in the return on investment in the future, which makes risk-averse investors hesitate to both trade and invest, and hence reduces welfare improvement. The establishment of an area currency system and the introduction of a single currency can eliminate the fluctuation of the exchange rate in the area, making future income from investment more certain and thus stimulating investment and improving outputs as well as welfare in the region.

   Second, a regional currency system can lower the level of real interest rate. Prices are the key signal for producers and consumers. An unstable exchange rate can lead to fluctuations in the price of goods and services, which increases the adjustment cost for decision making in the economy. The establishment of an area currency system will reduce exchange rate premium and then the real interest cost, also helping to stimulate regional investment.

   In fact, price uncertainty may push the real interest rate higher, because when the expected return on an investment is uncertain, the risk-averse investor will ask for a higher risk premium by way of compensation. In a regional currency system, the single currency unifies the interest rate, and the cheaper cost of using the currency can help accelerate investment.

   Third, a regional currency system is helpful in extending the credit of the currency area. Countries with bad credit ratings in struggles against inflation can obtain credit from those countries with good ratings. So, the key currency in the regional currency system can help avoid the turmoil of external capital flows.

2. Costs of establishing a regional currency system: The main cost to member countries of participating in a regional currency system is the loss of exchange rate policy tools. The single currency in such a system weakens these tools, and with them the ability of member countries to employ effective measures to adjust and control the macro-economy. Moreover, the external equilibrium of a monetary cooperation framework hides the fact that some member countries may have a permanent deficit, while others may have a permanent surplus in international trade.

   The independence of individual monetary policy will also be weakened. In a floating exchange rate system, countries can use their own monetary policy tools to achieve their own macro-economy targets. Given that the establishment of currency cooperation is based on cross-country cooperation on monetary policy, individual member countries lose the independence of monetary policy.

8.3.2   Lessons learnt from the euro and the yen

There are three principal examples of currency internationalization. The first example is dollarization, which transformed the central currency of the international monetary system into the vehicle currency. The second is euro internationalization, which established the single currency system and was dependent on regional cross-country economic cooperation. The third example is the internationalization of the yen, which leaned on the development and deepening of a financial system in order to promote the conversion of a non-vehicle currency into a vehicle currency. From the experiences of the euro and the yen, there are lessons to be learnt for internationalization of the RMB.

First, under the international monetary system dominated by US dollar, establishing the system of Currency Area should conduce to the currency internationalization of developing countries. In such an international currency system, the currency internationalization of any country can hardly succeed without the cooperation of other regional currencies. As a modern country with the most developed financial system, the US naturally does not support the reform of the international currency system. This creates more difficulties for those countries attempting to internationalize another currency. The experience of the euro provides a very good example, but it applies only to those regional countries that have a common or close cultural background and commensurate economic development. Without this or a similar background, it seems difficult for the RMB to follow the internationalization route taken by euro. This explains why the Japanese yen chose a different route for its internationalization.

Second, it is necessary to integrate the building of the domestic market with reform of the external financial environment. As was the case with the yen, mismatching of the two will block the process of currency internationalization. In the long history of the internationalization of the yen, the Japanese finance authority, facing pressure from the US and internal factions, focused on how to protect the domestic market from external shocks. As a result, the development of the domestic financial market fell behind the offshore market, which led to the vulnerability of Japan in the international financial market. The lesson here is that the government needs to take measures to improve the reform of the domestic market to match the external financial environment.

Third, the finance authority should take measures to realize "path dependence" and "self-consolidation" through appropriate structuring of financial institutions. Path dependence is best achieved in the process of institution building; once established, changing institutional arrangements is hard, even where the external environment changes.

Thus, measures can be taken that will lead currency internationalization along the correct path, at two levels. The first level involves the institutional arrangement of the reform of the domestic financial system. By promoting the opening and reform of the system, such an arrangement can encourage non-residents to use assets priced in the pre-internationalized currency. In the third stage of yen internationalization, Japan followed such a path. The second level concerns the institutional arrangements of regional currency cooperation. By following such a path from the outset, the euro achieved success.

8.3.3 Interactive effects between RMB internationalization and the Chinese financial market

Some of the international functions already being performed by RMB include medium of exchange and unit of account. Furthering the process of RMB internationalization will depend on the development and opening up of the Chinese financial market.

8.3.3.1 Impacts of RMB internationalization on the Chinese financial market

1. Deepen the Chinese financial market: If the circulation of RMB continues to expand, and the currency gains more international functions in the global marketplace, China's financial markets will become more efficient and internationalized, and the RMB exchange rate will more accurately reflect the depth of the country's economic foundations. An economy with larger scales and less regulation of capital accounts and exchange markets may enjoy less transaction costs and more convenience for trade in assets in the local currency. Furthermore, international use of the currency can make the local market more efficient and internationalized. Importantly for the RMB in terms of the international trade in financial

assets, the Chinese financial market needs to achieve a higher standard and efficiency. This will help to deepen and promote innovation within the country's financial market.

2. Promote the development of the RMB offshore market: The increasing demand for RMB in overseas markets requires investment and finance channels for non-residents, so the establishment of an offshore RMB financial market is essential. Such a market will provide an important intermediary between the domestic and foreign markets, and can offer market-oriented index systems of both interest rate and foreign-exchange rate—key indicators of the liberalization of the RMB. Moreover, an offshore RMB financial market will boost cooperation between China and other countries in Asia and the Pacific region.

3. Increase the competitive ability of Chinese financial institutions: In the process of internationalization, RMB will be used more and more in international trade as the medium of exchange and unit of account. This will be of considerable benefit to Chinese financial institutions and increase the competitive ability of China's finance sector in the international market.

4. Ease the pressure of currency mismatch: If RMB becomes an international currency, China can use the RMB in international trade and financing—which at once can avoid or at least lighten the risk of currency mismatch. The internationalized RMB can be adopted both in asset and liability accounts, thus avoiding the risk of currency mismatch in international operations.

8.3.3.2 *Effects of the financial market development on RMB internationalization*

Let us now look at the other side of the coin: the reverse effects of the financial market development on RMB internationalization. Currency internationalization depends on the global financial markets of international trade and investment. The openness and development of the market directly determines the efficiency of international investment and trade, and thus the process of internationalization of the currency.

The functions of an international currency should be performed in a developed financial market. The more efficient the financial market, the more currency will be used in international trade and investment in the market, and hence the currency will be more internationalized.

The euro has been challenging the position of the US dollar in the international currency system since its appearance, but to some extent it is the segmented capital markets that are preventing the euro from becoming the main reserve currency. A developed financial market can also supply sufficient credit and liquidity for RMB to execute its international currency functions. In a word, it is the development of the financial market that supports RMB internationalization.

The interactive effects above show the relationship of mutual promotion between RMB internationalization and China's financial market.

8.4   Financial industry support for RMB internationalization at different stages

The process of RMB internationalization can be divided into different stages such as regionalization stage and globalization stage. But all of these stages missed some important characteristics, either in currency function or regional extension. We consider RMB internationalization as a gradual process, one that can be divided into three stages according to the status of cross-border use and circulation of RMB. The first stage is liberalization, which aims at freeing the RMB from government regulation on exchange with foreign currencies, the interest rate and exchange rate. The second stage is regionalization, which focuses on the circulation, use and acceptance of RMB in the Asian countries bordering China. The third stage is globalization, where the RMB will fulfill all of the functions of a fully internationalized currency.

8.4.1   The short-term goal: Liberalization

The liberalization of a currency here means the currency can be freely converted into foreign currencies, and the interest rate and exchange rate of the currency are priced by the market rather than by the government. Kenen (1998) stated that a sufficient supply of a currency was necessary for its internationalization. Only freely circulating capital can expand and deepen a market, and this is indispensable for the internationalization of a currency. Two points need to be made here.

The first point concerns free convertibility of the RMB—a precondition for the internalization of RMB. Only a fully convertible currency can circulate freely and execute the international currency functions required of it in the international market. All of the main current international currencies—the US dollar, the euro and the yen—are of course freely convertible. So, to promote the internationalization of RMB, the realization of its convertibility is the first step.

As early as the end of 1996, the RMB became convertible for current account transactions. But the ensuing financial crisis in Asia stopped the process of capital account liberalization in China. China's accession to the WTO in 2001 is often considered a catalyst. Since then, the RMB has become more and more convertible, but some substantial government control still remains, including limits on currency outflow and the verification of capital account transactions.

The second point concerns market-oriented reform of interest rate and exchange rate regimes. Although these reforms are occurring gradually, the domestic financial market is more and more standardized and transparent.

Once achieved, the RMB will face less risk of interference from the government, and China's financial market will gain trust and obtain a higher score in international credit rating.

In summary, the RMB is now deep into the liberalization stage, creating a solid foundation for the internationalization of the RMB.

8.4.2   The medium-term goal: Regionalization

The aim of regionalization of the RMB is to promote the circulation of RMB in surrounding countries, to develop the habit of people in these countries holding and using the currency, and to make RMB fulfill international currency functions for individuals and even governments in the region. That the RMB has become one of the main reserve currencies in the region is a milestone on the route to full internationalization.

There are a number of optional approaches to promote the regionalization of RMB that will have beneficial effects on financial markets, and thus on the process of internationalizing the RMB.

The first is to develop cross-border trade. Because RMB is not at present convertible for capital account transactions, its performance in meeting international currency functions is very limited. Improving the regionalization of RMB through frontier trade is an important breakthrough in this direction (Ba, 2003).

There are a number of financial supporting conditions that can help to develop border trade. For example, Chinese banks can expand their branches overseas or develop RMB banking business in foreign banks so that RMB can circulate and be settled via a convenient financial channel. And through signing an agreement on bilateral settlement and cooperation with other countries, the Chinese government can promote RMB as the main currency in trade with these countries. In 2004, the percentages of cross-border trade between China and other countries settled in RMB were 81% for Vietnam, 90% for Mongolia and 45% for Korea. In these countries, RMB has become the main currency of settlement and pricing for border trade, so there is a good foundation and a bright prospect for RMB regionalization through cross-border trade.

The second approach is through a regional currency, which demands economic cooperation between countries in the region. For this, China first needs to expand its influence in the regional economy, and then upgrade the position of the RMB in the regional currency system. Meanwhile, the relationships between RMB and other international currencies in the region, such as the yen and the US dollar, should be dealt with appropriately. At the same time, for further development of regionalization of the RMB, China's evolving financial market and financial system need to achieve better integration.

The third approach is to accelerate foreign direct investment (FDI) in RMB. According to the IMF, FDI is an investment in enterprises in foreign countries, and hence the investors can get the right of control and return of profit from the enterprises.

Figure 8.5 shows that in 2005, China's FDI was US$12.26 billion, 1.68% of the world total, and an increase of 123% on the previous year. By the end of 2005, cumulative FDI stood at US$57.2 billion, 0.59% of the world total. We can also see that compared to other developing countries, China has supplied the largest amount of FDI.

However, most of the FDI is in US dollars rather than RMB. RMB has circulated and been widely accepted in some surrounding and nearby countries, including Mongolia, providing a good environment for direct RMB investment in these countries.

The fourth approach is to establish the offshore financial center in Hong Kong. As one of the key international financial centers, Hong Kong has unique economic influence in Asia. This is especially important for the RMB, which is regulated in its exchange and circulation, since Hong Kong boosts the potential for RMB to become a key currency in the region.

RMB has circulated widely and begun to be accepted as a medium of exchange and unit of account in China's neighboring countries, and it has also started to perform some of the primary international currency functions. What is more, the central banks of some countries like the Philippines have announced RMB as one of their foreign exchange reserve currencies. Thus, we can conclude that RMB is now at the beginning of the regionalization stage. Through the above and some other approaches, the regionalization of RMB will gradually improve in the years ahead.

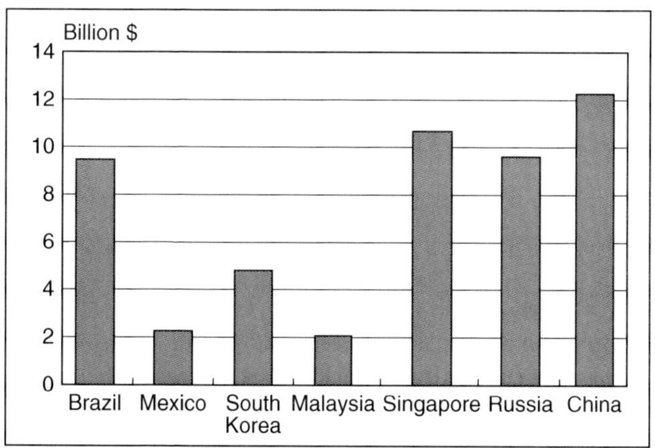

Figure 8.5   FDIs of some developing countries in 2005
Source: Ministry of Commerce of the P. R. China; Authors' calculation.

8.4.3 The long-term goal: Globalization

Globalization is the "high-grade" stage and the ultimate aim of RMB internationalization. Following on from its regionalization, the circulation of RMB breaks through its regional limitations and extends to a more worldwide market at a much larger scale. As a more widely functioning currency, besides the primary functions of medium of exchange and unit of account, the RMB can also perform advanced functions such as store of value in most countries of the world. Reaching this stage will be a long run for the RMB, but there are a number of approaches that can hasten globalization.

One approach is to issue international bonds denominated in RMB. As previously mentioned, the internationalization of RMB can benefit from the issuing of international bonds, and vice versa. This approach is the most important step to realizing the internationalization of RMB. Because issuing government bonds or corporate bonds in overseas financial markets can help RMB financial products to be accepted by foreign institutions as value reserve instruments. What is more, for domestic firms, this offers an international financing channel that is low cost and low risk. China can also improve its purchasing power. To a certain extent, this is the very mechanism by which the US avoids payment crises arising from the huge fiscal and trade deficits.

A second approach is FDI in RMB. FDI is a main form of capital internationalization. In the globalization stage, RMB will certainly be exported to a wider area of the world, and an increasing number of Chinese transnational corporations will participate in international markets. As Figure 8.6 shows, China's FDI has developed rapidly in recent years, particularly between 2004 and 2006. It increased from 5.5 to 21.2 billion US dollar, with a vigorous growth of 284.7% in two years.

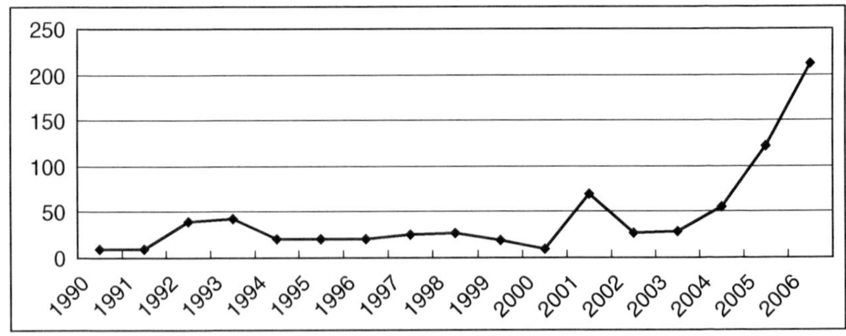

Figure 8.6 FDI flows of China (USD billion)
Source: Ministry of Commercial of the P. R. China; Authors' calculation.

But compared to the US, the scale of China's FDI is still very small. By the end of 2005, the cumulative FDI of the US was US$2,018.2 billion, while that of China stood at US$57.2 billion—less than 3% of that of the US. So, in the long run, China should encourage the transnational activities of its domestic corporations, which are the main investors in RMB assets in the international market. They can help expand the scale of Chinese FDI and in so doing improve the development of the internationalization of RMB.

A third approach is to establish a Chinese "transnational financial group." The overseas branches of commercial banks and other transnational financial institutions can offer support for the international business activity and for the wider circulation of RMB. Hence, a transnational financial group would provide a basic but important boost for the internationalization of RMB. However, at present China's finance market is only a emerging but underdeveloped market, which has little influence in the international market. It is nevertheless important for China to build strength in this area by expanding overseas branches or cross-border mergers and acquisitions in the international financial market.

Following the accession to the WTO, Chinese banks accelerated their transnational operations. The Bank of China (Hong Kong) was established on October 1, 2001, combining the businesses of ten of the 12 banks in Hong Kong originally belonging to the Bank of China Group. It has become a leading commercial banking group in Hong Kong. Another example is the Industrial and Commercial Bank of China Limited (ICBC) which announced that it had acquired a 79.9333% interest in Seng Heng Bank Limited (SHB) on August 29, 2007. The latter is the largest locally owned, independent bank in Macau.

8.5   Conclusion

It is convenient to give our conclusion in the form of the following table, which charts the process required to achieve the internationalization of the RMB (Table 8.3).

The three stages depicted in the table are not necessarily consecutive. For example, the reform of the foreign exchange market of RMB, which is part of stage one, is not the necessary precondition for the cross-border trade in stage two. It seems logically correct to split the process of internationalization of the RMB into the three stages, and it reflects the law of the forming of an international currency. A study of these stages in the two dimensions of currency function and regional extension will help us first understand and then promote the development of the internationalization of RMB.

In summary, the RMB has just started its marathon of internationalization. It is already deep into liberalization, and is at the threshold of

Table 8.3　Process characterizing the internationalization of the RMB

Stages	Regional extension	Currency functions and characters
Liberalization	Circulating freely across the border	• Free convertibility • Stable value • High credit rating in international market
Regionalization	Surrounding and adjacent countries	• In the region • A reserve currency in regional countries
Globalization	Worldwide market and countries	• Medium of exchange and unit of account in international trade • Loan and investment currency in international financial market • Store of value in many countries around the world

Source: Authors' compilation.

regionalization. The effects of the internationalization of the RMB on China's financial industry of China will be long-lasting, profound and will affect all stakeholders. There is still a long way to go and in such a process the innovation and reform of the financial sector in China is one of the most important supporting factors for the internationalization of RMB.

Notes

Ba, Shusong, Professor in the Department of Statistics and Finance, University of Science and Technology of China; research fellow in the Development Research Centre of the State Council of China. E-mail: bashusong@gmail.com.

Wu, Bo, PhD candidate in the Department of Statistics and Finance, University of Science and Technology of China, Hefei, Anhui, China. E-mail: seasunwu@gmail.com.

Yuan, Ping, PhD candidate at the School of Economics, Huazhong University of Science and Technology, Wuhan, Hubei, China; senior manager in the Department of Finance Budget, Bank of Communications.

Wang, Miao, Master's graduate of the Tianjin University of Finance and Economics, Tianjin, China.

Yin, Zhuqing, Master's graduate of the Central University of Finance and Economics, Beijing, China.

The authors acknowledge the Hong Kong Monetary Authority for their support for this research. The authors would also like to thank Professor Guonan Ma for his constructive comments on this chapter.

References

Adam, C., M. Goujon and S. Guillaumont Jeanneney (2004). "The Transactions Demand for Money in the Presence of Currency Substitution: Evidence from Vietnam," *Applied Economics*, Vol. 36, Issue 13, pp. 1461–70.

Aliber, R. Z. (1964). "The Costs and Benefits of the US Role as a Reserve Currency Country," *The Quarterly Journal of Economics*, Vol. 78, No. 3, pp. 442–56.

Aliber, R. Z. (1975). "Exchange Risk, Political Risk, and Investor Demand for External Currency Deposits," *Journal of Money, Credit and Banking*, Vol. 7, No. 2, pp. 161–79.

Areskoug, Kaj (1980). "Exchange Rates and the Currency Denominations of International Bonds," Economica, New Series, Vol. 47, No. 186, pp. 159–63.

Ba Shusong (2003). "Where can RMB Internationalization start?" *Finance and Economy*, No. 8, pp. 14–15.

Ba Shusong (2007). "Expanding the use of Insurance and the Development of Finance Market," *China Finance*, No. 4, pp. 22–3.

Bergsten, C. F. (1975). *The Dilemma of the Dollar: The Economics and Politics of United States International Monetary Policy*, New York: New York University Press.

Bird, G. and R. S. Rajan (2001). "International Currency Taxation and Currency Stabilization in Developing Countries," *The Journal of Development Studies*, Vol. 37, No.3, pp. 21–38.

BIS (Bank for International Settlements) (2003). "Guide to the international financial statistics," BIS Papers, No. 14, February 2003.

Boyer, R. S. and G. H. Kingston (1987). "Currency substitution under finance constraints," *Journal of International Money and Finance*, Vol. 8, pp. 235–50.

Chan, K. S. (2002). "Currency Substitution Between the Hong Kong Dollar and the Renminbi in South China," *Pacific Economic Review*, Vol. 7, Issue 1, pp. 37–50.

Chetty, V. K. (1969). "On Measuring the Nearness of Near-Monies," *American Economic Review*, 59, pp. 226–9.

Cohen, B. H. (2005). "Currency Choice in International Bond Issuance," *BIS Quarterly Review* (June), pp. 53–66.

Douglas, D. W. and P. H. Dybvigr (1983). "Banking Runs, Deposit Insurance and Liquidity," *Journal of Political Economy*, Vol. 91, No. 3, pp. 401–19.

Douglas, D. W. and R. G. Rajan (2001). "Liquidity Risk, Liquidity Creation, and Financial Fragility: A theory of Banking," *Journal of Political Economy*, Vol. 109, pp. 287–327.

Francis, B. B., I. Hasan and D. M. Hunter (2006). "Dynamic Relations between International Equity and Currency Markets: The Role of Currency Order' Flow," *Journal of Business*, Vol. 79, Issue 1, pp. 219–57.

Friedman, M. and A. J. Schwartz (1986). "Has the Government Any Role in Money?" *Journal of Monetary Economics*, Vol. 17, pp. 37–62.

Goldstein, M. and P. Turner (2005). *Controlling currency mismatches in emerging economies*, Washington, DC: Institute for International Economies.

Grubel, H. (2006). "The Economics of Monetary Unions: Traditional and New," Chapter 4, pp. 55–75 in *Regional Economic Integration*, Vol. 12 in the book series *Research in Global Strategic Management*, Bingley, UK: Emerald Group Publishing Ltd.

Heimonen, K. (2001). *Substituting a Substitute Currency: the Case Of Estonia*, Bank of Finland (BOFIT) Discussion Paper No. 11/2001.

Hu, Zhi (2003). "Study on financial opening and RMB internationalization." Xi'an: Xi'an Atlas Press.

Ingram, J. C. (1962). *Regional Payments Mechanisms,* University of North Carolina Press.

Kaufman, G. G. (1996). "Bank Failures, Systemic Risk, and Bank Regulation," *CATO Journal*, (Spring/Summer), Vol. 16, No. 1, pp. 17–46.

Kenen, P. B. (1980), "A model of the US balance of payments," *Journal of International Economics.* Vol. 10, No. 1, pp. 140–1.

Kenen, P. B. (1998). "Monetary Policy in Stage Three: A Review of the Framework Proposed by the European Monetary Institute," *International Journal of Finance & Economics,* Vol. 3 (1), pp. 3–12.

Krugman, P. (1980). "Vehicle Currencies and the Structure of International Exchange," *Journal of Money, Credit and Banking* 12, pp. 513–26.

Lei, Zhiwei (2000). "Theory and Mechanisms of European Monetary Union," Beijing: China Financial Publishing House.

Li, Jing and He, Fan. (2004). "The cost-benefit analysis and approach choice of RMB internationalization." http://www.doctor-cafe.com/detail1.asp?id=2540.

Ma, Ronghua and Rao, Xiaohui (2007). "The Estimation of Demand of Renminbi Abroad," Studies of International Finance, No. 2, pp. 50–59.

McKinnon, R. I. (1993). *The Order of Economic Liberalization: Financial Control in the Transition to a Market Economy,* 2nd edition, Baltimore, Maryland: Johns Hopkins University Press.

Minsky, H. P. (1982). "The Financial Instability Hypothesis: Capitalist Processes and The Behavior of The Economy," in C. P. Kindleberger and J-P. Laffargue (eds), *Financial Crises: Theory, History, and Policy*, Cambridge: Cambridge University Press.

Mundell, R. A. (1961). "A Theory of Optimum Currency Areas," *The American Economic Reviews,* Vol. 51, No. 4, pp. 657–65.

Ramirez-Rojas, C. L. (1985). "Currency substitution in Argentina, Mexico, and Uruguay," International Monetary Fund Staff Papers, Paper No. 32 (4), 629–67.

Remmers H. L. (1980). "A Note on Foreign Borrowing Costs," *Journal of International Business Studies*, Vol. 11, No. 2, pp. 123–34.

Rose, A. K. and C. Engel (2002). "Currency Unions and International Integration," *Journal of Money, Credit and Banking*, Vol. 34, No. 4, pp. 1067–89.

Rose, A. K., B. Lockwood and D. Quah (2000). "One Money, One Market: The Effect of Common Currencies on Trade," *Economic Policy*, Vol. 15, No. 30, pp. 7–45.

Xia, Jianwei, Shi, Anna and Cao, Guangxi (2006). "Research Development of the Currency Mismatching Theory," *Economic Perspectives,* No. 5, pp. 86–90.

Xu, Mingqi (2005). "The experience of Yen internationalization and regionalization of RMB," World Economy Study, No. 12.

9
Internationalization of the Renminbi and Its Implications for Monetary Policy

Haihong Gao

9.1 Introduction

The rise of China and its growing economic influence in the world has sparked consideration of the possibility of Chinese currency becoming internationalized. Although the renminbi (RMB) is currently far from being an international currency, its position internationally is steadily using. In the long term, the currency's internationalization is not only likely but also desirable for China and for the rest of the world.

To begin with, the need for the renminbi's internationalization is rooted in China's increasing importance in the world economy. In the coming years, China's share of global GDP will increase significantly. More importantly, the development of China's financial sector and financial market will accelerate and the capital account will be further liberalized, further strengthening China's financial influence in the world and enhancing use of the renminbi in international transactions.

Secondly, the current dollar standard has both pitfalls and inherent risks. The current situation of over-reliance on the US dollar in the world market has allowed the United States to adopt a policy of "benign neglect" toward foreign exchange markets. As the US continues to register massive deficits in its current account balances and stands as the world's largest net debtor country, the viability of the virtual single key-currency system based on the dollar has been implicitly threatened. The launch of the euro was expected to be a challenge to the dollar's status as an international currency. It is widely believed that the rise of the euro will be a balancing factor in the international monetary system. However, whilst the dollar and euro support the world's two major economic regions, America and Europe, the third major region, Asia, lacks its own principal currency. In fact, the US dollar has dominated the Asian region for decades. Asia is facing risks and losses under the current *de facto* dollar standard system. A third key currency, such as the renminbi, to stand alongside the US dollar and the euro is necessary, and can contribute to the establishment of a stable international monetary system supported by the sound economic policies of the US, the euro area and China.

Thirdly, China's increasing influence on the other economies in East Asia, in terms of trade and investment integration, will become a strong supporting factor in the regional use of the renminbi. And fourthly, the renminbi's internationalization will benefit China as well, by helping to reduce the exchange rate risk facing Chinese firms, strengthening the international competitiveness of Chinese financial institutions, allowing the Chinese monetary authority to reap seigniorage, and preserving the asset value of China's savings. However, internationalization of the renminbi is not cost-free. Moreover, it will challenge the Chinese Central Bank to carry out its monetary policy effectively.

The following section (9.2) discusses the implications of the international use of the renminbi for monetary policy, with the emphasis on how the channels through which the international use of the currency flows impacts on monetary policy. Section 9.3 investigates the relationship between renminbi internationalization and Asian monetary cooperation, suggesting that the regional use of the currency should be the first step towards international use. The chapter concludes with suggestions for the possible path and practical stages for internationalization of the renminbi.

9.2   Implications for monetary policy

The importance of considering the monetary implications of renminbi internationalization lies in the fact that the international use of a currency does impact on monetary policy by way of affecting monetary transmission mechanisms. Historical experience shows that when a country's currency starts being used internationally, it is likely to bring about difficulties for the central banks in controlling aggregates and the intervening inter-bank market. The initial resistant attitude of monetary authorities, such as the German central bank in the 1970s and the Japanese central bank in the 1980s, towards their currencies' internationalization reflected the worry about the negative impact of an increasing international use of the currencies.

It is also important to be aware of the difficulties of addressing the monetary implications of international use of the renminbi. Firstly, it is always difficult to distinguish the impact of the internationalization of a currency from other factors that have an impact on monetary policy – for instance, the development of financial markets, the liberalization of financial sectors and increasing trade and financial integration. Secondly, although it is assumed that the internationalization of currencies has impact on monetary policy mainly by way of affecting the transmission mechanism of monetary policy, a sound and well-established analytical framework is still absent. Thirdly, as far as general conditions for being an international currency are concerned, the renminbi is far from being able to play any role internationally.

The usage of the renminbi in trade invoicing, financial transactions and other official uses, such as foreign reserve, official intervention or currency pegging, is nearly zero, although there is a limited scale of use as a circulating currency in China's neighboring economies. Regardless of its current limited international usage, the renminbi is barely a fully convertible currency. So, any discussion of the relationship between the non-existing internationalized renminbi and China's monetary policy suffers from the problem of absence of data. It is thus difficult to carry out empirical study and give reasonable implications from statistical findings. Therefore, the discussion on this subject is mainly conceptual with regard to the renminbi.

Nevertheless, it is generally believed that the usages of a currency in the form of official reserves, financial transactions, derivatives transaction, trade invoicing and as a pegging or hard-fix anchor outside the country by non-residents and residents have an impact on domestic financial markets. For example, in the case of the euro, an enhanced international role for the currency has become a catalyst for the creation of a deep, broad and liquid financial market in the euro area, which in turn has lowered transaction costs and reduced transmission lags (Duisenberg 2000). The feedback effect also existed when the financial market became more liquid, attractive and convenient for foreign holders of euro assets, and thus increased the international use of the euro. This two-way relationship is likely to occur when the renminbi is widely used by international investors and China's financial markets become more advanced. Since financial markets play an important role in monetary policy transmission where interest rate, exchange rate and wealth effects are the key elements, the internationalization of a currency will have an impact, via domestic financial markets, on the monetary transmission mechanism (Cassola, 2000).

9.2.1   The impact channels

The impact channels of international use of the renminbi on monetary policy are as follows.

Firstly, internationalization of the renminbi would stimulate the development of direct finance by way of increasing its private usage in bond and other debt securities and equity markets, which brings about quicker adjustment of market interest rates than official interest rates. This is because an enlarged usage of the renminbi's financial instruments can help create a liquid and sophisticated financial market. For instance, when the Chinese monetary authority decides to tighten its monetary policy, it usually increases the official rate or reduces base money supply. In the case of interest rate hiking, given price stickiness, market interest rates would react to the policy change. Real short-term exchange rates and even the longer-term exchange rate would rise in response to tight policy. As a result, investment or consumption demand is likely to decline, as are aggregate demand and output. International use of the renminbi will enlarge renminbi debt securities and equity markets and thus enhance the effectiveness of this transmission mechanism. The more liquid the financial market is, the more sensitive market interest rates are in reacting to the official rate changes. In other words, internationalization of the renminbi will reinforce the effectiveness of monetary policy.

However, one key issue related to the interest rate channel in China is its limited degree of interest rate flexibility and its constraints in fully determining market interest rates. There is no effective yield curve carrying sufficient information to the market. The freedom of adjustment by the market rate, retail rate and loan rate in response to changes in the official rate is very limited. So, before taking full advantage of quicker responses in interest rate changes resulting from greater international use of the renminbi, a more liberalized interest rate mechanism should be put in place. Having said that, China's interest rate liberalization has been on the policy agenda, but given the many constrains, there is still a long way to go.

Secondly, internationalization of the renminbi may have impacts on money aggregates and hence weaken the Central Bank's monetary control. International use of the currency can take the form of increased holdings by residents and non-residents of yuan and yuan-denominated deposits and result in currency substitutions in third countries. Such currency substitution may send signals of changes in monetary aggregates and hence impact on the Central Bank's control over money aggregates. For example, when tight monetary policy is carried out and the interest rate rises so as to control inflation, demand for the renminbi in third countries will increase and thus enlarge the money aggregates. Therefore, the effectiveness of tight monetary policy might be weakened.

However, to what degree the impact of international use of a currency has on domestic money aggregates lacks clear-cut explanations. Furthermore, some mitigating factors do exist, especially when the following two aspects are considered.

One factor is related to the significance of monetary impacts of non-residents and residents holdings of domestic currency. From the experience of the euro area, non-resident holdings of euro-denominated deposits had a weak link to the money demand. This was because non-resident euro deposit holdings did not affect the information content of broad monetary aggregate (M3) used by the European Central Bank and hence was unlikely to have direct impact on stability of monetary demand in the euro area. The resident holdings of euros in third countries might impact on monetary aggregates because it was part of M3. However, the coverage of M3 had a wide range of financial assets in the euro area. The share of resident euro holdings abroad was relatively small in M3 and its impact on monetary aggregates was limited (Cassola, 2000).

Generally, historical experiences suggest that for economies with a sufficient large scale, like the euro area and the US, their currencies used in third countries would be only a relatively small part of domestic monetary aggregates, and thus unlikely to have significant impact on domestic monetary control.

Another factor lies in the fact that the central banks are, after all, in control of domestic credit and interest rates. The reason that the Japanese monetary authority changed its attitude towards the yen internationalization in the early 1990s was largely due to the fact that the Bank of Japan finally realized that the impact of flows of the yen in third countries had limited impact on domestic monetary policy, because the external flow of yen was determined by domestic monetary policy and not vice versa.

Thirdly, internationalization of the renminbi will allow increased access to the currency in third countries and hence is likely to invite arbitrage activities when monetary policy changes. In the case of tightening of monetary policy, an interest rate hike would cause currency appreciation, given the free flow of capital across the border. If the interest rate or spot exchange the rate deviates from the anticipated interest rate and exchange rate, or the real exchange rate deviates from the nominal exchange rate – which, in the case of monetary tightening, is presumed to be favorable for renminbi assets holdings – international investors may have the chance for interest rate arbitrage by buying more renminbi assets. The feedback effect also exists. Changes to monetary policy in other countries may also impact on interest rate and exchange rate arbitrage because they change the interest rate differentials between foreign countries and the home country, as well as changing expected exchange rate levels. In the short term, the consequence of interest rate arbitrage is likely to be short-term speculative capital flows and disturbance to central banks' monetary operations. In the long term, however, arbitrage would narrow the interest differentials between countries and between currencies, which would have an offset effect on domestic monetary policy changes.

Again, the intensity of the effects of interest rate arbitrage depends on the degree of flexibility of interest rates and exchange rates, and on the degree of capital account liberalization. On the one hand, it is fair to say that the basic conditions for large-scale arbitrage against the renminbi do not exist as things stand at the moment, given the limited flexibility of the interest rate and exchange rate and the absence of full convertibility of capital account transactions. Liberalization of capital transactions is indeed on the policy agenda, but short-term flows are still basically controlled, which to a large degree limits the arbitrage activities against the renminbi.

Fourthly, internationalization of the renminbi can also have an impact on the effectiveness of monetary policy via wealth effects. A decline in the official interest rate aimed at stimulating investment spending will induce a hike in asset prices by increasing earnings from holding renminbi assets. Correspondingly, the market value of firms will go up, so firms will have more incentives for investment spending. In such cases, international use of the renminbi will allow extra funds to flow into the renminbi equity market and hence enlarge the wealth effects of loose monetary policy.

Lastly, international use of the renminbi can take the form of growth of a euro- yuan market, even though China's capital controls are in place. The development of the euro-dollar market began during the time when the US government enforced restrictions on international lending and investments in the 1960s. A similar experience happened in the 1970s when the German monetary authority restricted non-residents from issuing Deutsche mark bonds, such that the euro-DM market developed outside Germany grew rapidly. Why did they do this? The most important reason was the real and fundamental factors in terms of an enlarged economy and growing influence in their international trade, investment and financial transactions. Such experience suggests that where real factors grow strongly enough, a currency market, in this case the euro-currency market, would eventually come to exist (as the euro-market did in 1999). What is relevant for monetary implications is that the existence of a euro-currency market might raise the concern that it would have a disturbing effect on the central bank's monetary control. The German government used to worry about arbitrage transactions between the domestic market and the euro-DM market, because it might place extra burden on its monetary policy, in particular on intervention in the inter-bank markets. The Japanese government used to worry that arbitrage between domestic and euro-yen markets could disturb its policy, for instance complicating its intervention in the bill and call markets and its "window guidance." Hence, the Japanese monetary authority resisted internationalizing the use of the yen over a long period of time before the 1990s. However, with the recognition that the interest rates and transaction amounts in the euro-yen market were determined by the domestic monetary policy and not vice versa, the Bank of Japan progressively changed its attitude and the "window guidance" was officially terminated in 1991 (Iwami and Sato, 1996).

9.2.2 Does renminbi circulation in neighboring economies matter?

With the rapid development of China's foreign trade, greater amounts of the renminbi are flowing out of Mainland China which leads to overseas circulation and exchange of the currency in neighboring areas. The major channels for offshore renminbi circulation include: Mainland China tourist and family visits abroad, Hong Kong being the most attractive place for mainlanders; the use of the renminbi in cross-border trade; capital outflows resulting from Chinese capital project-development contracts and Chinese Central Bank loans; and other channels such as the Qualified Domestic Investment Institutions (QDII) scheme that officially allows capital to flow out of China through capital account.

However, since the renminbi is not a fully convertible currency, it cannot be deposited in the banking systems of most neighboring economies.

Table 9.1   Renminbi inflows to Hong Kong in 2004 (in RMB million)

	Item	Through bank	Total
RMB inflow	New deposit	11,233	
	RMB bought from merchants and individuals	2,634	138,720
	Mainland card spending in Hong Kong	2,930	

Source: Hong Kong Monetary Authority; author's compilation.

This causes the problem of unavailability of data and the difficulty of reaching a reliable estimate of the scale of renminbi circulating in neighboring countries. There are a number of estimates of the size of the renminbi in circulation overseas; however, the figures differ considerably, ranging from CYN41 billion to CYN313 billion. For statistical reasons, a better way to carry out an estimate is to focus on the renminbi business in the Hong Kong banking system, which was launched jointly by Mainland China and Hong Kong SAR in February 2004. However, a problem with the Hong Kong data is a possible underestimation of the actual amount of the renminbi in circulation. Apparently, there is still a big gap between the flows through banks and other means of renmimbi exchange in Hong Kong. As shown in Table 9.1, total renminbi inflows to Hong Kong were about CYN138.72 billion in 2004, of which only 12.1% involved the banking sector.

The difficulty of quantifying the circulation of the renminbi outside China creates a problem in estimating the potential impact on China's monetary policy. The major concern at present is the risk of a sudden flow of the renminbi back to Mainland China, which is to a large extent determined by changes in renminbi appreciation expectations and changes in the monetary policy of China's Central Bank.

9.3   Relationship between renminbi internationalization and Asian monetary cooperation

China has been actively involved with the regional monetary arrangement since the outbreak of the financial crisis in 1997–8. For instance, China has become an important fund supplier of the bilateral swap arrangements (BSAs) under the Chiang Mai Initiative (CMI) framework and has also engaged in multiple policy dialog and economic surveillance mechanisms in the region. The involvement of the renminbi in the regional monetary arrangement has been strengthened, in part by acting as a payment currency in the BSAs and being the denominating currency in bond issuance. Moreover, the circulation of renminbi in neighboring countries has increased significantly. Some Asian countries, like India and the Philippines, use the renminbi as one component of the currency basket or in the official reserve portfolio. It is widely recognized that the renminbi's role as a regional currency has begun to take place, and this will have a significant impact on the process of the currency's internationalization.

As far as Asian regional monetary arrangements are concerned, what matters for the strategy of the renminbi's internationalization is the degree to which the currency is involved. So far, the existing monetary arrangements in Asia remain at a low level in terms of institutional framework. This gives China greater flexibility in originating routes for the renminbi's internationalization at the regional level. In other words, the process of internationalization of the renminbi will start with the currency's internationalization in East Asia.

9.3.1   The renminbi and regional self-supporting mechanisms

Currently, the CMI is the most important regional arrangement in the monetary sphere in East Asia. China is the second biggest contributor to the BSAs under the initiative. By the end of July 2007, China had signed BSAs with Japan, Korea, Thailand, Malaysia, the Philippines and Indonesia, respectively, totaling up to US$23.5 billion (Table 9.2).[1]

Table 9.2   Bilateral swap arrangements between China and other ASEAN+3 countries (as of July 2007)

BSA	One/Two way*	Currency	Total size	Status
China–Thailand	One-way	USD/Baht	US$2 billion	Concluded 6 Dec 2001 Expired 5 Dec 2004
China–Japan	Two-way	renminbi/yen yen/renminbi	US$6 billion	Concluded 28 Mar 2002
China–Korea	Two-way	renminbi/won won/renminbi	US$ 8 billion	Concluded 24 Jun 2002
China–Malaysia	One-way	US$/ringgit	US$1.5 billion	Concluded 9 Oct 2002
China–Philippines	One-way	renminbi/peso	US$2 billion	Concluded 29 Aug 2003 Amended 30 Apr 2007
China–Indonesia	One-way	US$/rupiah	US$4 billion	Concluded 30 Dec 2003 Amended 17 Oct 2006

Note: *The two-way BSA is the bilateral swap arrangement where each party can request the other to enter into the swap transaction to provide liquidity support when necessary to overcome balance of payments difficulties in the specified currency up to the agreed amount. In a one-way BSA, for instance, should Indonesia require short-term liquidity assistance, the country may propose a short-term loan to China through a swap mechanism between the Indonesian rupiah against the US dollar, up to a total of US$4 billion.

Source: Bank of Japan; author's compilation.

However, the major currency used in the arrangements has been dominated by the US dollar. The renminbi has been involved with just a few, with China–Japan, China–Korea and China–the Philippines among them. The limited usage of local currencies in the BSAs brings about extra risks for both fund providers and receivers. The ongoing discussion on multi-lateralization of the BSAs and the undertaking of a reserve pooling program will enable the CMI to become a more effective mechanism, with enlargement of the swap funding availability coupled with a collective prompt activation and joint decision-making process. China's currency will hopefully be one of the key currencies in the new multilateral swap arrangement.

9.3.2   Renminbi and the regional bond market

Another regional arrangement in the financial area is the development of the regional bond market. The second stage of the Asian Bond Fund (ABF2) was launched in June 2005 with seed money of up to US$2 billion. While bonds issued by sovereign and quasi-sovereign issuers under ABF1 were denominated only in the US dollar, ABF2 allows local currencies to denominate bond issuances in the eight markets, namely those of China, Hong Kong, Indonesia, Korea, Malaysia, the Philippines, Singapore and Thailand (EMEAP. 2006). The renminbi is correspondingly used in the China Fund issuance.

Given the limited size and immaturity of the Chinese domestic bond market, Mainland China should take full advantage of the well-developed market in Hong Kong to promote China's involvement in the development of the regional bond market. The recent issuance of government bonds denominated in the renminbi in Hong Kong can be seen as the first step in promoting the renminbi's involvement in the bond market outside Mainland China.

9.3.3   Renminbi and the regional exchange rate arrangement

Apart from the yen, which remains an independent floating currency, all the emerging economies in East Asia now have a similar exchange rate policy framework. The policy authorities of these economies, including China, adjust their dollar exchange rates with changes in the bilateral exchange rates of currencies in their baskets, which comprise the dollar, euro and yen, in order to keep their nominal or real effective exchange rates stable. This incurs the need for them to coordinate their exchange rate policies so as to avoid competitive devaluation among themselves. With a new regime in place, and its growing economic influence, China holds a key position in exchange rate policy coordination.

There are, in fact, several proposals circulating regarding regional currency arrangements for East Asia. The Asian Monetary Unit (AMU) proposed by Ogawa and Shimizu (2005), or the Asian Currency Unit (ACU) proposed by the Asian Development Bank (ADB), allows their respective units to serve as an index of volatility among the concerned countries' exchange rates.

This type of basket arrangement actually follows the footsteps of European monetary integration. Instead of creating a basket of outside currencies, the participating countries create the ACU, a numeraire, which will only consist of their own currencies. The difficult part of the proposal is the determination of weights for each currency in the basket; for example, what elements should be used to determine the weights of the individual currencies? As far as the trade share and GDP are concerned, the renminbi and the Japanese yen would dominate the basket. However, if financial transactions and some institutional elements, such as capital account liberalization, are taken into account, the Japanese yen would occupy the largest share in the ACU. Since there has been no consensus on the solutions to the technical difficulties with the ACU, its planned launch by the ADB in May 2006 was postponed. Nevertheless, the acceptance of the idea of the ACU will be largely dependent on agreement among the major players, such as China and Japan, on various details regarding the creation of the ACU. As far as China is concerned, as long as the country's growth is sustainable and its capital account continues to be liberalized, the likelihood of the renminbi's share in the regional currency arrangement growing is very high.

9.3.4   Renminbi and the yen

One key element with regard to China's role in regional monetary cooperation is the relationship between the renminbi and the Japanese yen. China's relationship with Japan is the key to the smoothness of the process of renminbi internationalization. Japan is no longer keen on the yen's internationalization. Instead, Japan is pursuing a regional exchange rate arrangement in which the yen is fully involved, such as the G3 pegging basket proposal and the AMU proposal. Japan's enthusiasm for regional monetary cooperation to some extent reflects the fact that the country is sensitive to its relationship with the rising China. China's continuing rapid growth and development will surely reinforce its economic influence in the region. The issue of the relationship between the yuan and the yen will inevitably stand out. How to reconcile the roles of the two key currencies? With regard to the relationship of the two currencies in the East Asia region, market forces will be the determining factor. However, the strategic consideration of policymakers is equally important.

9.4   Conclusion: The possible path for internationalizing the renminbi

Is there any model that China could follow in internationalizing the renminbi? The US dollar, the dominant currency in the world economy, and the euro, created as an alternative to the dollar, are the two successful examples of currency internationalization. However, the two currencies have experienced different routes to becoming an international currency. We roughly classify the two examples as: the German model and the American model.

The German model refers to the approach that Germany adopted in establishing the status of the Deutsche mark (before 1999) and the euro (since 1999) as the second most important international currency. The model can be viewed as the two-step approach: first, join the regional arrangement, known as the European Currency Unit (ECU), and second, create a new single regional currency to replace individual member countries' currencies, including the Deutsche Mark. The international position of the new currency, the euro, has been strengthening significantly since 1999, reinforcing the Euro area as the second largest economic bloc in the world. What applies to China, is that, given the fact that such an approach brings about the eventual elimination of individual currencies, China would be likely to involve itself in a fully pledged monetary union in East Asia such that the renminbi would be self-eliminated and ultimately replaced by a new, single Asian currency.

The American model is basically a monopoly one, meaning that the US dollar, as a key currency, plays a dominant role independently and globally. The status of the US dollar as an international currency was determined by economic and political factors. Unlike the euro, which was initiated through an institutional arrangement, the international position of the US dollar has been driven mainly by market forces since the collapse of the Bretton Woods system in the 1970s. In opting to follow the American model, China would need to pursue a strategy that results in the renminbi being used as a totally independent international currency, presumably parallel to the US dollar, the euro and, perhaps, the yen.

At the moment, it is far too premature to say which model, the American or the German model, is more suitable for China. The choice of alternative models is, of course, determined by China's own interest, which is clearly dependent on the perceived costs and benefits to China. However, external factors are equally important. One of the key conditions for being an international currency is acceptance by other countries. Moreover, the relationship between China and Japan is crucial in the process of internationalization of the renminbi. The domestic conditions for the role of the renminbi being used in international market are not well prepared at the current stage. Therefore, the feasible road map for China to adopt is to encourage the renminbi's regional utilization first by way of both market need and policy motivation, and then, gradually, to move the renminbi towards wider, international usage. A more radical way of internationalizing the currency would very likely have high risks and negative impact on China's economy.

The success of achieving an internationalized renminbi is dependent on market forces and on well-designed routes and sound strategic thinking. The process of kick-starting internationalization of the renminbi can begin by boosting usage of the currency by denominating cross-border trade and financial transactions in renminbi. Region-wide usage of the currency would be the natural outcome of its initial use by China's immediate neighbors. Renminbi regionalization can also result from a policy-driven process which includes, for example: issuing renminbi bonds (government bonds and private firm bonds); encouraging usage of the renminbi as the invoicing currency in China's Free Trade Areas (FTAs); signing up to currency swap (bilateral and multilateral) agreements using the renminbi as the settlement currency under the mechanism of the CMI; and ensuring that the renminbi will be actively involved in a regional monitoring system. In the medium to long term, renminbi regionalization will be an inevitable step towards use of the renminbi as a fully internationalized, vehicle currency.

Parallel developments domestically are also critical for the success of renminbi internationalization, including full convertibility; greater flexibility of the renminbi exchange rate regime; a strengthened domestic financial system in general and banking sector in particular; well-developed domestic money, bond and equity markets; an established advanced settlement system; and necessary adjustment of the legal system.

Apart from the economic aspects, political elements are equally important for achieving renminbi internationalization, which to a large degree depends on domestic harmony, Japan's reaction to China's increased influence in Asia, and the United States' reaction to China's rise in the world.

Notes

Professor and Director of the International Finance Section, Institute of World Economics and Polities, Chinese Academy of Social Sciences. The chapter has benefited from the valuable discussions of participants at the conference on "Currency Internationalization: International Experiences and Implications for the renminbi," organized by the Hong Kong Monetary Authority in Hong Kong on 15–16 October 2007. The author would like to thank Dr Yongidng Yu for his inspiring comments and Dr Zhongmin Li for his research assistance. The author is also indebted to Dr Wensheng Peng for his helpful suggestions on refining the chapter. Any errors are the author's alone.

1. By comparison, Japan's BSAs with its partners totaled US$75 billion.

References

Cassola, Nuno (2000). "Monetary Policy Implications of the International role of the Euro," International Financial Markets and the Implications for Monetary and Financial Stability, BIS Conference Papers No. 8, pp. 75–91. http://www.bis.org/publ/confer08d.pdf.

Duisenberg, Willem F. (2000). "The International Role of the Euro," Keynote address at the European Banking Congress, Frankfurt, November 17, 2000.

EMEAP (2006). "Working Group on Financial Market: Review of the Asian Bond Fund 2 Initiative, June 2006." http://www.emeap.org/ABF/ABF2ReviewReport.pdf.

Iwami, Toru and Kiyotaka Sato (1996). "The internationalization of the yen: with an emphasis on East Asia," Journal: International Journal of Social Economics, Vol. 23, Issue 10/11, 192–208.

Ogawa, E. and Shimizu J. (2005). "A Deviation Measurement for Coordinated Exchange Rate Policies in East Asia," RIETI Discussion Paper Series 05-E-017.

10
Impact of the Renminbi Exchange Rate on Asian Currencies

Chang Shu

10.1   Introduction

With the growing importance of the Chinese economy, it is widely believed that China's currency is having increasing impact on Asian currencies. Foreign exchange traders and analysts frequently attribute movements of Asian currencies to those of the renminbi.[1] A China dominance hypothesis has surfaced in academic research papers, suggesting that the sheer size of the Chinese economy will ensure that the renminbi will gradually play a central role in the region, and may become an anchor currency in Asia (Colavecchio and Funke, 2007; Greenaway et al., 2006). The knock-on effects that the renminbi can have on regional currencies have also been noted by policymakers worldwide. Yam (2007), for example, remarks that a large (stepwise) appreciation of the renminbi against the US dollar would trigger substantial movements in the exchange rates of developing economies, particularly those in Asia.

While the influence of the renminbi on Asian currencies has been frequently referred to, there have been few formal studies to examine the issue. One study by Colavecchio and Funke (2007) examines the spill-over effects from the renminbi to Asian currencies in the onshore and offshore forward markets. However, there does not appear to be any work undertaken on the spot market.

This study modifies a method introduced by Frankel and Wei (1994) to examine the spot exchange rate data with a view to addressing empirically the following two questions: Has there clearly been an impact from the renminbi on Asian currencies in recent years? Has the renminbi displaced the US dollar as the dominant driver of Asian currencies?

This chapter is organized as follows. Section 10.2 discusses possible reasons for the renminbi to drive Asian currencies. Section 10.3 follows the Frankel and Wei (1994) framework to examine empirically how Asian currencies are affected by the renminbi along with a number of major currencies including the US dollar, Japanese yen and euro. Section 10.4

discusses policy implications of the empirical findings on developments of exchange rate regimes in the region and financial stability globally.

10.2 Reasons for the renminbi's regional impact

The majority of Asian economies, mainland China included, have had a long-standing exchange rate policy of closely following the US dollar, *de jure* or *de facto*. In an earlier study by Frankel and Wei (1994), the US dollar is shown to dominate all other currencies in its influence on Asian currencies between the period 1979–92. The dollar standard broke down for a short period during the Asian crisis in 1997–8, but was quickly re-established by 2002 as the day-to-day volatility of Asian countries' exchange rates against the dollar became negligible (McKinnon and Schnabl, 2004). These findings are corroborated by Benassy-Quere and Coeure (2003) who identify a number of Asian currencies, including the Korean won, Philippines peso, Singapore dollar and Thai baht, as being pegged to the US dollar, which is at variance with the International Monetary Fund's official classification of these countries' exchange rate regimes.

There is, however, a sense among many quarters that developments in the renminbi exchange rate have been influencing regional currencies in recent years. The influence was even detected before the major exchange rate regime reform that took place in July 2005. Ho et al. (2005) noted that due to rising speculation on renminbi appreciation, the renminbi non-deliverable forward rates affected the spot rates of Asian currencies in 2003–4.

The impact of the renminbi spot rate on Asian currencies first became visible after July 2005, when China shifted away from a strict peg to the US dollar. With a reference to a basket and a daily trading band of ±0.3%, or ±0.5% since May 2006, around the central parity against the US dollar, the renminbi has been on an appreciating trend against the US dollar, and its volatility has generally been rising since the reform. During the same period, the majority of the Asian currencies also appreciated against the US dollar, with the exception of the Hong Kong dollar and New Taiwan dollar (Figure 10.1). Among the other currencies, the Indonesian ruphiah only saw a very modest gain of less than 1%. Four currencies – the Korean won, Malaysian ringgit, Philippines peso and Singapore dollar – appreciated by 10–13%. The Thai baht recorded the largest gain of over 20%. While some of these currencies were following an appreciating trend even before July 2005, Figure 10.1 shows that the changes in the renminbi exchange rate regime seem to have precipitated their further appreciation.

This influence is reflected by a general rise in bivariate correlation between the renminbi and individual Asian currencies after July 2005 (Table 10.1). The Malaysian ringgit, which followed the renminbi in de-linking with the US dollar, has the highest correlation with the renminbi with a correlation coefficient of over 0.9. As noted above, the Hong Kong dollar and

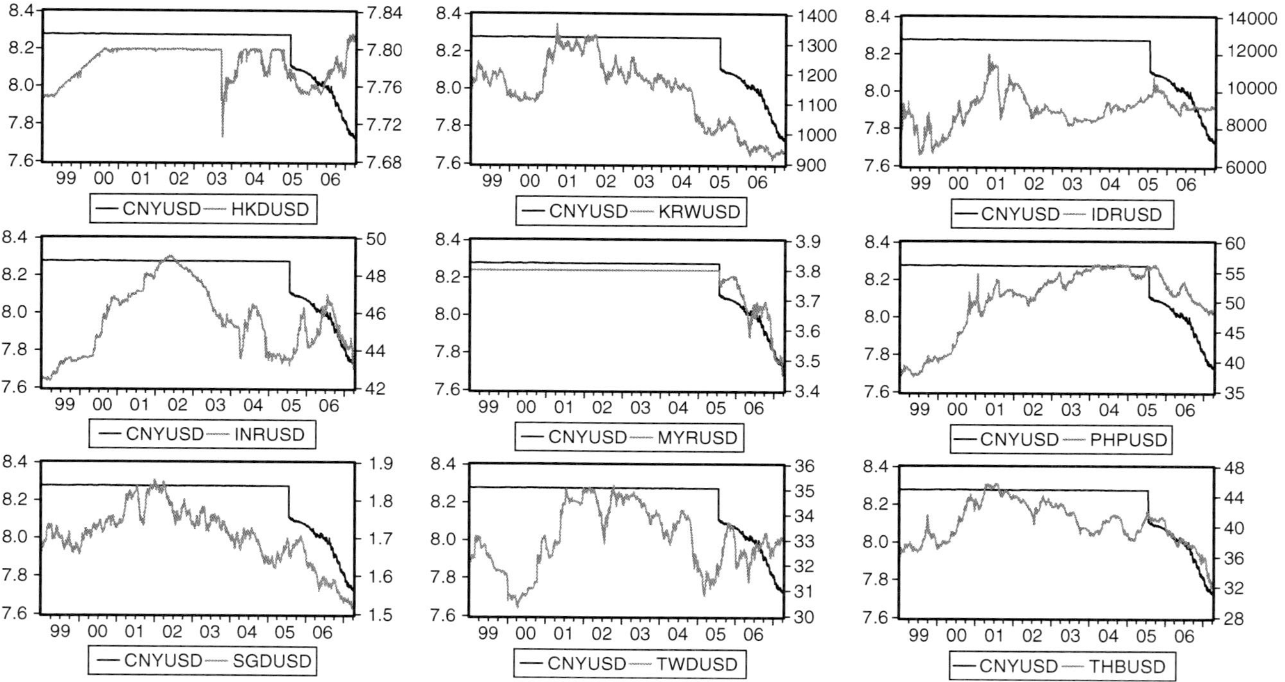

Figure 10.1   Co-movements between renminbi and Asian currencies
Source: Bloomberg; Author's compilation.

Table 10.1 Correlation between the renminbi and Asian currencie

	Before reform (5/1/1999–20/7/2005)	After reform (21/7/2005–2/4/2007)
Hong Kong dollar	–0.339	–0.875
Indian rupee	–0.392	0.118
Indonesian rupiah	–0.436	0.625
Korean won	–0.040	0.764
Malaysian ringgit	–0.186	0.927
Philippine peso	–0.730	0.890
Singapore dollar	–0.083	0.893
New Taiwan dollar	–0.453	–0.160
Thai baht	–0.391	0.955

Source: Bloomberg; Author's calculations.

New Taiwan dollar defied the appreciation trend in the region, and have been negatively correlated with the renminbi in the period since the renminbi exchange rate reform.

The correlation with the renminbi may be the result of government policies and/or market forces. Asian economies have often pursued an export-driven strategy for economic growth. It has been suggested that Asian currencies may be moving away from a dollar bloc to tracking a broad-basket effective exchange rate in order to maintain competitiveness of their exports (Kawai, 2002; Ho et al., 2005). If this is the case, the renminbi may have started to feature in the currency baskets that Asian economies track because of the competitive relationship between China and these economies in export markets. Branson and Healy (2005) show that the structure of the China's exports, both in terms of market and commodity distributions, is similar to that of a number of Asian economies. Asian economies therefore have the incentive to keep a close watch on renminbi movements in managing their currencies in order not to lose competitiveness against China exports.

Apart from government policies, market forces may also give rise to the renminbi's influence. The importance of the Chinese economy may lead the market to believe that the Asian currencies should follow the renminbi movements. In addition, some Asian currencies such as the Singapore dollar have been used as proxies for renminbi trading in the global foreign exchange markets (Yam, 2007). In view of the China's large trade surpluses, there have been wide expectations of renminbi appreciation in recent years. However, as the renminbi is unconvertible and access to renminbi trading is restricted, it is difficult for international investors to position themselves to directly benefit from renminbi appreciation. Under the circumstances, there are reports of the practice in the currency market of using Asian currencies as proxies to take a position for renminbi appreciation, on expectations that these currencies will follow suit if the renminbi appreciates.

10.3 Empirical analysis

Following some cursory observations of co-movements between the renminbi and Asian currencies, this section examines more formally whether the renminbi has an influence on Asian currencies by estimating a modified version of the method introduced by Frankel and Wei (1994).

10.3.1 Methodology and data

The Frankel and Weil (1994) framework takes the general form of:

$$\Delta e_j = \alpha_0 + \sum_{i=1}^{k} \alpha_i \Delta e_i . \tag{1}$$

In equation (1), e_j and e_is are, respectively, exchange rates of the currency under study and those which might influence it. They are measured against a common currency, typically the Swiss franc. A significant α_i would suggest that currency i has an impact on e_j, and α_i is interpreted as the importance or weight of currency i in the currency basket. The sum of the α_i s should be close to one if all the relevant currencies are included in the basket currency j is targeting. The approach has been widely used in estimating weights in a currency basket and for classifying *de facto* exchange rate regimes, including a number of applications on Asian currencies. For example, Eichengreen (2006) and Frankel (2007) apply it in an attempt to unveil the composition of the currency basket in the new renminbi exchange rate regime. McKinnon and Schnabl's (2004) application is to demonstrate the evolving role of the US dollar in influencing Asian currencies after the 1997–8 financial crisis.

For this study, we focus on the impact of the renminbi and G3 currencies on Asian currencies, and thus estimate the equation in the following form:

$$\Delta e_{Asiancurrency/SwissFranc} = \alpha_0 + \alpha_1 \Delta e_{Usd/SwissFranc} + \alpha_2 \Delta e_{Yen/SwissFranc}$$
$$+ \alpha_3 \Delta e_{Eur/SwissFranc} + \alpha_4 \Delta e_{Rmb/SwissFranc} \tag{2}$$

The exchange rates are taken logs and transformed into first differences. For the estimation, daily data for nine Asian currencies between 1 January 1999 and 2 April 2007, obtained from Bloomberg and CEIC, are used. The sample is split into two periods – before and after the renminbi exchange rate reform in July 2005 – to investigate whether the role of the renminbi has changed over time.

As the first pass of the estimation, the renminbi exchange rate against the Swiss franc is directly used. The results are not reasonable. In a number of cases, including the Hong Kong dollar which is known to be pegging to the US dollar, the coefficient on the US dollar, α_1, is not statistically significant, and/or carries a wrong sign. The results may be explained by the high correlation between the renminbi and US dollar, even after the *de jure* de-linking of the two. Peng and Shu (2006) show that significance was still attached to the stability of the RMB/US$ exchange rate for their sample period of between end-July 2005 and 2006 Q2. Eichengreen (2006) and Frankel (2007) also reveal that although declining, the weight of the US dollar remained very high in 2006 in the currency basket the renminbi had been tracking.

To circumvent the multi-collinearity problem, we ran an auxiliary regression of the changes in the renminbi on those of the US dollar. The residual from this regression is taken to be renminbi movements independent of the US dollar. We therefore use this residual to represent the renminbi exchange rate in estimating equation (2).[2] In this modified framework, α_4 can still indicate how much the renminbi exchange rate influences movements of an Asian currency, but it can no longer be interpreted as the weight in a currency basket. As will be seen later in our estimation results, the α_i s do not sum up to one as in the original framework of Frankel and Wei (1994).

Following the majority of the studies using the approach, the equation is estimated by the Ordinary Least Squares (OLS). However, there could be a simultaneity problem as conceivably the renminbi exchange rate is also influenced by Asian currencies, and hence endogenous to the system, leading to biased estimates. To check this, we undertook the Hausman specification test. The results showed that for the periods both before and after the exchange rate regime reform, the renminbi can be treated as an exogenous variable in the equation, and thus the OLS can be used for the estimation.[3] These findings may be explained intuitively. While the renminbi exchange rate is said to be set according to a basket of currencies, the US dollar is found to have a dominant weight (Eichengreen, 2006; Frankel, 2007). Other currencies, including the euro, Japanese yen and other Asian currencies, do not appear to have a strong impact on renminbi movements.

10.3.2 Estimation results

Tables 10.2 and 10.3 report the estimation results for two sample periods – before and after the exchange rate reform. The overall results point to a clear rise in the importance of the renminbi in influencing other currencies after the regime shift. The US dollar continues to have a dominant effect on Asian currencies, and the Japanese yen is also a component in currency baskets that many Asian currencies track. We now discuss the details of the estimation results for the two periods.

Before the exchange rate regime reform: The estimation over the period shows that among the nine currencies, the Hong Kong dollar and Malaysian ringgit were strict dollar peggers. The coefficient on the US dollar is almost

Table 10.2 Asian currencies' regimes before the renminbi exchange rate reform (1 January 1999–20 July 2005)

	Constant α_0	Dollar α_1	Yen α_2	Euro α_3	Rmb α_4	Adjusted R^2
Hong Kong dollar	0.000 (0.340)	0.994*** (536.921)	0.005*** (3.227)	0.004** (2.156)	0.002 (0.015)	0.998
Indian rupee	0.001 (0.354)	0.987*** (130.578)	0.022*** (3.330)	0.032* (1.858)	0.459 (0.371)	0.951
Indonesian rupiah	0.011 (0.444)	0.879*** (16.920)	0.188*** (3.579)	0.083 (0.674)	–13.295 (–1.438)	0.314
Korean won	–0.008 (–0.785)	0.851*** (39.795)	0.177*** (9.022)	0.014 (0.330)	–1.397 (–0.373)	0.706
Malaysian ringgit	0.000 (0.017)	1.001*** (2151.299)	0.000 (–0.641)	–0.001 (–1.558)	–0.075 (–0.950)	1.000
Philippine peso	0.021* (1.820)	0.920*** (50.471)	0.080*** (2.892)	0.032 (0.773)	–3.512 (–0.986)	0.672
Singapore dollar	0.001 (0.252)	0.723*** (60.609)	0.201*** (19.024)	0.048 (1.623)	1.373 (0.806)	0.877
New Taiwan dollar	0.000 (–0.047)	0.934*** (82.627)	0.040*** (3.255)	–0.007 (–0.291)	–0.226 (–0.111)	0.890
Thai baht	0.009 (1.048)	0.786*** (45.052)	0.178*** (11.569)	0.045 (1.209)	0.960 (0.319)	0.774

Note: t-values are in ( ). *, ** and *** indicate that coefficients are significant at the 10%, 5% and 1% levels respectively.
Source: Author's estimation.

one in the equation for the two currencies, and so is the adjusted R^2. Apart from these two officially pegged to the US dollar, other Asian currencies were also heavily influenced by the US dollar. In the equation for the Indian rupee and Indonesian rupiah, the US dollar also has a coefficient close to one. The coefficient for the US dollar, α_1, is around 0.9 for the Korean won, Philippine peso and New Taiwan dollar. The US dollar's influence on the Singapore dollar and Thai baht was slightly smaller, with a weight of around 0.7–0.8.

The Japanese yen's influence was noticeably smaller, but present in a number of cases. It did not impact on the Malaysian ringgit. In the equation for the Hong Kong dollar, α_2 is somehow statistically significant, but its magnitude is too small to exert any material impact. α_2 is significant in the other seven equations, and around 0.2 for the Indonesian rupiah, Singapore dollar and Thai baht – higher than for other Asian currencies. The euro virtually had no impact on Asian currencies.

The renminbi did not show any impact during this period, with its coefficient, α_4, being statistically insignificant in all the equations.

Table 10.3 Asian currencies' regimes after the renminbi exchange rate reform (21 July 2005–2 April 2007)

	Constant α_0	Dollar α_1	Yen α_2	Euro α_3	Rmb α_4	Adjusted R^2
Hong Kong dollar	0.001 (0.917)	0.990*** (420.209)	0.009*** (3.520)	–0.002 (–0.333)	0.051*** (4.934)	0.998
Indian rupee	–0.001 (–0.086)	0.870*** (25.732)	0.086* (1.942)	0.038 (0.4093)	0.388*** (3.695)	0.763
Indonesian rupiah	–0.016 (–0.578)	0.846*** (11.211)	0.032 (0.474)	0.015 (0.094)	0.334** (2.081)	0.394
Korean won	–0.025 (–1.528)	0.832*** (20.756)	0.134*** (2.898)	–0.019 (–0.190)	1.062*** (12.994)	0.660
Malaysian ringgit	–0.022** (–2.254)	0.948*** (36.721)	0.028 (1.180)	0.016 (0.254)	0.210 (1.138)	0.866
Philippine peso	–0.031** (–2.253)	0.924*** (25.527)	–0.005 (–0.111)	0.023 (0.247)	0.198 (1.331)	0.747
Singapore dollar	–0.021*** (–2.616)	0.644*** (32.472)	0.186*** (7.696)	0.272*** (5.154)	0.585*** (4.660)	0.864
New Taiwan dollar	0.006 (0.516)	0.888*** (26.080)	0.113*** (3.070)	–0.043 (–0.557)	0.672*** (5.959)	0.797
Thai baht	–0.060*** (–2.717)	0.724*** (18.465)	0.216*** (3.724)	0.115 (0.847)	0.683*** (4.510)	0.489

Note: t-values are in ( ). *, ** and *** indicate that coefficients are significant at the 10%, 5% and 1% levels respectively.
Source: Author's estimation.

Goodness of fit is generally reasonable for most of the equations. Apart from the two US dollar peggers with adjusted R^2 close to 1, the adjusted R^2 for other equations is mostly between 0.71 and 0.95. However, the equation for the Indonesian rupiah has relatively low explanatory power with its adjusted R^2 being 0.31.

After the renminbi exchange rate reform: The Hong Kong dollar is the only currency whose regime has remained unchanged from before the reform period. The coefficient on the US dollar, α_1, is close to 1, and the adjusted R^2 is virtually 1. This suggests that the Hong Kong dollar has maintained a strict peg to the US dollar. α_2 on the Japanese yen is statistically significant, but small, while the euro has had no impact on the Hong Kong dollar. Renminbi movements that were uncorrelated with those of the US dollar appear to influence the Hong Kong dollar. Rather than reflecting government policy, this may be capturing market forces at play. Upon strong upward pressures on the renminbi in recent years, some investors speculated that Hong Kong might abandon the link with the US dollar and eventually link to the renminbi. Also, the Hong Kong dollar has been used as a proxy for the unconvertible renminbi for placing bets on renminbi appreciation. These factors drove the Hong Kong dollar to be traded on the strong side of its target zone for considerable periods of time, for instance in late 2005 and the first half of 2006.

For most of the other currencies, the US dollar has continued to dominate in its impact, but its coefficient, α_1, has generally declined compared with the period before July 2005. Notably, α_1 drops from close to 1 to 0.95 in Malaysia's case. Shortly after mainland China announced the changes in the exchange rate regime, Malaysia also officially abandoned the dollar peg, which is captured by the decline in the US dollar weight in the estimated equation for the Malaysian ringgit.

The impact of the Japanese yen is broadly similar to that prior to the renminbi exchange rate regime reform with two exceptions. Its coefficient is no longer significant in the equation for the Indonesian rupiah and Philippine peso. The euro has continued to play no part in influencing movements of all Asian currencies except one – the Singapore dollar.

The distinctive change comes from the impact of the renminbi, which appears to have started to play a role in regional currency movements. Apart from the Malaysian ringgit and Philippine peso, the coefficient for the renminbi, α_4 has become statistically significant in other equations. Among the currencies, the renminbi's impact is the highest, almost one-for-one, for the Korean won; that is, a 1% change in the renminbi exchange rate independent of US dollar movements will lead to a corresponding 1% change in the Korean won.

10.3.3 Robustness check

The results reported above are based on data series that have included all non-missing observations. However, it is known that including observations with unusually large movements may change the relationship among variables. One noteworthy outlier, for example, is the announcement day of the renminbi exchange rate reform (21 July 2005) when most Asian currencies recorded unusually large movements (Figure 10.2).

Table 10.4 presents a different set of estimation results for the period after the renminbi exchange rate reform, using data series that have excluded outliers (defined as observations that are more than two standard deviations from the mean), including 21 July 2005. The estimates change somewhat compared to Table 10.3. While the influence of G3 currencies is virtually unchanged, there are some differences in the renminbi's impact. α_4 becomes insignificant in the equations of the Hong Kong dollar and Thai baht, but turns significant for the Malaysian ringgit and Philippine peso. For the remaining five currencies, the estimates of α_4 are largely robust and in the ballpark of those in Table 10.3, showing significant impacts of the renminbi. The results broadly support our earlier finding that the role of the renminbi has risen distinctively since the regime reform.

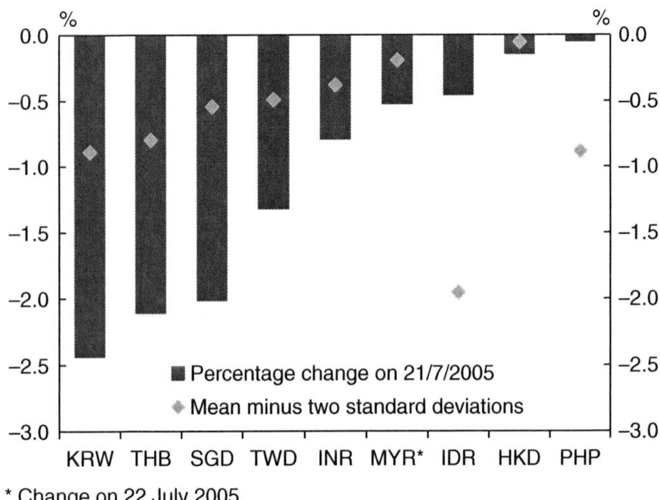

Figure 10.2   Asian exchange rate movements on 21 July 2005
Source: Bloomberg; Author's calculation.

10.3.4   Major findings

Overall, there are a number of main findings from our empirical analysis:

- With the exception of the Hong Kong dollar which maintains a strict peg to the US dollar, major Asian currencies have been moving towards a regime targeting some measure of an effective exchange rate in recent years. This finding corroborates with observations by Ho et al. (2005).
- In the currency basket that Asian currencies are tracking, the US dollar has continued to dominate in its impact, having a weight in the region of 0.8–0.9 in over half of the currencies, but its importance has declined somewhat since the renminbi exchange rate reform/in July 2005. In the case of the Singapore dollar, the US dollar has a lower weight of around 0.65 (Figure 10.3a).
- Movements of the Japanese yen have non-negligible impact on regional currencies, particularly for the Singapore dollar and Thai baht (Figure 10.3b). The euro only features in Singapore's currency basket.
- One distinctive development in recent years has been the rising importance of the renminbi on regional currencies. Since the exchange rate reform on 21 July 2005, the renminbi has had statistically significant impact on the movements of Asian currencies (Figure 10.4). Changes in the renminbi that are independent of those of the US dollar tend to lead to movements in other Asian currencies in the same direction. Nevertheless, it needs to be pointed out that the renminbi's independent

Table 10.4   Asian currencies' regimes after the renminbi exchange rate reform (22 July 2005–2 April 2007)

	Constant α_0	Dollar α_1	Yen α_2	Euro α_3	Rmb α_4	Adjusted R^2
Hong Kong dollar	0.001 (1.085)	0.990*** (393.510)	0.010*** (3.800)	–0.008 (–1.082)	0.025 (1.330)	0.998
Indian rupee	–0.004 (–0.353)	0.865*** (24.001)	0.091** (2.521)	–0.005 (–0.053)	0.588*** (2.814)	0.750
Indonesian rupiah	–0.043* (–1.942)	0.848*** (15.087)	0.089 (1.439)	0.008 (0.058)	0.671** (2.195)	0.467
Korean won	–0.028* (–1.668)	0.814*** (19.905)	0.151*** (3.223)	–0.093 (–0.940)	1.056*** (4.435)	0.607
Malaysian ringgit	–0.023** (–2.563)	0.896*** (37.493)	0.058** (2.452)	0.043 (0.670)	0.763*** (5.171)	0.854
Philippine peso	–0.040*** (–3.051)	0.887*** (25.980)	–0.007 (–0.191)	–0.049 (–0.534)	0.642*** (3.052)	0.717
Singapore dollar	–0.022*** (–2.754)	0.643*** (32.247)	0.197*** (8.464)	0.197*** (3.656)	0.220* (1.749)	0.838
New Taiwan dollar	0.005 (0.408)	0.858*** (26.237)	0.127*** (3.393)	–0.035 (–0.455)	0.971** (5.877)	0.769
Thai baht	–0.058*** (–3.718)	0.681*** (19.415)	0.220*** (4.684)	0.054 (0.573)	0.131 (0.437)	0.599

Note: t-values are in ( ). *, ** and *** indicate that coefficients are significant at the 10%, 5% and 1% levels respectively.
Source: Author's estimation.

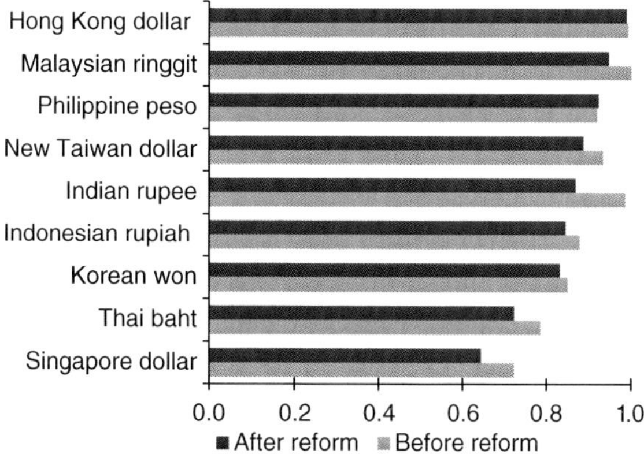

Figure 10.3a   Weights of the US dollar
Source: Author's estimation.

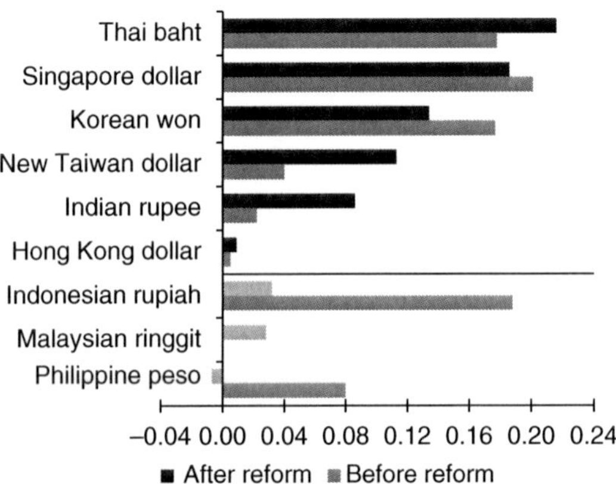

Figure 10.3b   Weights of the Japanese yen
Note: A grey bar suggests that the coefficient is not statistically significant.
Source: Author's estimation.

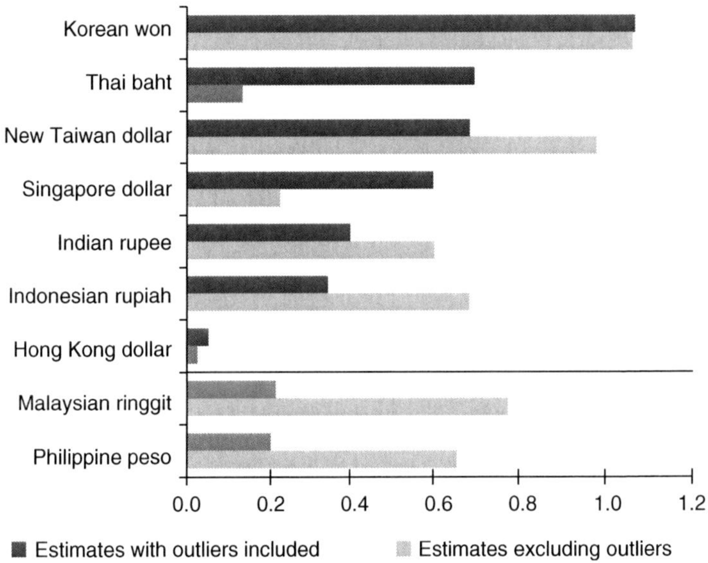

Figure 10.4   Coefficients on the renminbi
Note: A grey bar suggests that the coefficient is not statistically significant.
Source: Author's estimation.

movements are relatively modest so far given the heavy weight
attached to the stability of the RMB/US$ exchange rate. In particular,
as renminbi movements independent of the US dollar have been fairly
limited, the renminbi did not have as much impact as the Japanese yen

on regional currencies during the period under study, despite bigger estimated coefficients on the renminbi variable than on the yen in some cases.

10.4   Conclusion

The finding that the renminbi exchange rate has indeed had increasing impacts on Asian currencies should be interpreted with caution for two reasons. As already noted, the renminbi's impact is in fact constrained by the heavy weight attached to the US dollar in the currency basket that the renminbi itself is tracking. Also, it is difficult to assess whether the impact is the result of government policy of Asian economies or market forces, or both.

These important considerations aside, the empirical findings indicate that the renminbi exchange rate has assumed an international dimension, alongside the key currencies in the global marketplace such as the US dollar and Japanese yen. It has been widely argued, as well as accepted by the mainland China authorities, that greater exchange rate flexibility is beneficial to the China, especially in the medium to longer term. The renminbi exchange rate has indeed been gaining flexibility after the regime shift, particularly since the second half of 2006, with increased variations against the US dollar in both directions observed. The authorities also announced in May 2006 a widening of the daily trading band for the RMB/US$ exchange rate from ±0.3% to ±0.5%, signalling that greater flexibility is a policy goal. This, coupled with the increasing importance of the Chinese economy in the region, suggests that the renminbi's role in the region is likely to grow over time.

Appendix

Hausman Specification Test

When some regressors in an equation are endogenous and thus likely to be correlated with the error term, the OLS estimator will not be consistent. A version of the Hausman specification test can be used to find out whether there is a simultaneity issue. Assume that we are interested in estimating the following equation:

$$y_t = \alpha_1 x_t + \beta_1 z_t + e_t, \tag{A1}$$

where z_t and e_t are a set of totally exogenous variables and residuals respectively, and x_t is a suspect endogenous regressor. To detect the presence of simultaneity is essentially to test whether x_t is correlated with the error term, which can be carried out in two steps. In the first step,

Table 10A.1   Hausman specification tests

	Before reform		After reform	
Hong Kong dollar	0.856	[0.392]	–0.643	[0.521]
Indian rupee	–0.534	[0.594]	–0.410	[0.682]
Indonesian rupiah	0.708	[0.479]	–1.177	[0.240]
Korean won	0.432	[0.666]	0.032	[0.974]
Malaysian ringgit	0.993	[0.321]	1.007	[0.314]
Philippine peso	0.010	[0.992]	0.735	[0.463]
Singapore dollar	–0.415	[0.678]	0.667	[0.505]
New Taiwan dollar	0.307	[0.759]	–0.632	[0.528]
Thai baht	–1.465	[0.143]	0.119	[0.906]

Note: t-statistics are reported with associated p-values in [ ].
Source: Author's estimation.

regress x_t on the set of exogenous variables z_t and relevant instrumental variables iv_t:

$$x_t = \alpha_2 z_t + \beta_2 iv_t + u_t. \tag{A2}$$

Then in the second step, include the calculated residual from the first step $\hat{u}_t$ in the original equation for y_t, and estimate:

$$y_t = \alpha_3 x_t + \beta_3 z_t + \gamma_3 \hat{u}_t + w_t. \tag{A3}$$

If the coefficient on $\hat{u}_t$ is statistically significant, x_t is correlated with the error term e_t in equation (A1), and thus the simultaneity issue is present, while an insignificant γ_3 will indicate absence of simultaneity problems.

Following this procedure, we test whether the renminbi exchange rate variable is an endogenous variable in equation (2). Lagged renminbi exchange rates are used as instruments in the procedure. The test results are reported in Table A1. They show that the residuals are not significant for all the currencies for both sample periods of before and after the renminbi exchange rate reform. This suggests that the renminbi exchange rate can be treated as an exogenous variable in the regression for all the currencies, and the OLS estimator can be used.

Notes

1. See, for example, Jen (2006).
2. We have also estimated auxiliary regressions which include all G3 currencies as regressors. However, the coefficients on the euro and yen are not significant.
3. Details of the Hausman specification test can be found in the Appendix.

References

Benassy-Quere, A. and B. Coeure (2003). 'On the Identification of De Facto Currency Pegs', mimeo.

Branson, W. H. and C. N. Healy (2005). 'Monetary and Exchange Rate Policy Coordination in ASEAN+1', *NBER Working Paper* No. 11713.

Colavecchio, R. and M. Funke (2007). 'Volatility Dependence Across Asia-Pacific On-shore and Off-shore US Dollar Futures Markets', Hamburg University Mimeo.

Eichengreen, B. (2006). 'China's Exchange Rate Regime: The Long and Short of It', University of California Berkeley mimeo.

Frankel, J. A. (2007). 'Assessing China's Exchange Rate Regime', mimeo.

Frankel, J. A. and S. Wei (1994). 'Yen Block or Dollar Bloc? Exchange Rate Policies of the East Asian Economies', in T. Ito and A. Krueger (eds), *Macroeconomic Linkage: Savings, Exchange Rates, and Capital Flows*, Chicago: University of Chicago Press, 295–333.

Goldstein, M. (2007). 'Assessing Progress on China's Exchange Rate Policies', Testimony Before the Hearing on 'Risks and Reform: The Role of Currency in the US-China Relationship', Committee on Finance, US Senate, 28 March 2007.

Greenaway, D., A. Mahabir and C. Milner (2006). 'Has China Displaced Other Asian Countries' Exports?' Leverhulme Centre for Research on Globalisation and Economic Policy, Nottingham University, Research Paper No. 2006/21.

Ho, C., G. Ma and R. N. McCauley (2005), 'Trading Asian Currencies', *BIS Quarterly Review*, March 2005, 49–58.

Jen, S. (2006). 'My Thoughts on Currencies', *Currency Economics*, Morgan Stanley Equity Research, 16 January 2006.

Kawai, M. (2002). 'Exchange Rate Arrangements in East Asia: Lessons from the 1997–98 Currency Crisis', *Monetary and Economic Studies*, Bank of Japan, Institute for Monetary and Economic Studies, 20 (S-1).

McKinnon, R. and G. Schnabl (2004). 'The East Asian Dollar Standard, Fear of Floating, and Original Sin', *Review of Development Economics*, 8 (3), 331–60.

Peng, W. and C. Shu (2006). 'The Renminbi Exchange Rate and Its Role in Macroeconomic Control', *China Economic Issues*, 02/06, Hong Kong Monetary Authority.

Yam, J. (2007). 'Political Pressure on the Renminbi Exchange Rate', *Viewpoint*, 27 April 2006, Hong Kong Monetary Authority.

Index

Bold page numbers indicate figures and tables